Visual QuickStart Guide

Internet Explorer 3

for Windows 95/NT

Steven Schwartz

Peachpit Press

Visual QuickStart Guide
Internet Explorer 3 for Windows 95/NT
Steven Schwartz

Peachpit Press
2414 Sixth Street
Berkeley, CA 94710
510/548-4393
800/283-9444
510/548-5991 (fax)

Find us on the World Wide Web at: http://www.peachpit.com

Peachpit Press is a division of Addison Wesley Longman

Editor: Jeremy Judson
Copyeditor: Janet Schwartz
Cover design: The Visual Group
Production: Steven Schwartz

Colophon
This book was created with Adobe PageMaker 6.0 on a Radius 81/110. The fonts used were Concorde and Kabel from Adobe.

ISBN 0-201-68827-1

9 8 7 6 5 4 3 2 1

Printed and bound in the United States of America

Printed on recycled paper

Table of Contents

Introduction

About This Book

The intent of this book (and every other title in the *Visual QuickStart* series) is to get you up and running as quickly as possible. This book makes only a few assumptions about you:

- You understand the fundamentals of using a computer, such as how to use a mouse and how to choose menu commands. You do not have to be an expert computer user or an Internet maven.
- You have some form of Internet access. It doesn't matter whether you use an *ISP* (Internet Service Provider) or a major information service, such as America Online or CompuServe.
- You have or can obtain a copy of Internet Explorer 3.

  If you don't already have a copy of the program, you can download it from Microsoft's Web site at:

  `http://www.microsoft.com/ie/`

The Philosophy of This Book

Internet Explorer is a special breed of software. It is a full-featured suite of Internet programs. Like many current programs, though, Internet Explorer does not include a manual. Although extensive help files are provided, you'll find that many of your questions and problems are not addressed.

The purpose of this book is to provide you with answers to those questions—in the succinct, step-by-step, visually rich style for which the *Visual QuickStart* series is known.

Parts of the Book

This book is divided into three parts, each corresponding to a component of the Internet Explorer package:

- Internet Explorer (web browser).
- Internet Mail (e-mail program).
- Internet News (newsgroup reader).

If you stumble across a term that you don't understand, look in the Glossary (Appendix A) for a definition. You can find keyboard shortcuts for the three programs in Appendices B–D.

About the Author

I began writing professionally in 1978 as a contributing editor for *Nibble*, a popular Apple II magazine. In the past 18 years, I've written hundreds of reviews and computer-related articles, in addition to more than 30 books. I was also the chief methodologist and a founding editor for *Software Digest*, the Business Applications Editor for *MACazine*, and Technical Services Director for Funk Software.

I have a Ph.D. in psychology and live with my family and pets in the little town of Lizard Spit, Arizona. (At 128 degrees, it doesn't *matter* if it's a dry heat!)

Special Thanks

To Jeremy Judson and Kate Reber of Peachpit Press for their assistance and support.

Part I:
Internet Explorer

1

Browser Basics

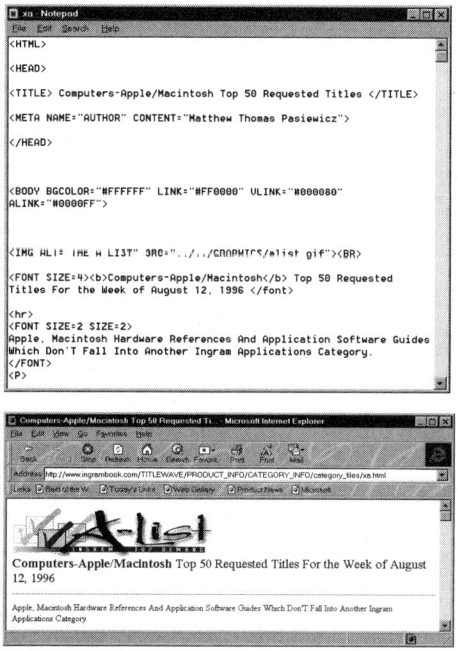

Figure 1.1 *When viewed in a browser, this HTML code (top) generates a banner and some introductory text (bottom).*

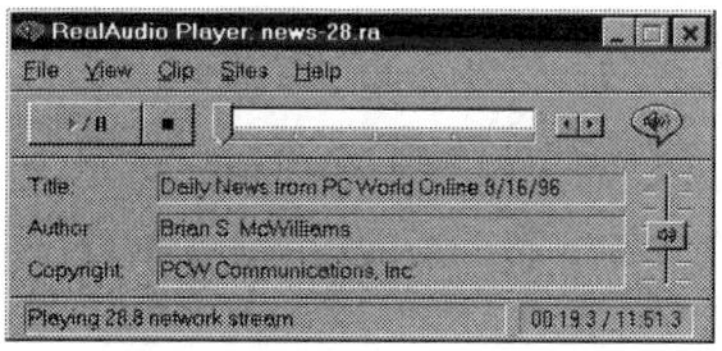

Figure 1.2 *When you download a RealAudio clip, a built-in player appears.*

About Web Browsers

A *browser* is an application used to view and experience the rich text, graphic, audio, and video content of the World Wide Web. Each document (or *page*) on the Web is created with a computer language called HTML (*Hypertext Markup Language*). **Figure 1.1** shows how HTML is used to create a Web page.

Unlike most languages, HTML was designed to work on multiple computer platforms. It doesn't matter whether a particular Web page was designed on a PC or a Mac. The page will display the same information and still be presentable regardless of the platform on which it was created or is ultimately viewed.

The capabilities of your browser, however, *do* have an impact on how some advanced page elements are handled. Whether or not you can hear an audio clip (see **Figure 1.2**) or view a movie depends on whether your browser supports these options—either via built-in capabilities or helper applications. Some browsers can only display text, for instance. Any graphic, audio, or video elements are simply ignored.

These aren't issues for *your* chosen browser, though. Internet Explorer 3 is a state-of-the-art browser, capable of presenting graphics, frames, movie clips, sound effects, and music as Web page components.

About Browsing

The process of using a browser to view and interact with pages on the World Wide Web is commonly referred to as *browsing*. The "surfing" aspect of using the Internet comes largely from the way a browser is often used to jump from page to page—much like using a television remote control to channel surf.

Web pages frequently contain *links*—either text or graphics—that tie the current page to other Web pages. When you click a link, you are instructing the browser to go to the Web page that is represented by the link (see **Figure 1.3**). If you like, you can jump from link to link, viewing a seemingly endless series of pages devoted to almost any topic under the sun.

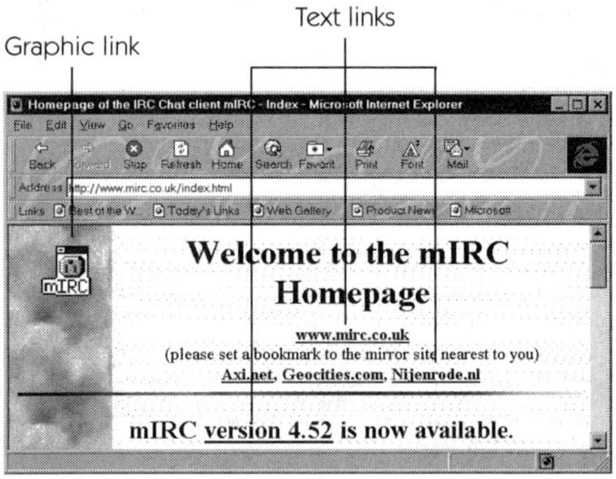

Figure 1.3 *Text links are usually underlined. Graphics, such as pictures and buttons, can also be links.*

Some Web pages also contain *forms*, such as the one shown in **Figure 1.4**. By filling in the blanks and clicking a Submit button, you can apply for a password to a Web site; order a book, program, or pizza; or check out the holdings in your stock portfolio.

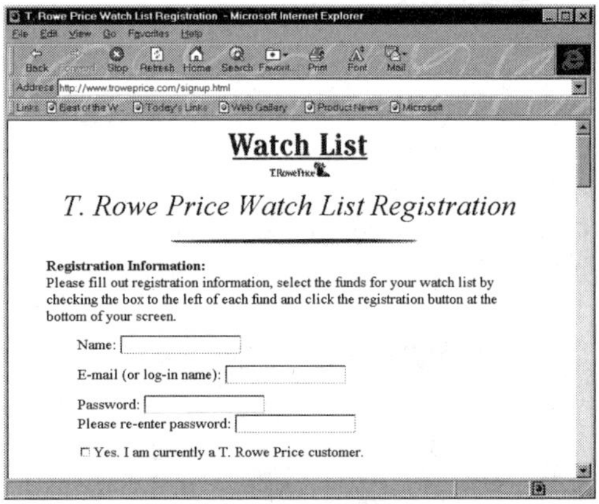

Figure 1.4 *Fill-in-the-blank forms require an advanced browser, such as Internet Explorer. The form shown here is used to register for a service provided by the site.*

The Internet is also a great source of software. Shareware, freeware, and program updates are readily available, for example. Using your browser, you can download all the data files and programs that you want. In fact, if you are still using an earlier version of Internet Explorer or another browser, you can download version 3 from:

`http://www.microsoft.com/ie/`

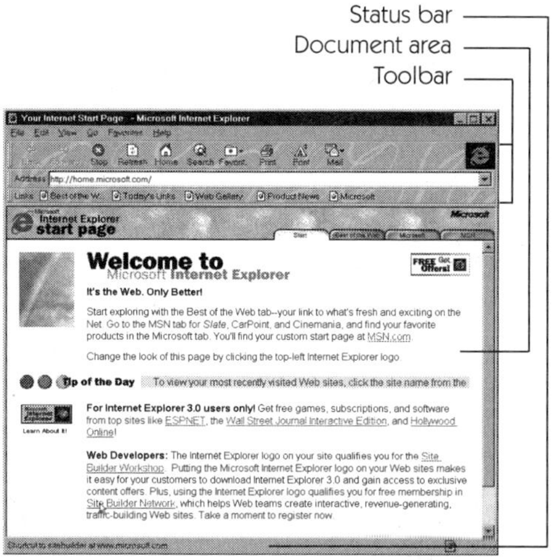

Figure 1.5 *The three parts of the browser window.*

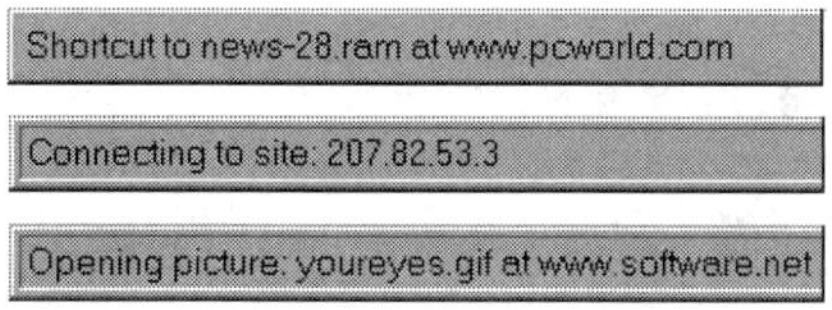

Figure 1.6 *As long as you keep an eye on the status bar, you can always tell what's happening. These messages show that the cursor is being passed over a link to another page in the site (top), Internet Explorer is connecting with the chosen Web site (middle), and a picture is downloading so it can be viewed as part of the current page (bottom).*

The Browser Window

The browser window is divided into three parts, as shown in **Figure 1.5**. The *toolbar* has buttons for performing basic commands related to browsing, such as returning to previously viewed pages or displaying your home page. Page addresses (also called *URLs*) can be typed in the Address box, enabling you to visit any page of interest. The icons below the Address box are called Quick Links. Clicking any Quick Link instantly transports you to the Web page that it represents.

The *document area* displays the contents of each Web page. As shown in **Figure 1.5**, pages often combine text and graphics. Other elements can include hypertext or graphic links to other pages, buttons, frames (dividing the window into multiple sections), tables, and fill-in-the-blank forms. Some elements, such as audio and video players, appear in their own windows rather than as part of the browser window.

The *status bar* is at the bottom of the window. Messages appear in the status bar (see **Figure 1.6**). You may note that a particular Web or FTP (*File Transfer Protocol*) site is being sought or that a graphic is loading.

✔ Tip

- You can have multiple browser documents open simultaneously—to view another site while waiting for a slow-loading page to appear, for example. To create another window, choose New Document from the File menu.

The Toolbar Buttons

The buttons on the top row of the toolbar (see **Figure 1.7**) provide convenient access to basic browser functions. Clicking the appropriate button during an on-line session can accomplish the tasks described below.

Figure 1.7 *Click the toolbar buttons to perform common browser functions. The Explorer icon at the right side of the toolbar shows whether the current page is still loading (active) or is fully displayed (inactive).*

Moving Backward and Forward

The Back and Forward buttons (see **Figure 1.8**) and these commands in the Go menu enable you to move backward and forward through the pages viewed during the session. Each click of the Back button moves you back one page. When the Back button is inactive, it means that you are at the first page visited during the session.

Figure 1.8 *Click the Back and Forward buttons to move through pages already visited during the current session.*

Click the Forward button to move forward through the pages you've viewed during the session. When the Forward button is inactive, you are already on the last page visited during the session.

Stopping a Page from Loading

The Stop button (see **Figure 1.9**) and Stop command in the View menu enable you to stop the current page from loading—or *finishing* loading. (Note that as long as the Explorer icon at the end of the toolbar is in motion, elements of the page are still loading.)

Figure 1.9 *Click the Stop button to tell Internet Explorer to halt the present action, such as downloading graphics for the current page.*

There are many instances when you will not want a page to complete the loading process, such as the following:

- A page is loading slowly, and you don't want to wait for it to finish.
- You discover that the *wrong* page is loading.

- The information needed from the page (such as a link or company phone number) is already visible, so there is no reason to wait for the rest of the elements to appear.

✔ **Tip**

- If you want to go immediately to a site represented by a link on the current page, you don't have to click Stop (to halt the download) before clicking the link. This is true for all types of links, such as those for viewing a full-size image of a thumbnail graphic, downloading a file, and so on.

Refreshing the Current Page

Figure 1.10 *Click the Refresh button to reload the current Web page.*

Click the Refresh button (see **Figure 1.10**) or choose Refresh from the View menu to force the current page to reload. Here are two reasons why you might want to refresh a page:

- You believe that the information on the page has been updated. (Clicking Refresh automatically displays the most current information for a page.)
- The page is displaying incorrectly or is incomplete.

Going to Your Home Page

Figure 1.11 *Click the Home button to return to your start page; that is, the page that you automatically go to at the start of each normal browser session.*

At the start of every Explorer session, your start (or *home*) page automatically loads. You can return to the home page at any time during a session by clicking Home (see **Figure 1.11**) or choosing Start Page from the Go menu.

The Microsoft Web site is the default home page, but you can change it to another page, if you prefer.

To set a new home page:

1. Go to the page that you intend to make your new home page (by typing its URL in the Address box or selecting the page from the Favorites menu, for example).

   or

1. Make a note of the URL of the page that you intend to make the new home page.
2. Choose Options from the View menu. The Options dialog box appears.
3. Click the Navigation tab at the top of the Options dialog box.
4. Choose Start Page from the Page pop-up menu (see **Figure 1.12**).
5. Click Use Current to make the current Web page your home page.

   or

5. Type the URL of the page into the Address box.
6. Click OK.

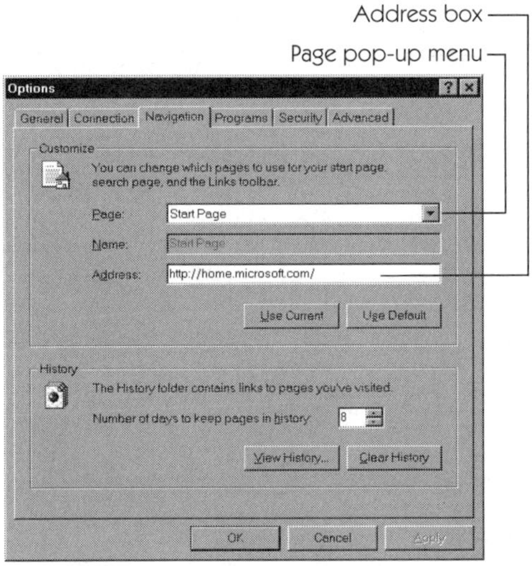

Figure 1.12 *You can set a home page, search page, and Quick Links in this part of the Options dialog box. Refer to Chapters 3 and 4 for information about the search page and Quick Links.*

✔ Tips

- You can restore the Microsoft page (see **Figure 1.13**) as the home page by clicking Use Default in the Options dialog box.
- After spending some time on the Web, you'll learn which sites you visit most. You may want to set your favorite site as the home page. Or if you like to begin the day by checking out the Dow-Jones Industrials or reading the headlines, you can set your home page to an investment site or one of the many on-line newspapers.

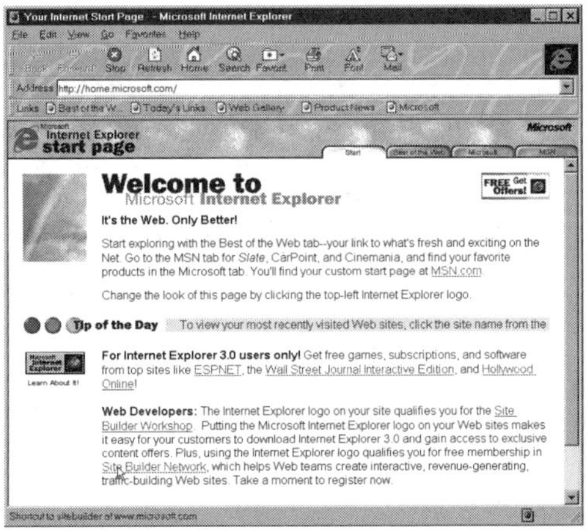

Figure 1.13 *While the Microsoft home page shown here can serve you well, you may want to change the start page to one that more closely matches your needs.*

Figure 1.14 *Click the Search button to go to your default search page, enabling you to search the Internet for many types of information.*

Going to Your Search Page

When you click the Search button (see **Figure 1.14**) or choose Search the Web from the Go menu, you go to your default search page. A search page is designed to help you search the Internet for information. The types of information that can be found vary according to the purpose of the search site. You can search for topic-specific material (all mentions of the words Congress, iguana, or James Brown, for example); a company's Web site; or a friend's phone number.

To set a new search page:

1. Go to the page that you intend to make your new search page (by typing its URL in the Address box or selecting the page from the Favorites menu, for example).

   or

1. Make a note of the URL of the page that you intend to make the new search page.
2. Choose Options from the View menu. The Options dialog box appears.
3. Click the Navigation tab at the top of the Options dialog box, as shown previously in **Figure 1.12**.
4. Choose Search Page from the Page pop-up menu.
5. Click Use Current to make the current Web page your search page.

   or

5. Type the URL of the page into the Address box.
6. Click OK.

✔ Tip

- You can restore the Microsoft page as your search page by clicking Use Default in the Options dialog box.

Displaying the Favorites List

Click the Favorites button to display a menu of all Web page locations that you've stored (see **Figure 1.15**). Favorite sites can be revisited by choosing them from the Favorites menu. For information on adding and managing favorites, see Chapter 3.

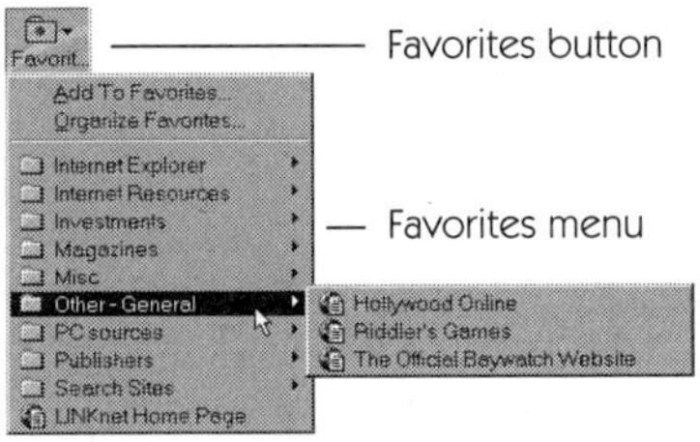

Figure 1.15 *Click the Favorites button to display the Favorites menu, enabling you to choose a Web page to revisit.*

✔ Tip

- The menu that appears when you click Favorites is identical to the one displayed when you open the Favorites menu.

Printing

Using the printers that you've defined for Windows 95, you can print the current Web page. While saving a page to disk stores only its text, printing uses *all* the information that's on the page—graphics, buttons, and text.

Note that there is no length limit imposed on Web pages. A single page can be one or thousands of lines long.

Figure 1.16 *Click the Print button to print the current Web page.*

To print a Web page:

1. Display the Web page that you want to print.
2. Click the Print button, as shown in **Figure 1.16**. The Print dialog box appears (see **Figure 1.17**).
3. Select a printer to use from the list of currently installed printers.

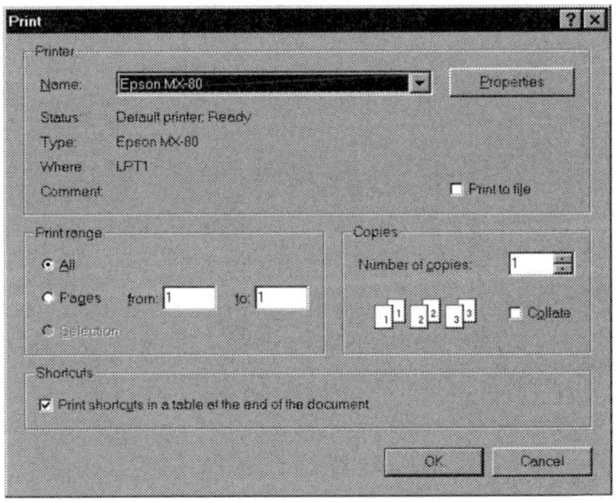

Figure 1.17 *Prior to printing, set options in the Print dialog box.*

4. *Optional:* To specify properties for this print job, such as the type and size of paper, graphics quality, and so on, click the Properties button.

5. Set a print range by clicking All or by entering numbers in the From and To boxes.

   Note that the From/To range refers to the number of pieces of paper to print rather than to the number of Web pages. The All choice prints the entire Web page, regardless of the number of sheets of paper needed.

6. Specify the number of copies to be printed.

7. *Optional:* If you're printing several copies, you can automatically collate the copies by clicking the Collate check box.

8. *Optional:* To print the addresses of all hypertext and graphic links embedded in the Web page, click the Print Shortcuts check box.

9. Click OK to begin printing.

For more information about printing and print options, see Chapter 6.

✔ Tips

- You can also print by choosing Print from the File menu or by pressing [Ctrl][P].
- If you just want to print a page using your default printer and standard print options, choose Print and press [Return].
- To print more pages from the same or another Web site, display each page and issue the Print command for each one.

Changing the Display Font Size

To squeeze more information onto each Web page or to increase its readability, you can vary the font size of all text (see **Figure 1.18**). You can choose from five sizes.

To change the display font size:

- Click the Font button, as shown in **Figure 1.19**. Each click cycles to the next font size.

  or

- Choose a size from the Fonts submenu of the View menu, as shown in **Figure 1.20**.

✔ Tip

- Changing the size of the display fonts affects all Web pages, not just the one you're viewing. You can change this setting as often as you like.

Working with Mail and Usenet Newsgroups

Although they are separate programs, Internet Explorer is integrated with Internet Mail (e-mail) and Internet News (newsgroup reader). You can compose and send e-mail messages from within Internet Explorer, as well as choose commands to launch either Internet Mail or Internet News.

If you did a full install of Internet Explorer or manually installed Mail and News, you can click the Mail button to reveal a pop-up menu of newsgroup and e-mail commands (see **Figure 1.21**). The commands have the following effects:

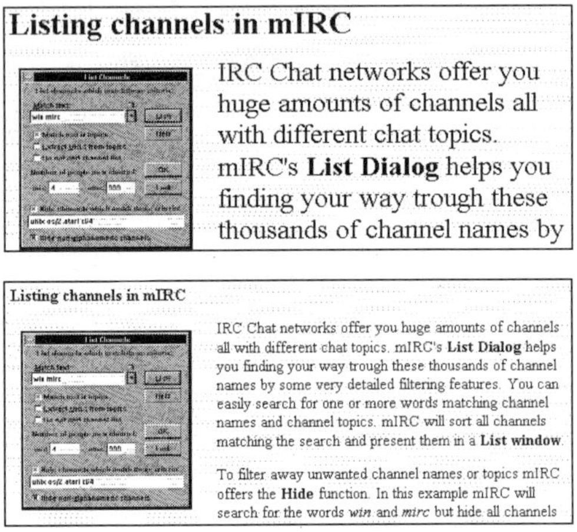

Figure 1.18 *You can vary the font size for all text from Largest (top) to Smallest (bottom)—or any size in between.*

Figure 1.19 *Each click on the Font button cycles to the next font size.*

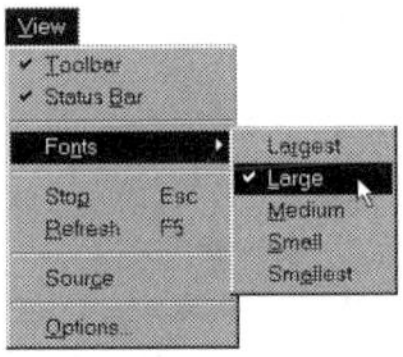

Figure 1.20 *If you want a specific font size, it is often quicker to choose it from the Fonts submenu.*

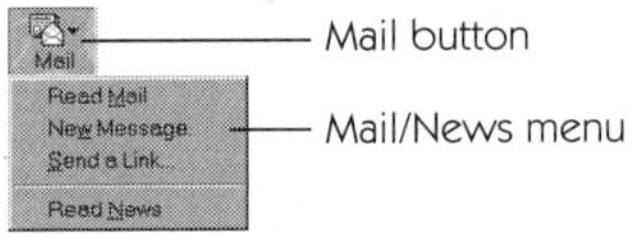

Figure 1.21 *If you have installed the Mail and News components of Internet Explorer, you can click the Mail button to access features of either program.*

Figure 1.22 *Choose the New Message command to open a blank message form.*

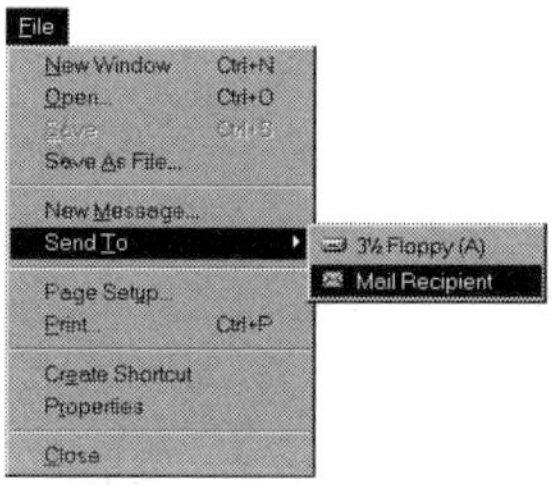

Figure 1.23 *With Internet Mail installed, a Mail Recipient command appears in the Send To submenu. You can use it to send URL shortcuts or files as e-mail attachments.*

- *Read Mail.* Use this command to launch Internet Mail. (It is the same as choosing Read Mail from the Go menu or choosing Internet Mail from the Start menu on the taskbar.)
- *New Message.* This command opens a New Message window (see **Figure 1.22**), enabling you to compose and send e-mail to an individual. (It is the same as choosing New Message from the File menu.)
- *Send a Link.* This command sends a URL shortcut for the current Web page as e-mail.
- *Read News.* Use this command to launch Internet News. (It is the same as choosing Read News from the Go menu or choosing Internet News from the Start menu on the taskbar.)

✔ Tips

- You can also send a URL by choosing Mail Recipient from the Send To submenu of the File menu, as shown in **Figure 1.23**. You can also achieve this effect by right-clicking a shortcut icon and choosing the same command.
- You can compose a message and send a more substantial attachment (such as a word processing document, graphic, or program) by right-clicking a file icon and then choosing Mail Recipient from the Send To submenu of the File menu.

More About the Toolbar

The toolbar contains two other major sections: the Address box and the Quick Link buttons.

The Address Box

The Address box (see **Figure 1.24**) displays the address of the current page. You can also type addresses into the Address box to visit pages.

Examples of addresses include:

- `http://www.tips.com/list.html`
  [a specific page within a Web site]
- `ftp://aclu.org/pub/`
  [the public directory of an FTP site, as shown in **Figure 1.25**]
- `c:\graphics\fish.jpg`
  [a file loaded from your hard disk]

Although you can type an address from scratch or edit the current one (to avoid some typing), you can also enter *simplified* URLs. You don't have to type *http://* as the address prefix, for example. If the prefix is omitted, it is filled in for you.

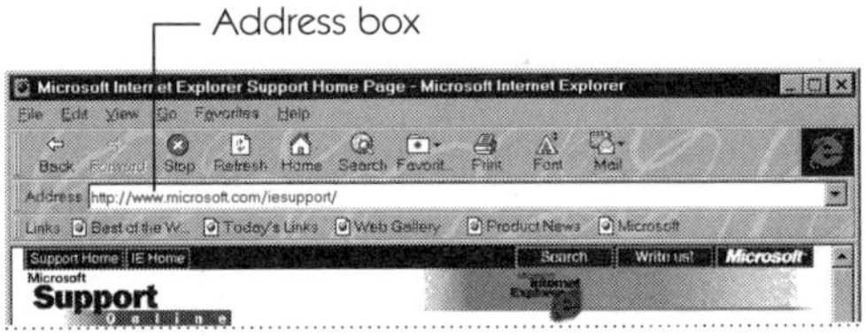

Figure 1.24 *The address (or URL) for the current page is listed in the Address box.*

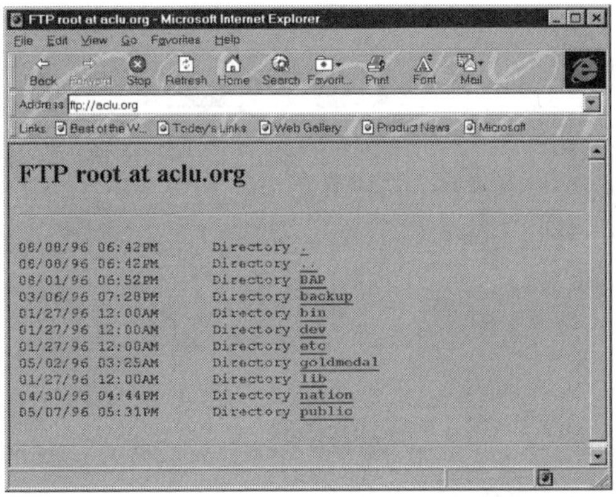

Figure 1.25 *FTP sites are often shown this way. You switch directories and choose files to download by clicking text or graphic links.*

The Quick Link Buttons

The purpose of the buttons (called Quick Links) in the Links section of the toolbar is to make it easy to get to important or favorite Web pages. Click any button to go to the Web page it represents (see **Figure 1.26**).

Although the Quick Links are preset for Microsoft sites, you can change them so they'll go to other pages, as explained in Chapter 3.

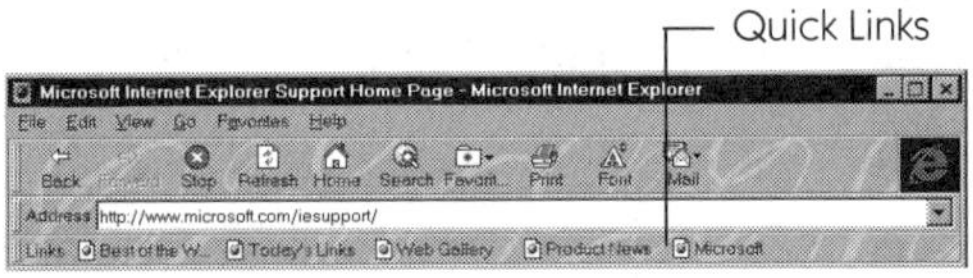

Figure 1.26 *Click any button in the Links section of the toolbar to go to that Web page.*

✔ **Tip**

- If the Quick Links aren't visible in the toolbar, click the word *Links*.

Customizing the Toolbar

Although you can't alter the main toolbar buttons (as you can in Internet Mail and Internet News), there are changes that you *can* make to the rest of the toolbar. You can alter the five Quick Link buttons (as mentioned previously) and reorganize the parts of the toolbar in the following ways:

- *Eliminate the toolbar.*

  Choose Toolbar from the View menu to remove or display the toolbar.

- *Hide one or more sections.*

  To hide the bottom section of the toolbar, move the cursor over the bottom edge of the section (it becomes a double-headed arrow), and then drag upward. To eliminate the next section, continue dragging. (Only the top section must remain.)

- *Change the order of the three sections.*

  Drag any of the vertical bars in the toolbar to the left, right, up, or down. **Figure 1.27** shows several possible arrangements.

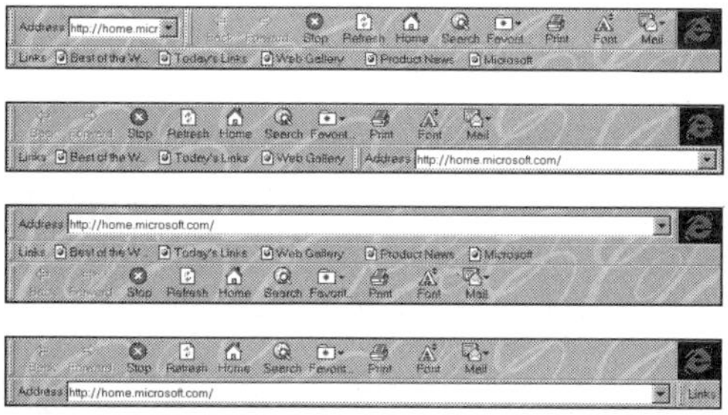

Figure 1.27 *By dragging the parts of the toolbar, you can create a variety of useful and pleasing arrangements.*

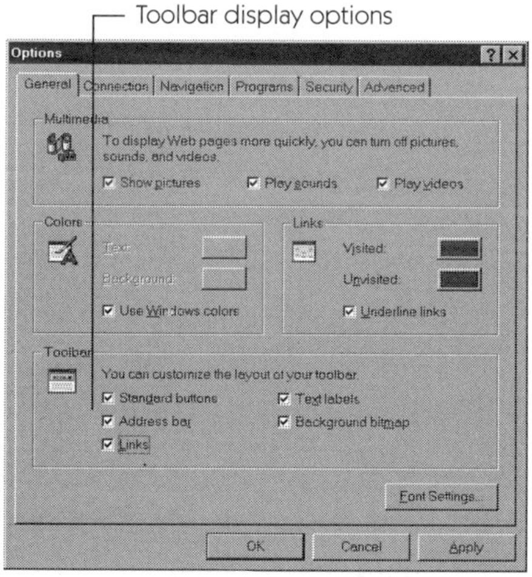

Figure 1.28 *Click check boxes in the Toolbar section of this dialog box to remove or restore toolbar features.*

✔ Tips

- You can also hide the status bar by choosing Status Bar from the View menu.
- If two toolbar sections are in the same row, you can expose the hidden one by clicking its name.
- To hide other parts of the toolbar, choose Options from the View menu and then click the General tab, as shown in **Figure 1.28**.

2 Navigating the Web

Moving from one Web site or page to another is an important part of almost every browser session. In this chapter, you will learn how to use Internet Explorer to navigate the World Wide Web.

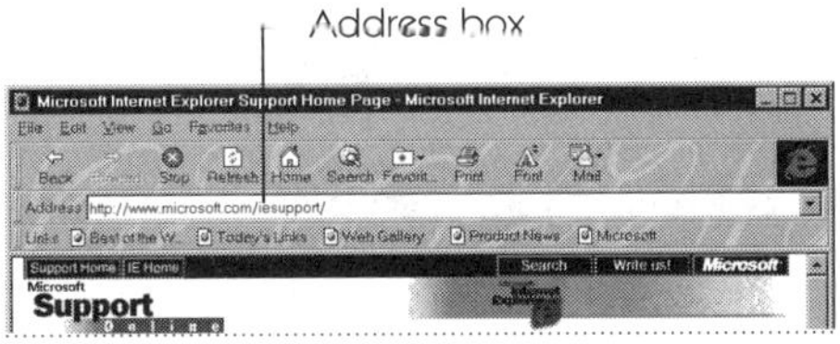

Figure 2.1 *To display a Web page, type or paste its address into the Address box and then press* Enter *or* Return.

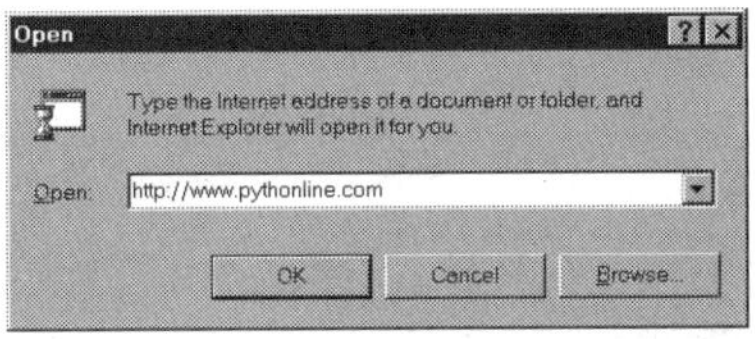

Figure 2.2 *You can also go to a page by typing or pasting an address into the Open line of the Open dialog box.*

Typing an Address (URL)

One of the most common ways to visit a Web page is by typing its URL into the Address box, and then pressing Enter or Return (see **Figure 2.1**). Or you can choose Open from the File menu, type the address in the Open dialog box, and click OK (see **Figure 2.2**).

✔ Tips

- It's often faster to edit the current URL than to type one from scratch. Addresses frequently start with *http://www* and end with *.com*. All you may have to do is change a few letters.
- Internet Explorer intelligently handles typed Web addresses. You don't need to include the *http://*, for example.
- If a URL is cited in a document, such as an e-mail message, you can copy and paste it into the Address box. (If you use Internet Mail as your e-mail program, all URLs in messages are automatically treated as hypertext links. Clicking such a link launches Internet Explorer and fetches the Web page.)

Clicking Links

When you're viewing a Web page, you can go to any link that is referenced in the page by clicking the hypertext or link object. Depending on the purpose of the link, you may be taken to a spot on the same page, another page in the same Web site, or a different Web site.

Hypertext links are usually underlined (see **Figure 2.3**). Objects, such as the graphic shown in **Figure 2.4**, can also be links. When you click a graphic link, a larger version of the graphic may be displayed (see **Figure 2.5**) or you might be taken to the page that is referred to by the graphic link.

✔ Tips

- You can easily tell which text strings and objects are links. Just move the cursor over them. When moved over a link, the cursor changes to a pointing hand, and the link information (a URL or page reference) is shown in the status bar (see **Figure 2.6**).
- You can keep your hands on the keyboard while Web surfing by pressing Tab to move from one link to the next. The currently selected link is surrounded by a thin dotted line (see **Figure 2.7**). Press Enter or Return to go to the chosen link.
- You can create shortcut icons for important links (as described in Chapter 3). Double-click or open the shortcut to go the Web page.

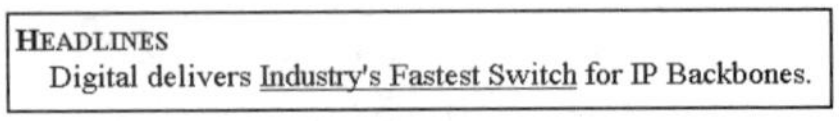

Figure 2.3 *When clicked, this hypertext link (the underlined text) takes you to another Web page.*

Figure 2.4 *Graphic images like this one (called an image map) may be used as links—often to multiple Web pages.*

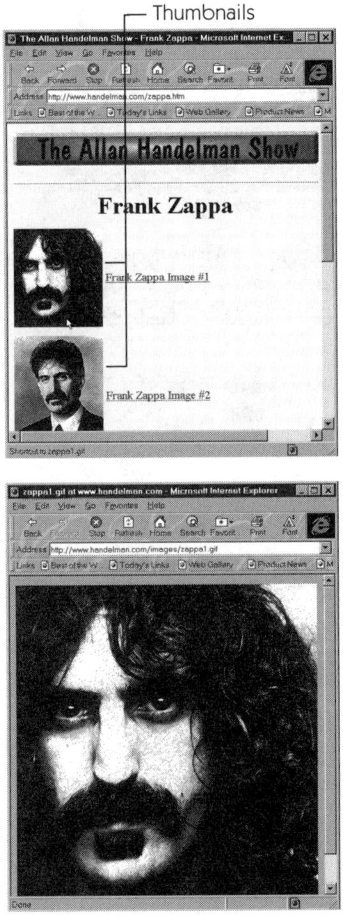

Figure 2.5 *Sometimes you can click a thumbnail (top) to display a full-size image on a new Web page (bottom).*

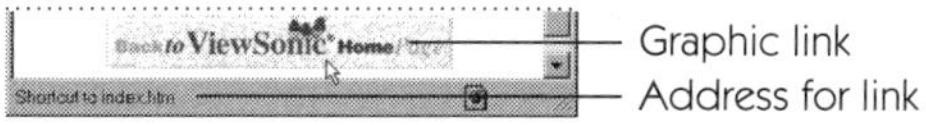

Figure 2.6 *When the cursor moves over a link, the link's address appears in the status area.*

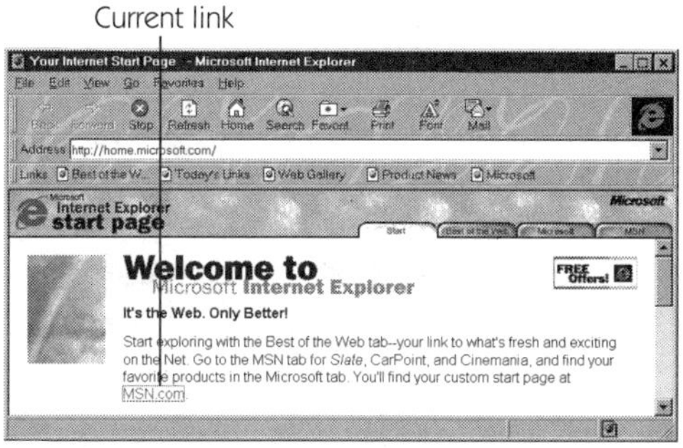

Figure 2.7 *When you tab from link to link, the current link is surrounded by a box.*

Figure 2.8 *Click the Back and Forward buttons to review recently visited pages.*

Revisiting a Web Page

Internet Explorer provides several ways to return to previously visited Web pages: the Back and Forward buttons, the History cache, and the Favorites folder and menu.

The Back and Forward Buttons

Click these buttons to flip through pages you've viewed during the current on-line session. Each time you click the Back or Forward button (see **Figure 2.8**), you move one page in the direction indicated.

To move between viewed pages:

- To view the last Web page visited, click Back or press Backspace.
- To view the next Web page, click Forward or press Shift Backspace.

✔ Tip

- You can only go forward if you have previously pressed the Back button; that is, you must be somewhere in the middle of the pages viewed during the session. If you can't move in a given direction, the appropriate button is disabled.

Using the History Cache

Internet Explorer maintains a History folder with the names and addresses of Web pages that you've recently viewed. (*All* viewed pages are tracked, even if they're not "favorites.") Unlike the way the Back and Forward buttons work, the History folder's contents can—and usually does—encompass multiple on-line sessions.

To go to a History page:

- Choose the page from the numbered list near the bottom of the Go menu (see **Figure 2.9**). Only pages viewed during the current session are listed.

  or

- Choose Open History Folder from the Go menu, and select the page to open (see **Figure 2.10**).

  or

- Click the pop-up menu at the end of the Address box, and choose a history page. (Only URLs that you previously typed in the Address box are listed.)

✔ **Tip**

- The length of time an entry remains in the History folder depends on the options you've set (see **Figure 2.11**). For information on altering this and other History settings, see Chapter 7.
- You can also open the History folder using Windows Explorer or by choosing Options from the View menu, clicking the Navigation tab, and then clicking View History (refer to **Figure 2.11**).

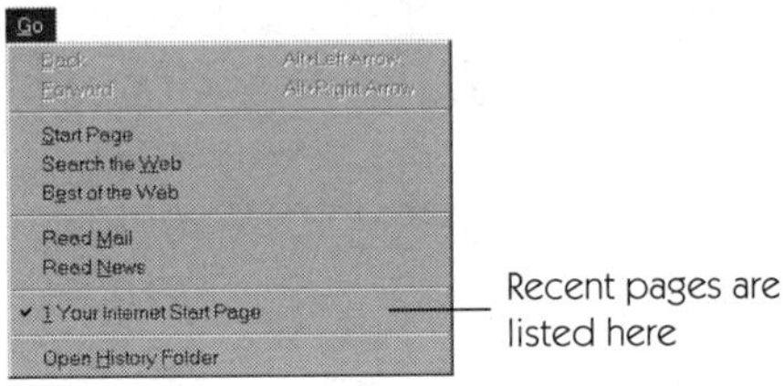

Figure 2.9 *Go to recently viewed pages by choosing a numbered entry from the Go menu.*

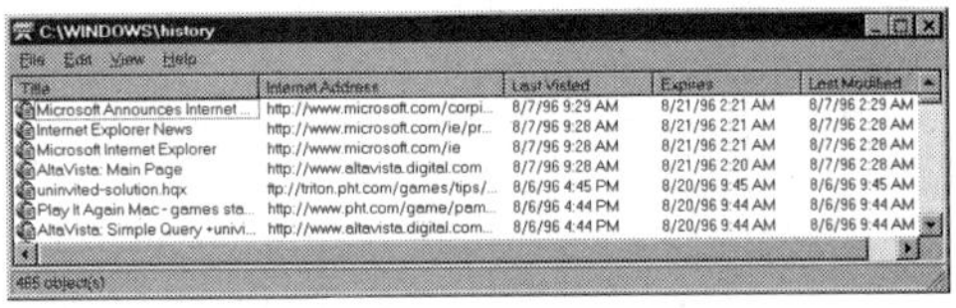

Figure 2.10 *You can visit any Web page in the History folder by double-clicking an item or by choosing Open from the File menu.*

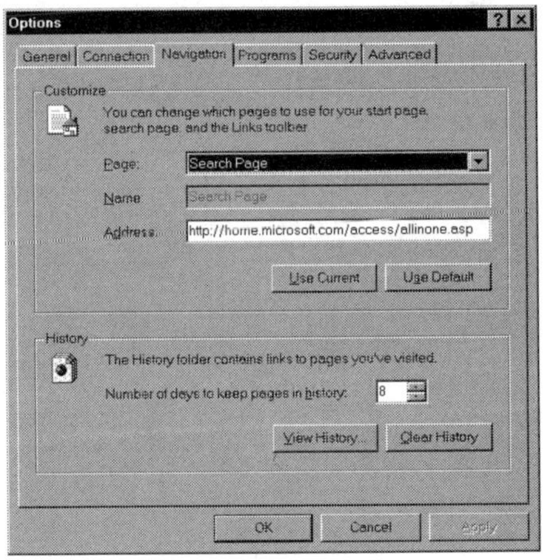

Figure 2.11 *You determine the number of days that visited pages are stored in the History folder. If you want to examine the contents of the History folder, click the View History button.*

Going to a Favorite Page

You can store the addresses of important Web pages in the Favorites folder (as described in Chapter 3) and go to those pages whenever you wish.

You can choose a page to visit from the Favorites menu or, if you prefer, you can click the Favorites button to display the Favorites menu and then choose a page.

Navigating within a Page

Not all Web pages can fit on one screen. In fact, there is no established length limit for Web pages. A page can sometimes span dozens of screens, for example. The following commands and procedures can be used to move within any Web page:

- To scroll to the top or bottom of the current page, press Home or End, respectively.
- To move up or down one screen of information, press Pg Up or Pg Dn, respectively.
- To scroll one line up or down, press ↑ or ↓, respectively.
- To move from link to link in the current page, press Tab to move forward and press Shift Tab to move backward. The screen scrolls automatically, as necessary.
- To switch from one frame on the current page to the next frame on the same page, press Ctrl Tab. **Figure 2.12** shows an example of a page with frames.

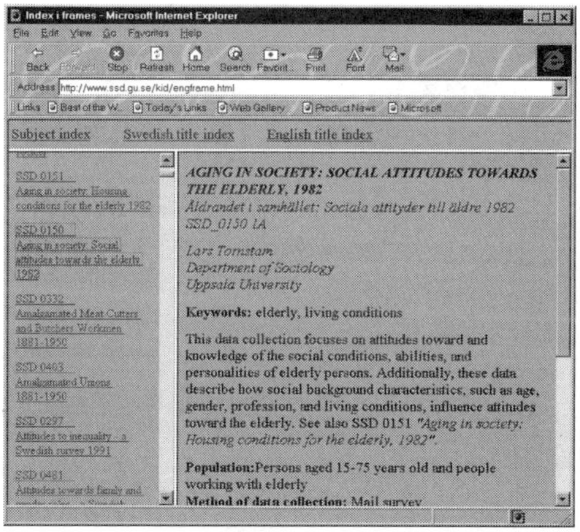

Figure 2.12 *This Web page uses frames to separate an index (left) from the articles that it references (right).*

✔ Tip

- You can also navigate within a page by using the scroll bars. To move a small distance, click an arrow button on the scroll bar. To scroll continuously in a direction, click an arrow button while holding down the mouse button. To move a greater distance, drag the scroll box or click in the blank area of the scroll bar.

Working with Favorites

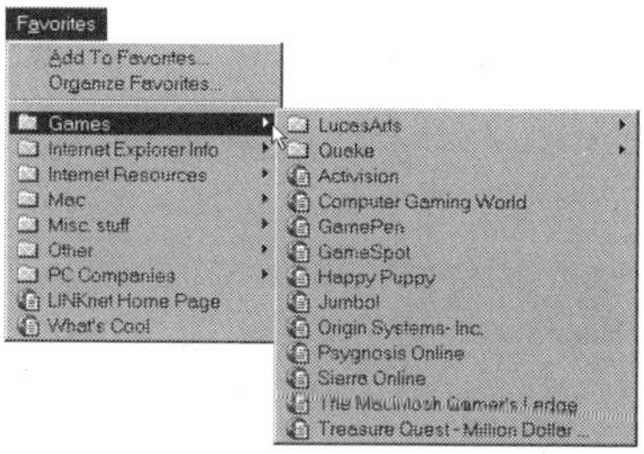

Figure 3.1 *The Favorites menu lists the names of Web pages that you may want to visit again.*

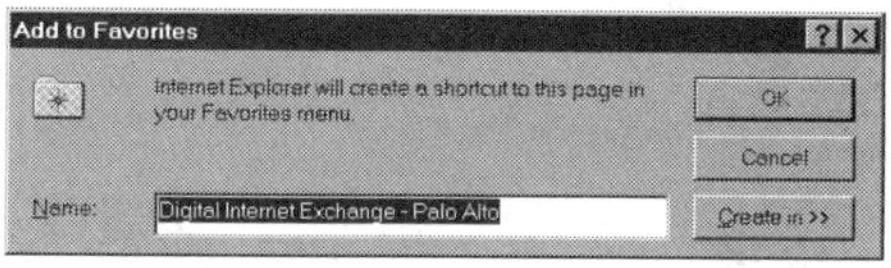

Figure 3.2 *When adding a favorite, you can change its name, and save it in an existing or a new folder.*

About Favorites

Whether you jump from one important link to the next or spend your on-line time roaming aimlessly about the Web, you're certain to find sites that you'd like to visit again. Internet Explorer calls such sites *favorites* and provides several tools for recording and organizing them. Once you've saved a favorite, you can quickly return to that site by choosing its name from the Favorites menu (see **Figure 3.1**).

Adding Favorites

The easiest way to create a favorite is to go to the Web page, and then add the page to the Favorites menu.

To add a Web page as a favorite:

1. Display the page that you want to make into a favorite. (It doesn't matter whether you reach the page by typing its URL in the Address box, choosing its name from the History folder or Go menu, or by clicking a link for the page.)
2. Choose Add to Favorites from the Favorites menu. The Add to Favorites dialog box appears, as shown in **Figure 3.2**.
3. *Optional:* The name for the Web page is shown in the Name box. You can edit the proposed name or type a new one, if you like.

4. The favorite can be added to the top level of the Favorites menu or stored in a folder within the menu.

   To save the favorite in the top level of the Favorites menu, click the OK button.

   or

   To save the favorite inside a folder, click Create In. The dialog box expands to show the folder list (see **Figure 3.3**). Select a folder in which to place the new favorite, and then click OK. If the folder doesn't already exist, click Create New Folder, name the folder (see **Figure 3.4**), and then click OK to save the favorite in the folder.

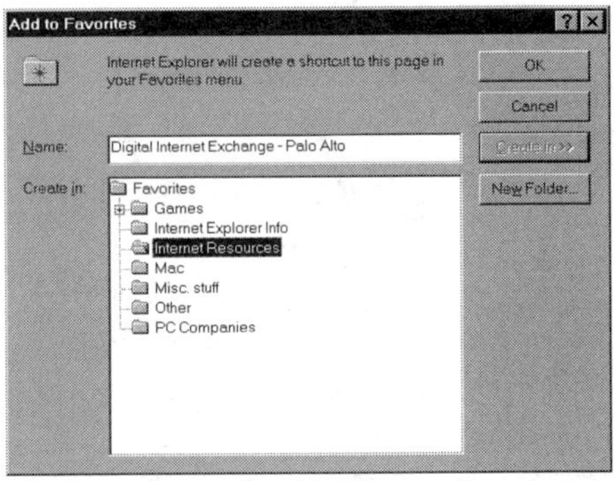

Figure 3.3 *To help you organize favorites, you can store them within folders. If you like, you can create a hierarchy of folders by nesting folders within other folders.*

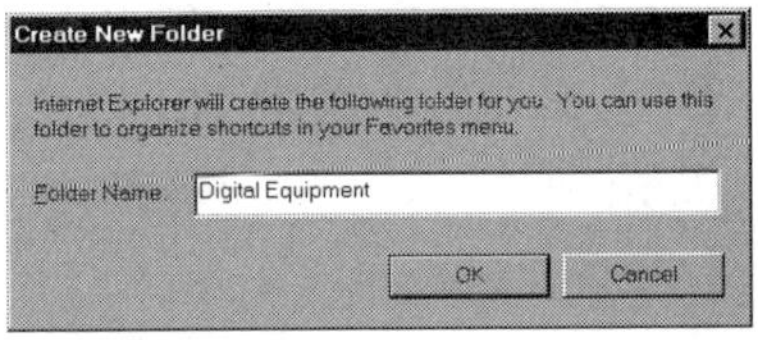

Figure 3.4 *Use the Create New Folder dialog box to name the new folder.*

✔ Tips

- You don't have to save a site's home or index page as a favorite. If there's another page in the site that interests you more, save *it* as the favorite. Or you can save both pages, if you prefer.
- New folders for favorites can be nested within other folders. For example, as shown previously in **Figure 3.1**, the Games folder contains two other folders: LucasArts and Quake.
- You don't have to organize a favorite the moment it's created. If you're in a hurry, choose Add to Favorites and then click OK. When time permits, you can rename the favorite and move it into a folder (see "Organizing Favorites" on page 26 for details).

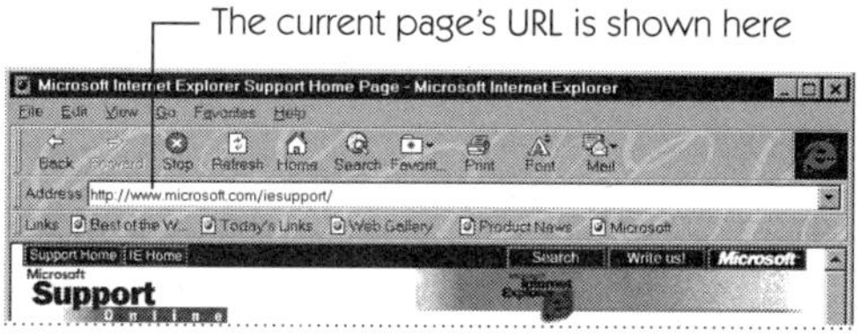

Figure 3.5 *The address (or URL) for the current page is listed in the Address box.*

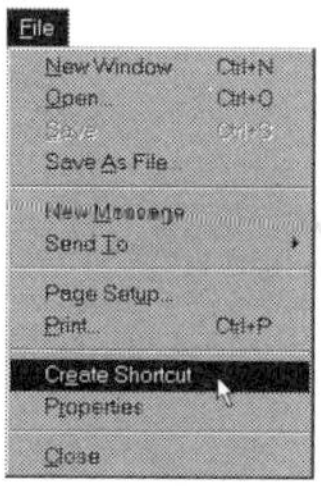

Figure 3.6 *Choose Create Shortcut from the File menu.*

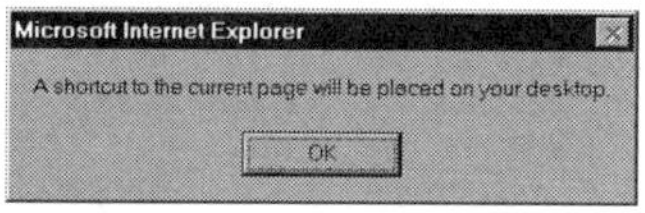

Figure 3.7 *Click OK to create a shortcut on your desktop.*

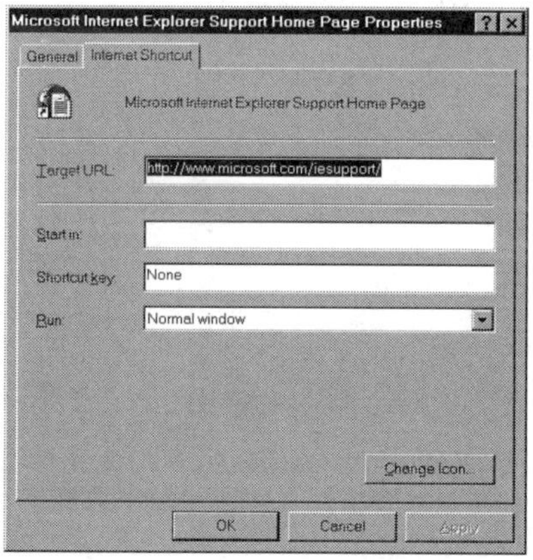

Figure 3.8 *The properties of a shortcut—including its URL—can be viewed or changed in the Properties dialog box.*

Creating a Desktop Shortcut for a Web Page

Some Web pages are more important than others. To avoid having to hunt for an important page in the Favorites menu, you may prefer to create a desktop shortcut for it. When you want to go to the Web page, you can double-click its shortcut icon.

To create a shortcut for a page:

1. In Internet Explorer, go to the Web page for which you want to create a shortcut.

   After the page loads, its URL is displayed in the Address box, as shown in **Figure 3.5**. The URL is saved as part of the shortcut's definition.

2. Choose Create Shortcut from the File menu, as shown in **Figure 3.6**. A dialog box appears (see **Figure 3.7**), stating that a shortcut is about to be created.

3. Click OK. A shortcut to the page's URL appears on the desktop.

✔ Tips

- You can examine and modify a shortcut's properties (see **Figure 3.8**) by right-clicking the shortcut icon and choosing Properties from the pop-up menu that appears.
- You can create a shortcut for any hypertext link found on a Web page by dragging the link text or object onto the desktop or into a folder.

Organizing Favorites

As mentioned earlier in this chapter, favorites can be organized in folders, making it easier for you to find them. In addition to creating folders and moving favorites between folders, Internet Explorer also has commands for renaming and deleting favorites.

To create a new favorites folder:

1. Choose Organize Favorites from the Favorites menu. The Organize Favorites dialog box appears, as shown in **Figure 3.9**.
2. Click the Create New Folder button. An empty folder named New Folder is created.
3. Type a name for the folder.
4. Press Enter, Return, or click the Close button.

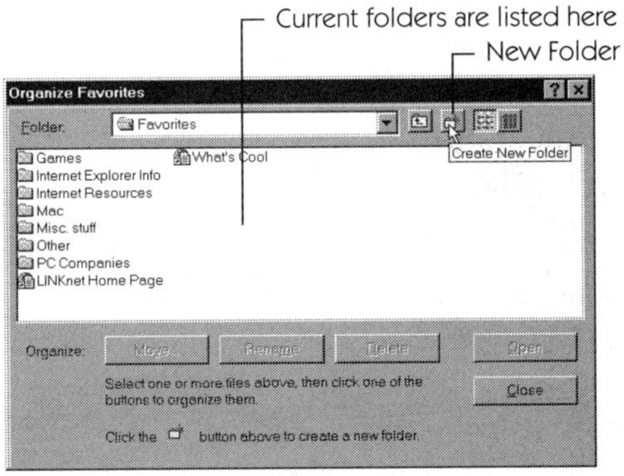

Figure 3.9 *Use the Organize Favorites dialog box to create new folders, as well as move, rename, and delete favorites.*

To move a favorite:

1. Choose Organize Favorites from the Favorites menu. The Organize Favorites dialog box appears, as previously shown in **Figure 3.9**.
2. Select the favorite(s) that you want to move, opening folders as necessary.
3. Click the Move button. The Browse for Folder dialog box appears, as shown in **Figure 3.10**.
4. Select a destination, opening folders as necessary. (To store the favorite(s) at the top level of the Favorites menu, select the Favorites folder.)
5. Click OK to complete the move or Cancel if you change your mind.

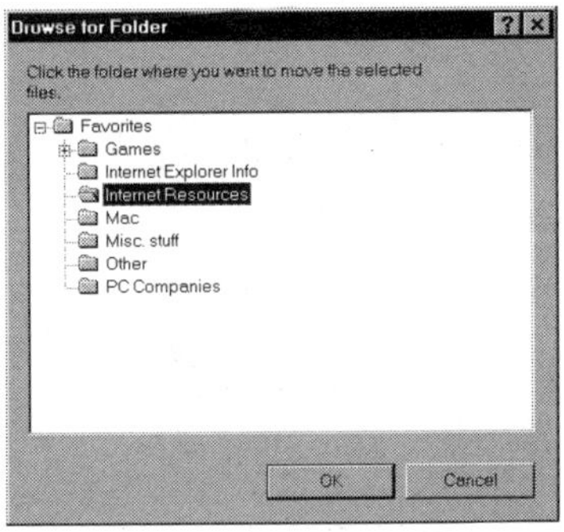

Figure 3.10 *Select a destination folder for the selected favorite in the Browse for Folder dialog box.*

To rename a favorite or folder:

1. Choose Organize Favorites from the Favorites menu. The Organize Favorites dialog box appears, as shown previously in **Figure 3.9**.
2. Select the favorite or folder that you want to rename.
3. Click the Rename button.
4. Edit the favorite's name.
5. To accept the new name, press Enter, press Return, or click the Close button.

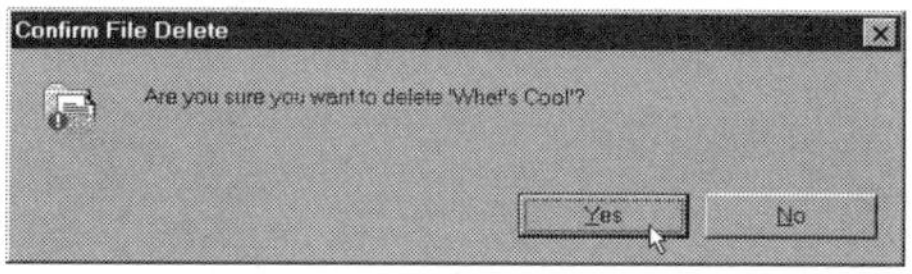

Figure 3.11 *All deletions (whether of a single favorite or an entire folder) must normally be confirmed. However, if you change the Recycle Bin properties so that "Display delete confirmation dialog box" is unchecked, all files and folders—including favorites—move directly into the Recycle Bin without displaying this dialog box.*

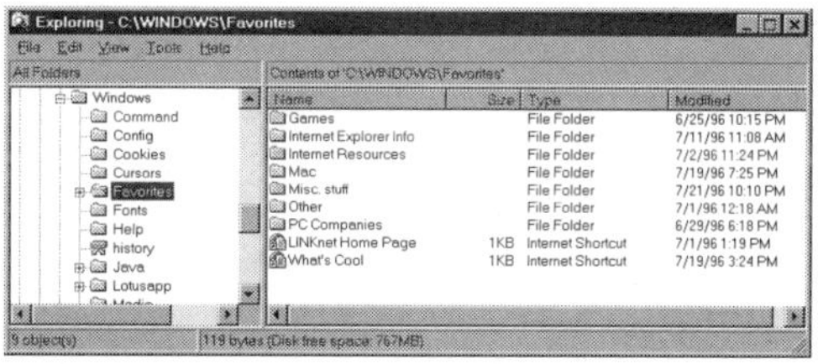

Figure 3.12 *You also can use Windows Explorer to move, rename, and delete favorites, as well as add new folders. The Favorites folder is located inside the Windows folder.*

To delete a favorite or folder:

1. Choose Organize Favorites from the Favorites menu. The Organize Favorites dialog box appears, as shown previously in **Figure 3.9**.
2. Select the favorite or folder that you want to delete.
3. Click the Delete button or press Del. The Confirm File Delete dialog box appears, as shown in **Figure 3.11**.
4. Click the Yes button to confirm the deletion, or click No to cancel.

✔ Tip

- Because each favorite is an actual file and the favorite folders are real folders, you can also manipulate favorites and folders with Windows Explorer (see **Figure 3.12**). For example, you can easily move favorites from one folder to another, create new folders, and rename or delete favorites.

Defining Quick Links

If you examine the third row of the toolbar (see **Figure 3.13**), you'll note a row of buttons. Click any Quick Link button to visit the Web page that it represents. Although Quick Links are initially linked to Microsoft Web pages, you can replace them with links of your own.

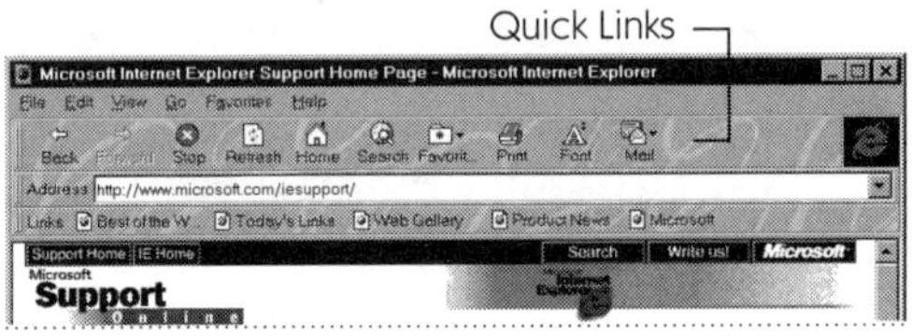

Figure 3.13 *Internet Explorer provides five Quick Link buttons in the toolbar that you can replace with your favorite Web pages.*

To replace a Quick Link:

1. Go to the Web page that you want to make into a Quick Link.

   or

1. Note the URL for the Web page.
2. Choose Options from the View menu. The Options dialog box appears.
3. Click the Navigation tab (see Figure **3.14**).
4. Pull down the Page menu, and select the number of the Quick Link (1–5) to be replaced.
5. To use the current Web page as the new Quick Link, click the Use Current button.

   or

5. Type the URL of the Web page into the Address box.
6. Click OK.

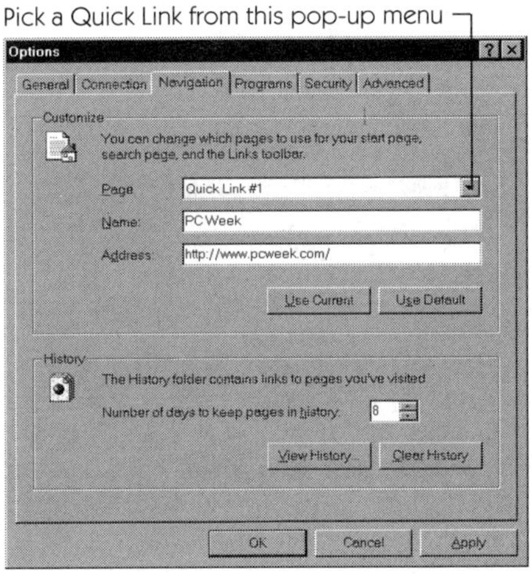

Figure 3.14 *Use the Options dialog box to create new Quick Links.*

✔ Tip

- To restore a Quick Link to its default setting, select it (as described in Step 4), and then click Use Default.

Going to a Favorite Page

There are several ways to go to a favorite Web page. After launching Internet Explorer, you can do any of the following:

- Choose the Web page from the Favorites menu.
- Click the Favorites button (see **Figure 3.15**) to reveal a copy of the Favorites menu, and then choose the Web page.
- Choose Organize Favorites from the Favorites menu, select a favorite, and then click Open.
- If there is a desktop shortcut for a favorite (as described on page 25), double-click the shortcut.
- If you have replaced any of the Quick Link icons with ones for your own favorite pages, click the appropriate icon to go to the page that it represents.

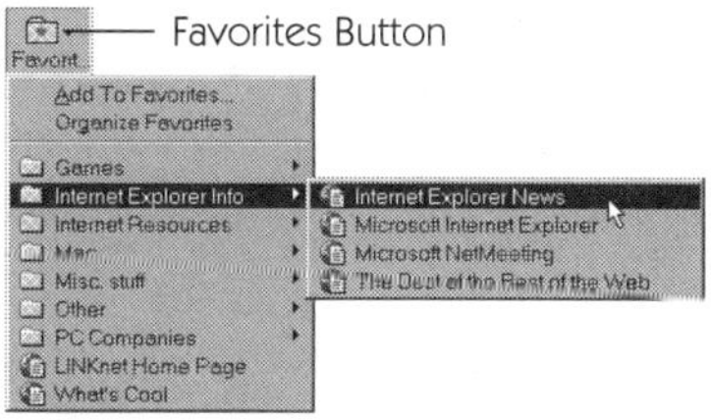

Figure 3.15 *A copy of the Favorites menu appears when you click Favorites.*

✔ **Tip**

- The same folders and commands appear regardless of whether you pull down the Favorites menu or click the Favorites button. When selecting or modifying favorites, use whichever method is most convenient.

4

Searching the Web

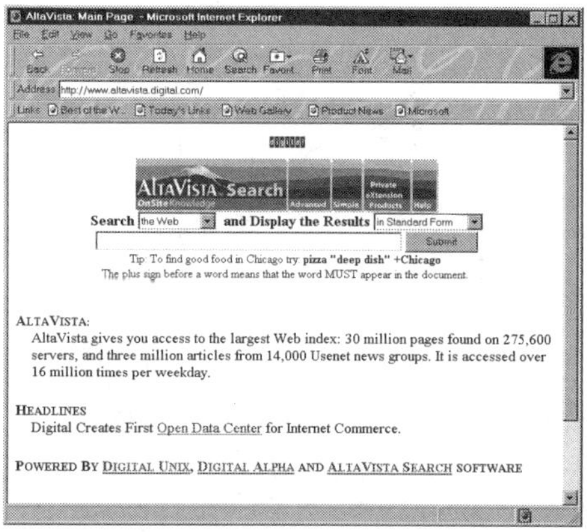

Figure 4.1 *Sponsored by Digital Equipment Corporation, AltaVista is one of the most powerful search sites on the Web.*

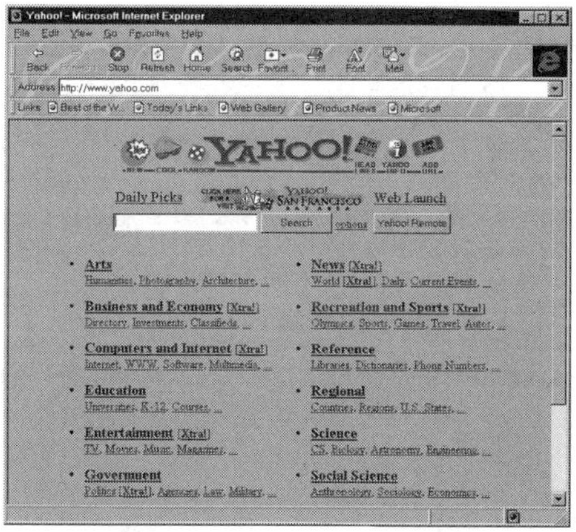

Figure 4.2 *In Yahoo!, you can browse the Web by just clicking categories that interest you.*

About Searching

Jumping from one known Web site to another is easy. You can click on links, type URLs, or select favorite sites from the Favorites menu. But what do you do when you don't know the name of a particular Web site or have no idea where some information can be found?

Unlike highly-organized services such as America Online and CompuServe, the Internet is a disorganized array of information distributed across millions of computers. No group is responsible for organizing the content of the Internet. If you want to learn something about butterflies, for example, it's up to you to find the relevant sites.

To impart some order to this data mish-mash, some sites are dedicated to the task of searching the Web—providing the equivalent of an electronic card catalog system. By entering keywords and phrases, you can use a search site to find information on almost any topic imaginable. **Figures 4.1** and **4.2** show two of the most popular search sites: AltaVista and Yahoo!

Internet Explorer helps you search for information in three ways:

- You can set a preferred search site, such as AltaVista or Yahoo!
- You can perform an AutoSearch by typing keywords into the Address box.
- You can search for keywords within any Web page.

Selecting a Main Search Site

Your preferred search site appears whenever you click the Search button (see **Figure 4.3**) or choose Search the Web from the Go menu.

Figure 4.3 *Click Search to go to your default search site.*

To set a preferred search site:

1. Choose Options from the View menu. The Options dialog box appears.
2. Click the Navigation tab, as shown in **Figure 4.4**.
3. Choose Search Page from the Page pop-up menu.
4. If the current Web page is the desired search site, click Use Current. (Change to the desired search site prior to Step 1.)

   or

4. If you know the URL of the site (http://lycos.cs.cmu.edu/, for example), you can type it into the Address box.

   or

4. To select Microsoft's search site (see **Figure 4.5**), click Use Default.
5. Click OK to record your changes and close the dialog box; click Apply if you want to make other changes; or click Cancel to close the dialog box without recording your changes.

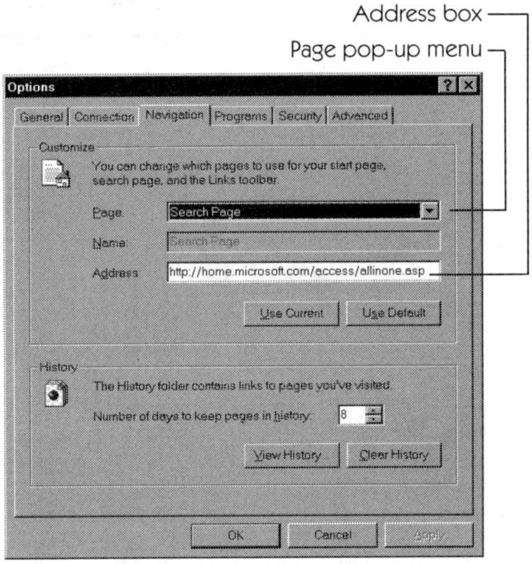

Figure 4.4 *To set a default search site, open the Options dialog box and click the Navigation tab. You can also use this section of the dialog box to set a home (start-up) page and Quick Links.*

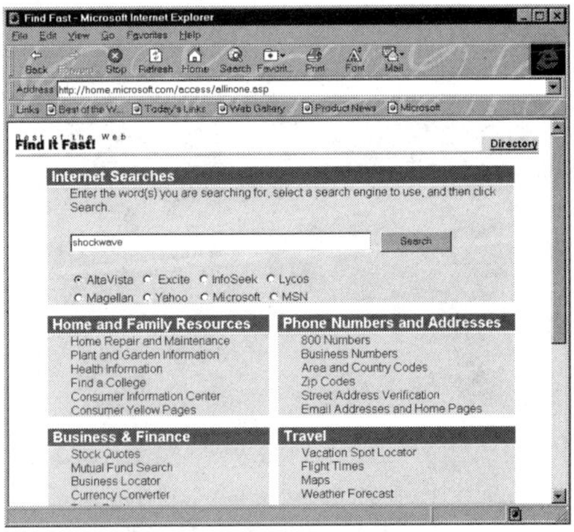

Figure 4.5 *If you want access to several search engines, click Use Default in the Options dialog box (see Figure 4.4) to choose Microsoft's Internet Searches as your preferred search site.*

✔ Tip

- As you try out different search sites, you may find others that are more powerful or easier to use. You can change your preferred site whenever you like. Add the other search sites to your Favorites list.

Table 4.1. AutoSearch Examples

Type of Search	Begin Search with...	Example
Single keyword	?	? elephant
Single keyword	Go	Go airmail
Single keyword	Find	Find baseball
Multiple keywords		Schwartz game books

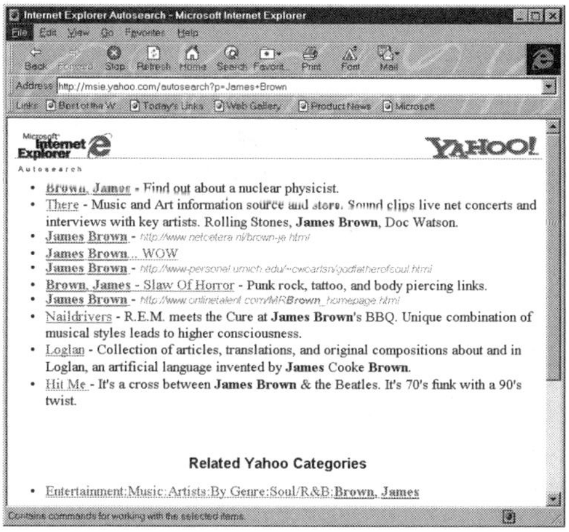

Figure 4.6 *A Microsoft Web page presents the results of each AutoSearch.*

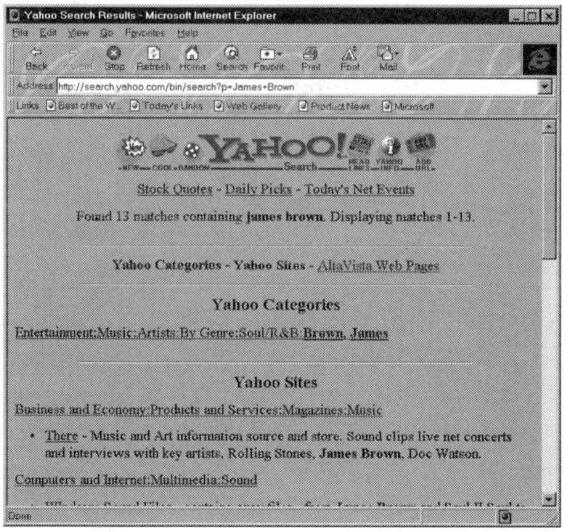

Figure 4.7 *You can view additional hits or expand the search by going to the Yahoo! Web site.*

Performing an AutoSearch

If you don't feel like summoning a search site, you can quickly perform a Web search by typing search terms directly into the Address box of the browser window. The procedure varies depending on whether you are searching for one or several keywords (see **Table 4.1**).

To search for a single keyword:

1. In the Address box, type ?, Spacebar, and the keyword.

or

1. In the Address box, type the word *Go*, Spacebar, and the keyword.

or

1. In the Address box, type the word *Find*, Spacebar, and the keyword.
2. Press Return or Enter to execute the search.

To search for multiple keywords:

1. In the Address box, type the keywords, separated by spaces.
2. Press Return or Enter to execute the search.

After executing the search, a new Web page appears and displays the hits, if any (see **Figure 4.6**). Click any hypertext link to go to the chosen page.

✔ Tip

- If you'd like to expand the search, click the Search Yahoo! button at the bottom of the page. You'll be taken to Yahoo! and shown any additional hits (see **Figure 4.7**).

Searching for Information within a Web Page

In addition to giving you quick access to your favorite search site (via the Search button), Internet Explorer also enables you to search for text in the current Web page—in much the same way as using a word processor's Find command.

To search within a Web page:

1. Choose Find (on this page) from the Edit menu. The Find dialog box appears (see **Figure 4.8**).
2. Enter the search string in the Find box.
3. *Optional:* To start the search from the top of the current Web page, click the check box for Start from top of page.
4. *Optional:* Click the Match Case check box to restrict matches to those with the same case as that of the search string.
5. Click Find Next to begin the search. If a match is found, Internet Explorer scrolls to display it (see **Figure 4.9**).
6. Click Find Next to continue searching, or click the Cancel button to dismiss the dialog box.

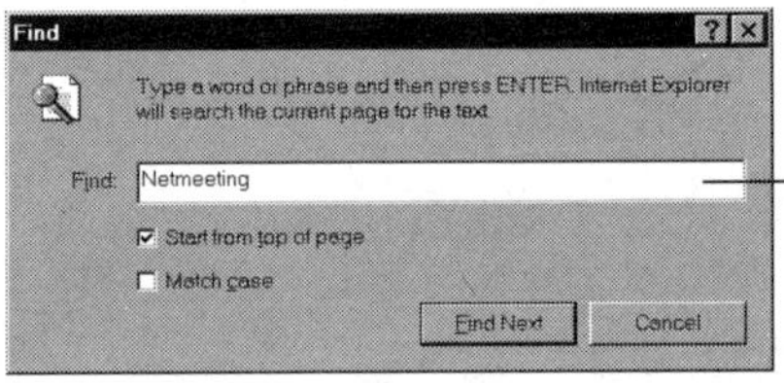

Figure 4.8 *Use the Find dialog box to search for information on the current Web page.*

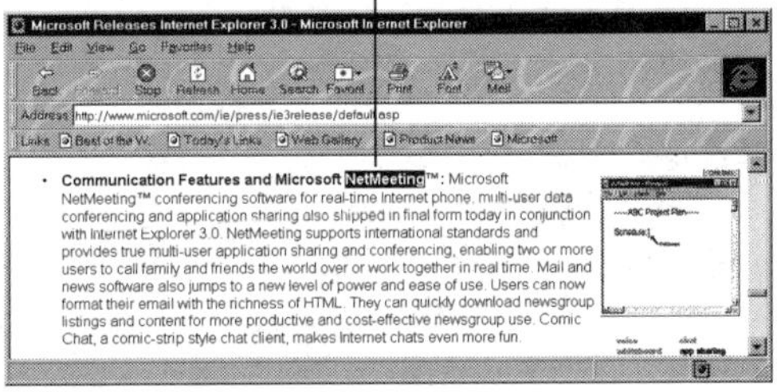

Figure 4.9 *If a match is found, Internet Explorer automatically scrolls to display the matching text.*

✔ **Tip**

■ The Find command can be very useful immediately after using a search site to locate a relevant Web page. Use Find to search for the same text string so you can quickly jump to the first instance of the text.

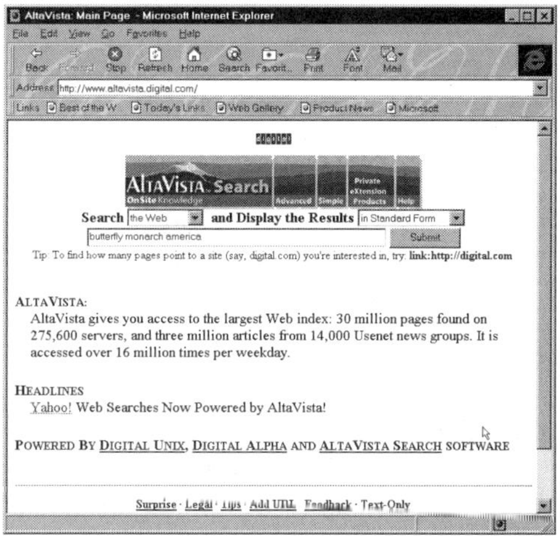

Figure 4.10 *To conduct a simple search, type keywords into the text box near the top of the page, and then click the Submit button.*

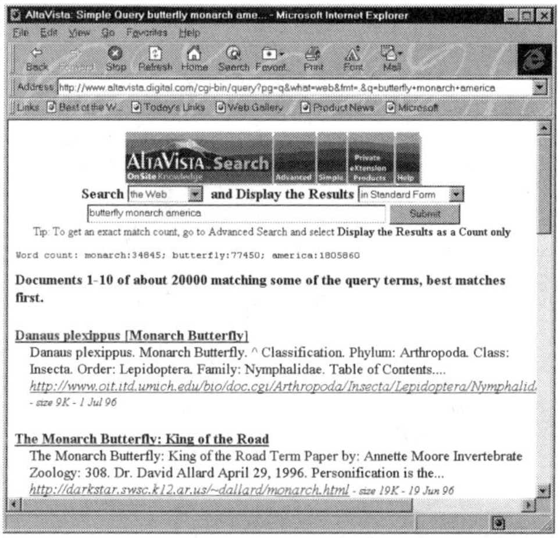

Figure 4.11 *Matches for the query are displayed as hypertext links. Click any link to go to the site described. (Other pages of matches may also be available. Click the numbers at the bottom of the page to view these matches.)*

Search Procedures

To give you a better idea of how to perform a search, I'll show you how it's done in AltaVista.

- *Type a list of keywords that you want to find. Separate keywords with spaces.*

  Entering *butterfly*, *monarch*, and *america* as keywords will present a list of hypertext links, as shown in **Figures 4.10** and **4.11**. The best matches—those that contain as many terms as possible—are listed first. (If you enter keywords in lowercase, it instructs AltaVista to ignore case when searching.)

- *To treat words as a phrase, enclose them in quotes.*

  When searching for a person's name, for example, you'll have better luck using *"Bob Smith"* than entering the name as separate keywords (i.e., *Bob Smith*). The former will find only Bob Smith, while the latter will identify all Bobs and all Smiths.

- *Search words can be required or prohibited.*

  To require a word, precede it with a plus (+) symbol; to prohibit it, precede it with a minus (-) symbol. For example, +*"Steve Schwartz"* -*music* will find links for Steve Schwartz, while omitting those for the composer by that name.

- *Use an asterisk as a wild card to identify variants of a word.*

  For example, enter *iron** to find iron, ironed, ironing, and ironclad.

Tips for Productive Searches

Following are some general strategies for improving the productivity of your searches.

- *Try, try again.*

  No search site covers all the information on the Internet. Each one can only find matches within the information stored in its index. If you can't find what you're looking for at a particular search site, try another one. As an alternative, you may want to use a search page that employs multiple search engines (see **Figure 4.12**).

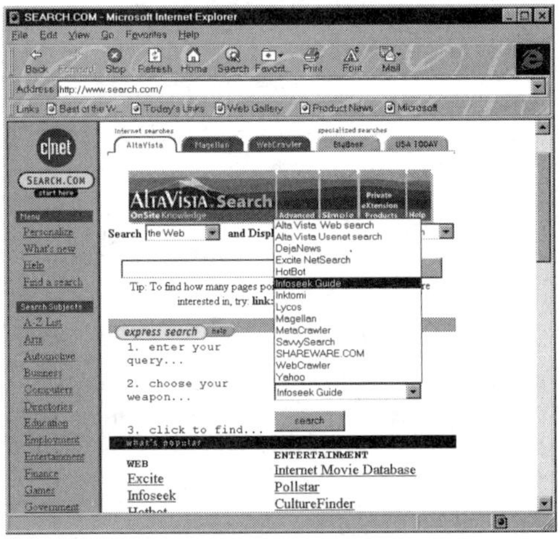

Figure 4.12 *A part of c|net, Search.com lets you execute searches using the search engines of other sites.*

- *Read the search instructions for the site.*

  Search procedures can vary dramatically from one site to the next. For example, although all search tools allow you to enter a single keyword, there are often special procedures for entering multiple words. Words may have to be typed in different boxes, separated by the words OR or AND, or enclosed in quotation marks. By phrasing your search in the correct manner, you have a greater likelihood of finding what you want (see **Figure 4.13**).

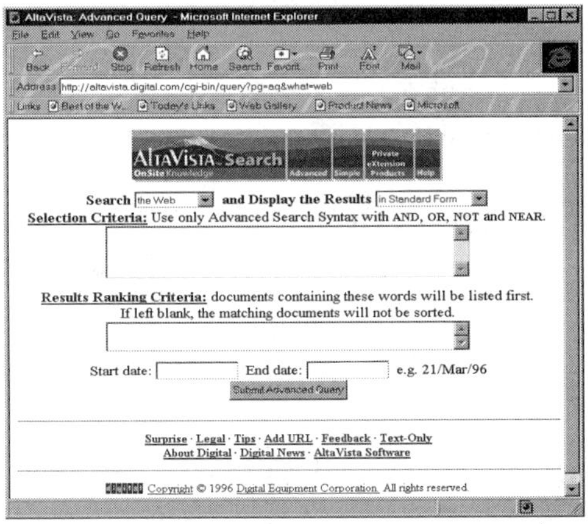

Figure 4.13 *In AltaVista, advanced searches can also be constructed. Click the Advanced icon at the top of the page to create such a search request.*

- *Be as specific as possible, but not too specific.*

  Most search tools are capable of performing *fuzzy searches* (finding matches that are close to the search terms). This means that searching for Steve Schwartz will also yield hits for Steven, Stephen, and S. Schwartz. Usually, the closest matches are listed first.

Figure 4.14 *You can't send a message if you don't know the recipient's e-mail address. WhoWhere? may be able to help.*

- *Use the appropriate search tool.*

  Search sites frequently specialize in the types of information that they cover (see **Table 4.2**). For example, areas of specialization may include Web pages; Usenet newsgroups; names, addresses, and phone numbers; and e-mail addresses (see **Figure 4.14**). Regardless of which search site you set as your default (see page 32), you'll probably want to use other search tools now and then.

✔ **Tip**

- If your *ISP* (Internet Service Provider) doesn't offer newsgroups, you can search for their names in AltaVista and then read the most recent articles. (Be sure to choose Usenet from the Search menu.)

Table 4.2. Web Search Sites

Site Name	Specialization	URL
AltaVista	Web and newsgroups	www.altavista.digital.com
InfoSeek	Web, newsgroups, e-mail addresses, category searches	guide-p.infoseek.com
Lycos	Web and category searches	lycos.cs.cmu.edu
Internet Searches	Multiple search engines	home.microsoft.com/access/allinone.asp
PeopleFind	Addresses and phone numbers	www.lycos.com/pplfndr.html
Search.com	Multiple search engines	www.search.com
WebCrawler	Web and category searches	webcrawler.com
WhoWhere?	Addresses, phone numbers, e-mail addresses, personal Web pages	www.whowhere.com
Yahoo!	Category searches	www.yahoo.com

Working with Files

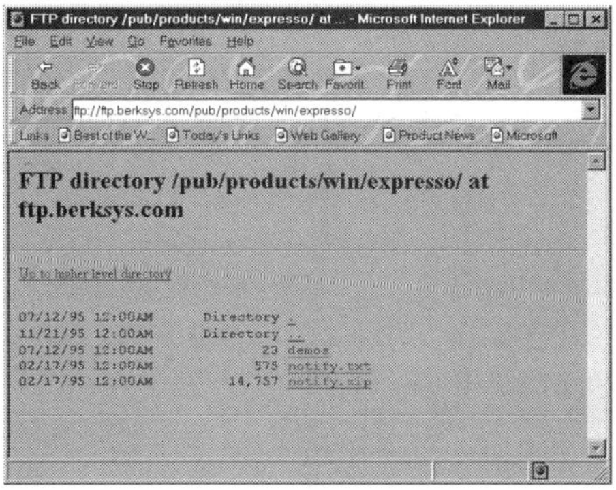

Figure 5.1 *Software and hardware companies often maintain FTP sites from which drivers, updates, demos, and templates can be downloaded. Click a directory name to move up or down a level. Click a file name to download that file.*

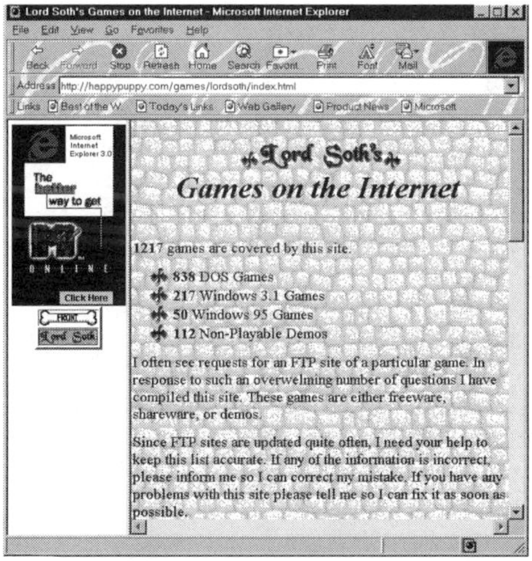

Figure 5.2 *Web pages often contain graphics. It's not unusual to find pictures, icons, and background patterns, for example. All of these elements can be saved to disk.*

About File Handling

One of the great things about using Internet Explorer is that you aren't restricted to just *looking* at the World Wide Web. You can also use a browser to accomplish the following file-related activities:

- Download files, such as drivers for computer equipment, program updates, templates, documentation, demos, shareware, and freeware (see **Figure 5.1**).
- Save the current Web page as a text or HTML file, and copy selected text from a Web page.
- Save any graphic image on a Web page as a file or as Windows wallpaper (see **Figure 5.2**).
- Save any background image from a Web page as a graphics file.
- Save audio and video files found on the Web.
- Open files from your own hard disk, such as HTML documents and graphics.

You can accomplish all of these file-handling activities by clicking links, choosing commands from the File menu, or right-clicking elements on the Web page.

Downloading Files

Downloading a file from the Internet is simple. Web and FTP sites often contain hypertext links or buttons you can click to download files. The only decision you must make is whether to save the file on disk or—in the case of an executable file—to open it at once.

The following example shows how to download Comic Chat (an *Internet Relay Chat client*) from Microsoft's Web site.

To download a file:

1. Go to the Web page or FTP site that contains the file you want to download.
2. Click the hypertext or graphic link for the file (see **Figure 5.3**). The download begins (see **Figure 5.4**).
3. The dialog box shown in **Figure 5.5** now appears. To save the file, click the Save it to disk radio button. To immediately launch the file (extracting its contents, in the case of an archive), click Open it.
4. If you are saving the file, **Figure 5.6** appears. Select a location on disk for the new file.

   The download continues. The File Download dialog box (see **Figure 5.7**) lets you track its progress.

   When the download finishes, the file is saved to disk or opened (depending on the option chosen in Step 3).

Click any link to download the file

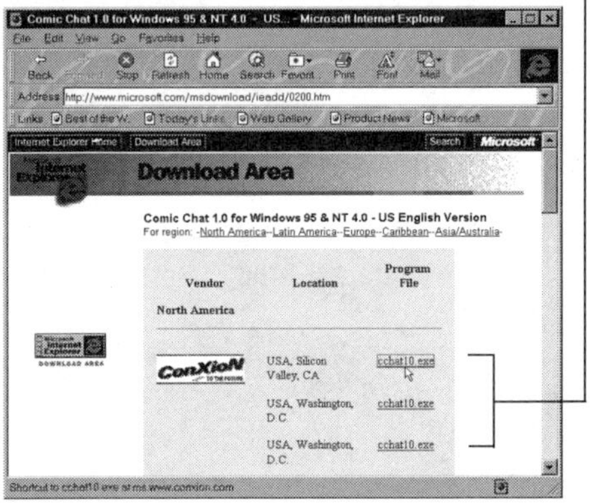

Figure 5.3 *To initiate a download, click a hypertext link or button (depending on what the page provides).*

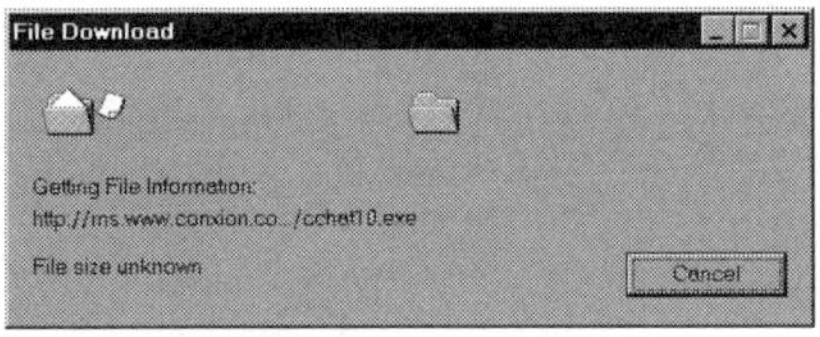

Figure 5.4 *The download process starts by retrieving information about the file.*

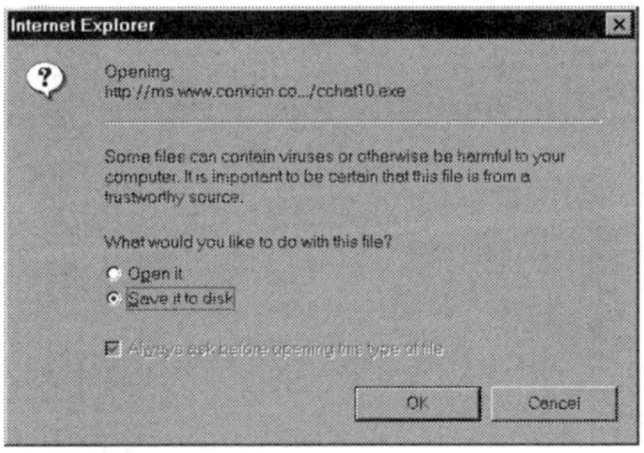

Figure 5.5 *Decide whether you want to open the file the moment it is received or save it to disk.*

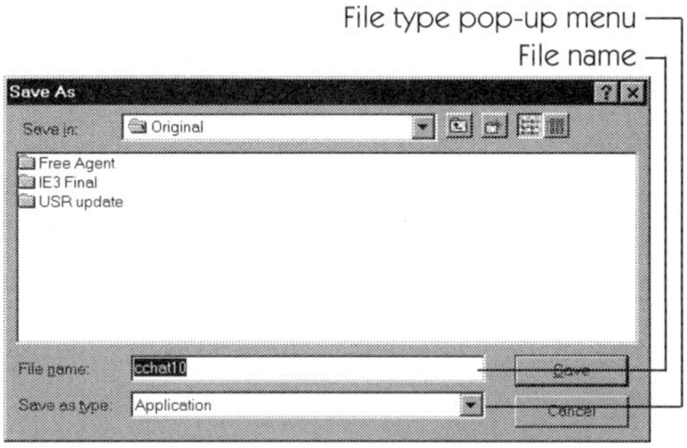

Figure 5.6 *When using the "Save it to disk" option for a downloaded file, you must choose a location on disk in which to save.*

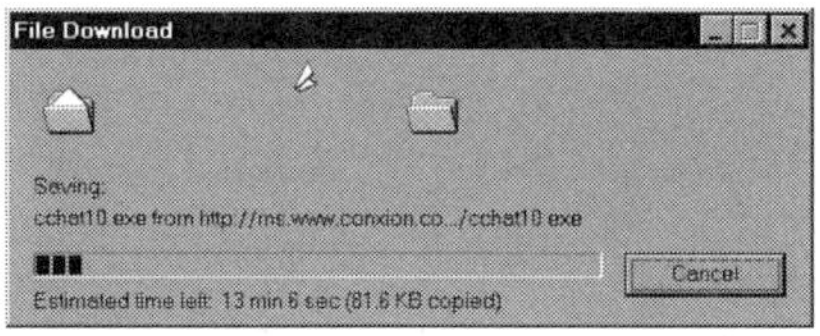

Figure 5.7 *As the download proceeds, you can track its progress. Watch the bar as it fills.*

✓ Tips

- You can download any file directly to disk by right-clicking its link and choosing Save Target As from the pop-up menu that appears. See "Saving Multimedia Files," later in this chapter, for instructions.
- Not all downloads are automatically saved to disk or launched. Some text files, for example, are displayed by Internet Explorer as Web pages. You can save the current page by choosing Save As File from the File menu.
- You can also download a file from an FTP site by typing the file's URL in the Address box, such as:

  `ftp.aznet.com/pub/test.exe`
- You can halt a download at any time by clicking the Cancel button in the File Download dialog box (refer to **Figure 5.7**).
- The amount of time that a download takes is directly affected by the amount of network traffic. If it seems to be taking much too long, try again at a different time of day. You may also find that the same file downloads faster from another site. In general, when you are offered a choice of download sites, choose the one closest to you.
- Some download attempts will be met with an error message of one sort or another. Don't give up too quickly. Not all errors are meaningful. It's often worth a second (or third) try.

Saving Files

By following the procedures in this section, you can save entire Web pages, graphics embedded in pages, graphic backgrounds, and multimedia files.

Saving a Web Page

You can save the current Web page in HTML or text format, depending on what you want to do with the file.

- If you intend to open the file in a browser or want to examine the code used to construct the page, save the page in HTML format.
- If you're only interested in the page's text (i.e., what the file *says*), save it in plain text format.

To save a Web page:

1. Display the page that you want to save.
2. Choose Save As File from the File menu. The Save As dialog box appears, as shown previously in **Figure 5.6**.
3. Enter a name for the file in the File name box.
4. Select a type for the file from the Save as type pop-up menu.
5. Click Save.

✔ Tips

- Another way to examine a page's HTML code is to choose Source from the View menu. The code is displayed in Notepad (see **Figure 5.8**), where it can be examined, edited, and saved.

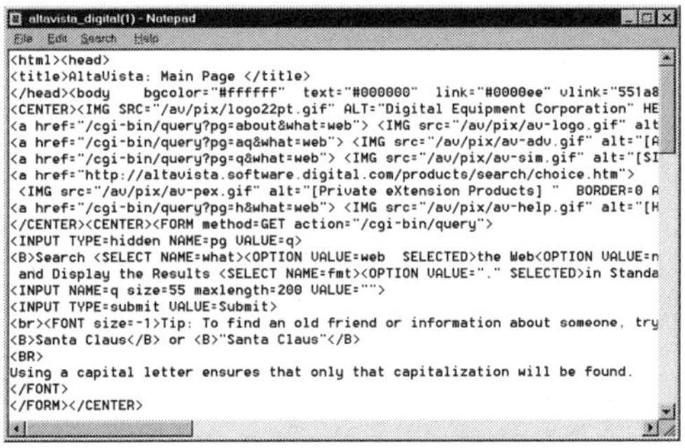

Figure 5.8 *You can also use the Source command to view the HTML code that was used to generate a Web page.*

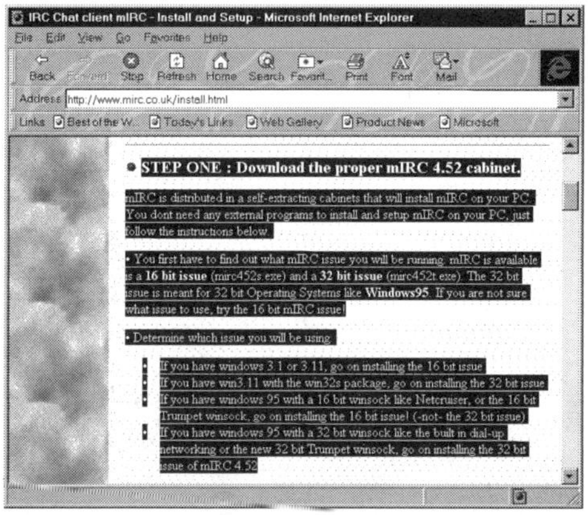

Figure 5.9 *You can select and copy any text that is on a Web page.*

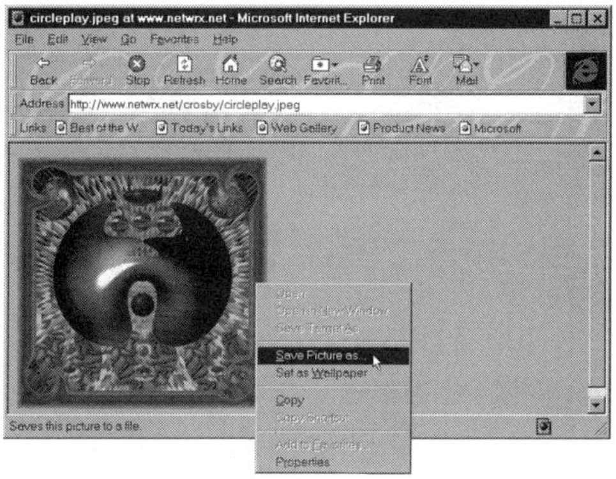

Figure 5.10 *Choose Save Picture as to save the selected element as a file.*

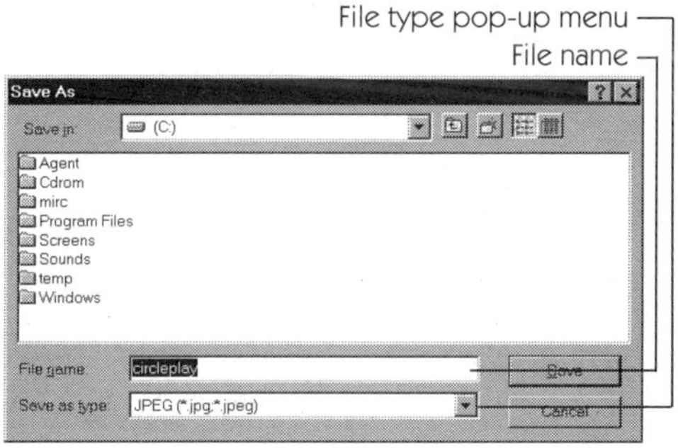

Figure 5.11 *Name and select a file type for the item.*

- Only the text portion of a Web page is saved. Graphics, such as pictures and buttons, are not saved. If you want to duplicate a Web page (including graphics), save the page in HTML format. Then save every graphic item on the page into the same folder as the HTML file.
- To save only selected text from a page (see **Figure 5.9**), highlight the text, choose Copy from the Edit menu, and then paste it into a Notepad or WordPad document.

Saving a Page Element

Any graphic element—a picture, icon, or advertisement, for example—can be saved on disk.

To save a page element:

1. Right-click the page element that you want to save. The pop-up menu in **Figure 5.10** appears.
2. Choose Save Picture as from the pop-up menu. The Save As dialog box in **Figure 5.11** appears.
3. *Optional:* The name proposed for the file is the name that the Web page creator assigned to it. You can rename the file, if you wish.
4. Select a file type from the pop-up menu at the right end of the Save as type box.
5. Click Save.

✔ Tips

- You can also copy a page element to the clipboard by choosing Copy from the pop-up menu. The item is then available for pasting into other documents.

■ If you right-click a hypertext or graphic link to another Web page or a link for downloading a file, a new choice appears on the pop-up menu: Save Target As. Choose this command to save a link as an HTML file or to download a file.

This command is especially useful when you want to capture a Web page and view it later—when you are off-line, for example. Note, however, that when saved in this manner, an HTML file will not display graphics unless they have been saved and stored in the same directory as the HTML file.

Saving a Graphic as Wallpaper

There are many eye-catching images on the Web. If you find one that really appeals to you, it's easy to capture and use it as your desktop wallpaper.

To save an element as wallpaper:

1. Right-click the page element that you want to use as wallpaper. The pop-up menu shown previously in **Figure 5.10** appears.
2. Choose Set as Wallpaper from the pop-up menu. The image is saved as Internet Explorer Wallpaper and becomes the current wallpaper (see **Figures 5.12** and **5.13**).

✔ Tips

■ You don't have to be connected to a Web site when saving an image as wallpaper. You can use Internet Explorer's Open command to view previously saved JPEG and GIF files, and then save them as wallpaper.

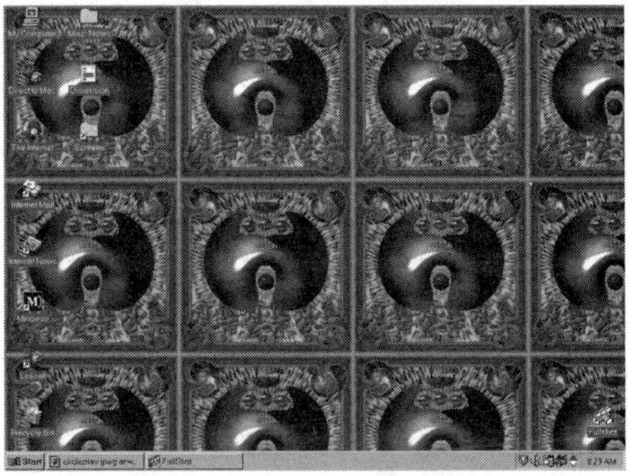

Figure 5.12 *You can convert many of the images on the Web into interesting wallpaper.*

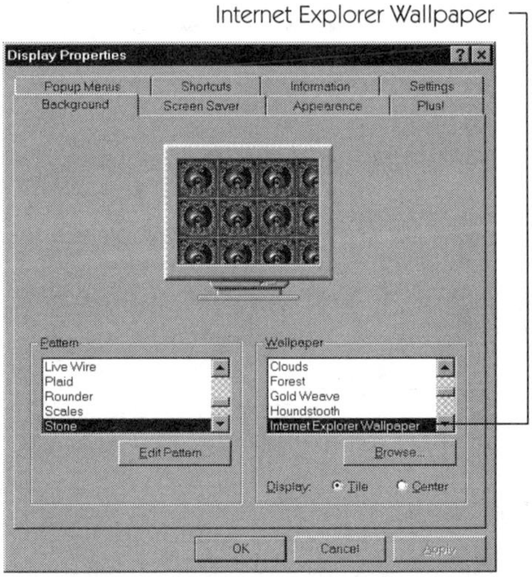

Figure 5.13 *When set as wallpaper, a Web graphic is named Internet Explorer Wallpaper. If you later replace the wallpaper with a new Web graphic, the old Internet Explorer Wallpaper is overwritten.*

- Even if you didn't save a particular image when you were on-line, there is a good chance that you can find it in the Temporary Internet Files folder. To use such a JPEG or GIF file as wallpaper, copy the file to another directory, open it in Internet Explorer, and then follow the procedure described earlier in this chapter ("To save an element as wallpaper").

Saving a Page Background

Many Web pages have decorative backgrounds. If you'd like to examine a background more closely or use it in your own page, you can save it as a graphic file.

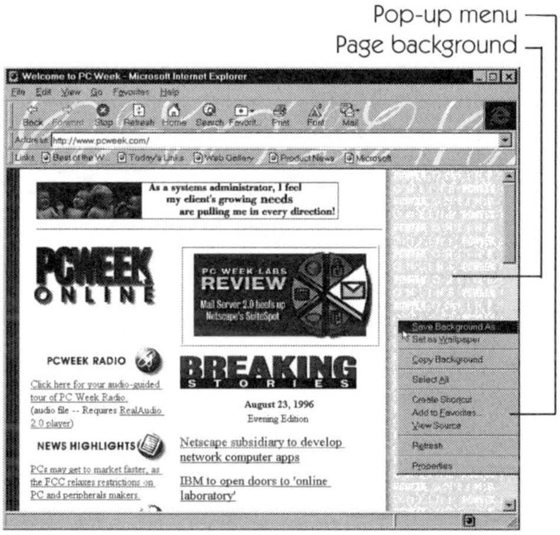

Figure 5.14 *To save a page background, right-click it to make this pop-up menu appear.*

To save a background graphic:

1. Right-click the background, and choose Save Background As from the pop-up menu that appears (see **Figure 5.14**). The Save As dialog box appears.
2. Choose a name, location, and type for the file.
3. Click Save.

✔ Tip

- You can copy a background to the clipboard by choosing Copy Background from the pop-up menu. After it has been copied, the background is available for pasting into other documents.

Saving Multimedia Files

You can save multimedia files directly to disk, or you can open and play them with the ActiveMovie control (see Figure 5.15).

Figure 5.15 When downloading or playing a movie file, an ActiveMovie control window appears.

To download a multimedia item directly to disk:

1. Right-click the hypertext or graphic link for the item. A pop-up menu appears (see Figure 5.16).
2. Choose Save Target As. The Save As dialog box appears.
3. Choose a name, location, and type for the file.
4. Click Save. When the download completes, the file is saved as directed.

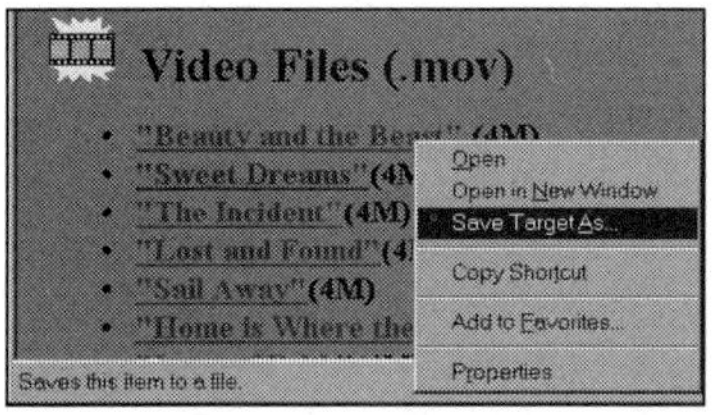

Figure 5.16 To download a file directly to disk (without opening or running it), right-click the file's link and choose Save Target As.

Although downloading an item to disk is the easiest way to save multimedia files, most users don't decide to save an item until after they have listened to or viewed it. The more common procedure is to open the item by clicking the link, listen to or view it, and then save it.

To save a previously opened multimedia item:

1. Open the Temporary Internet Files directory (normally found within the Windows directory).
2. Locate the multimedia file.
3. Copy the file to another disk or directory.

Opening Files

In Internet Explorer, you can open and display many of the files on your hard disk, including these types:

- Text (TXT) and HTML files
- Graphics (JPEG and GIF)
- Sounds (WAV, AU, and AIFF)
- Movies (AVI, MPEG, and MOV)

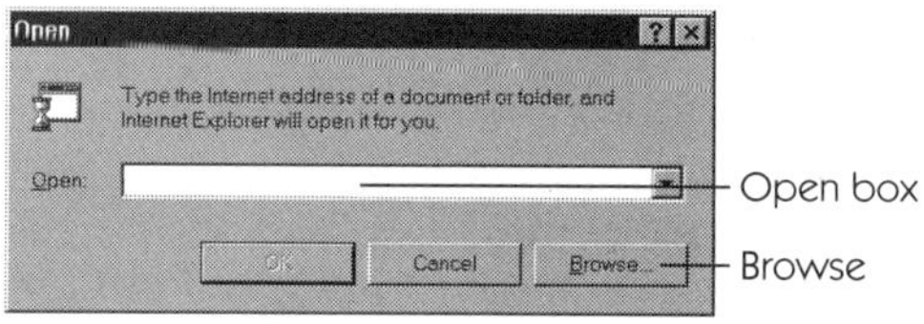

Figure 5.17 *You can open a file by typing its path in the Open box or by using the Browse button to manually find the file.*

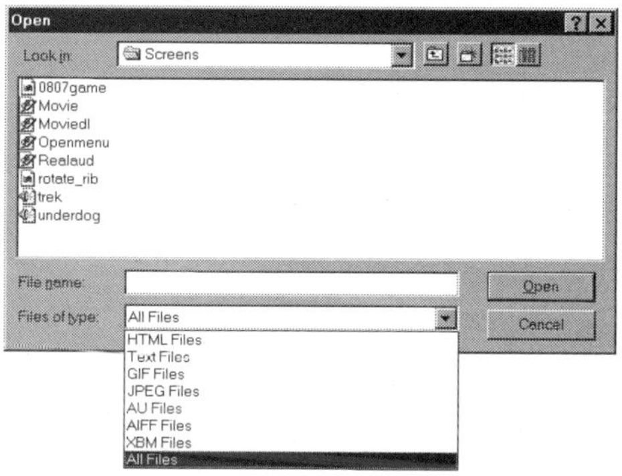

Figure 5.18 *To make it easier to find a file, you can specify which file types are included in the file list.*

To open a file from disk:

1. Choose Open from the File menu (or press Control O). The Open dialog box appears (see **Figure 5.17**).
2. In the Open box, type the path of the file you want to open (for example, *C:\Screens\Ball.jpg*).

   or

2. Click Browse. The Open dialog box expands to show the drives, directories, and files for your system, as shown in **Figure 5.18.** Navigate to the appropriate drive and directory, select a file, and click Open.
3. Click OK.

   Depending on the file type, the file is either displayed in the browser, opened in an ActiveMovie control window (refer to **Figure 5.15**), or opened by another program, such as WordPad or Paint.

✔ **Tip**

- If you double-click any type of file that is associated with Internet Explorer, the file is automatically opened in the browser.

  To see a list of the file associations, choose Options from the View menu, click the Programs tab at the top of the Options dialog box, and then click the File Types button (see **Figure 5.19**). If you'd like to associate a particular file type with a different program (linking JPEG files with a graphics viewer, for example), refer to "File icons, associating with programs" in Windows Help.

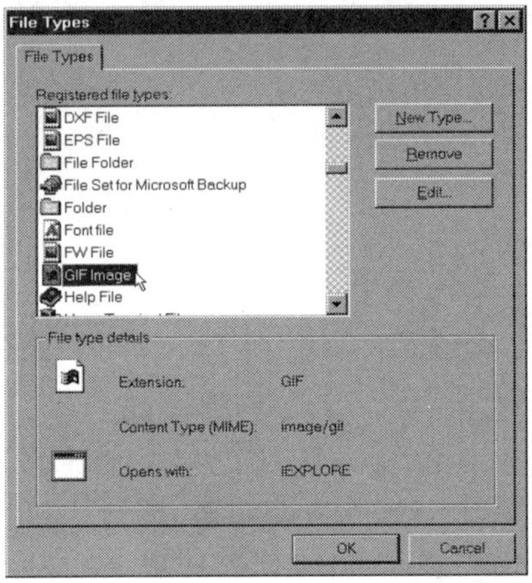

Figure 5.19 *You set file associations in the File Types dialog box. To view any current setting, select a file type from the scrolling list.*

6 Printing

About Printing

Although you can save a Web page as a text or HTML file (the latter option saves the code needed to re-create the page in a browser), you'll note that only the text portion of the document is actually saved. If you also want to see any graphics that are on the page, you must save them separately.

Printing a Web page, on the other hand, uses *everything* on the page—text and graphics. When dealing with Web pages that include graphics, the most convenient way to make a permanent record of the page is to print it.

Print options in Internet Explorer 3.0 are somewhat limited. You can only print a single Web page at a time—the one you're viewing. If you want to print several pages (all pages in a site, for example), you must visit and then issue the Print command for each page.

Future versions of Internet Explorer will have new printing capabilities, such as the following:

- *Drag-and-drop printing.* Drag a URL onto your printer icon to print the Web page.
- *Selective printing.* Print only the currently selected text from a page.
- *Recursive printing.* Print the current page, plus all pages to which the page links.

Installing a Printer

When printing Web pages, Internet Explorer uses the printer drivers you have installed for Windows 95. If you have not installed a driver for your printer, you can do so by following these steps:

To install a printer driver:

1. Open the Printers control panel and double-click the Add a Printer icon (shown in **Figure 6.1**). The Add Printer Wizard appears.
2. Click the Next button. The dialog box lists the supported printer manufacturers and models (see **Figure 6.2**).
3. Select the manufacturer and model of your printer.
4. *Optional:* If your printer came with its own driver, click Have Disk, and then indicate where the driver can be found, as shown in **Figure 6.3**.
5. Click Next to view the list of communications ports on your computer (see **Figure 6.4**).
6. Select the port to which your printer is connected. For a parallel printer, the correct choice is usually LPT1. Serial printers are connected to COM ports.
7. *Optional:* Click Configure Port to see how the port is configured or to change its settings.
8. Click Next. The dialog box shown in **Figure 6.5** appears.
9. Accept the proposed printer name or enter a different name.

Figure 6.1 *When you open the Printers control panel, you'll see an icon for every printer that is installed.*

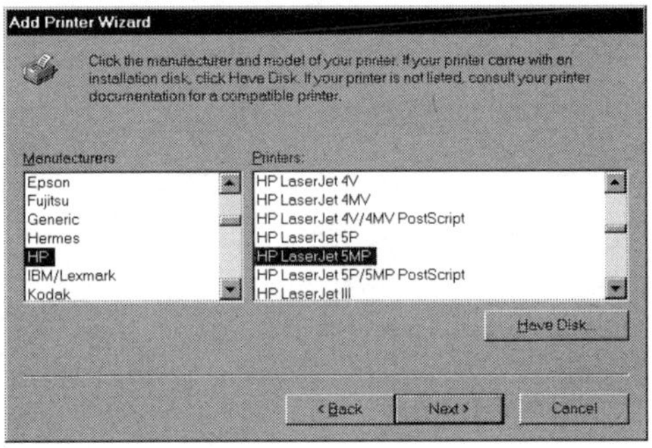

Figure 6.2 *Choose the manufacturer and model of your printer in the Add Printer Wizard dialog box.*

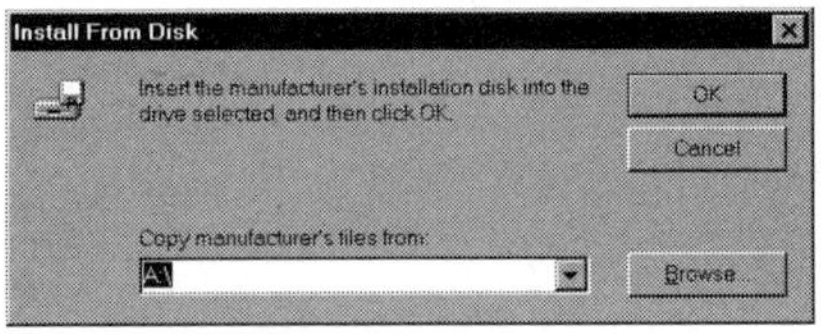

Figure 6.3 *To install new printer drivers from disk, you must indicate where they can be found.*

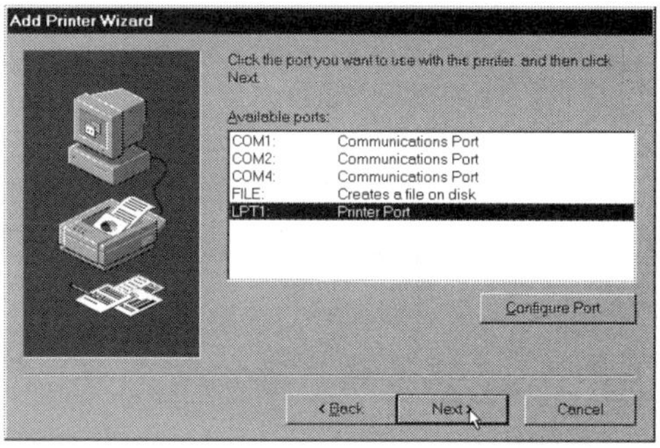

Figure 6.4 *Select the communications port to which the printer is connected.*

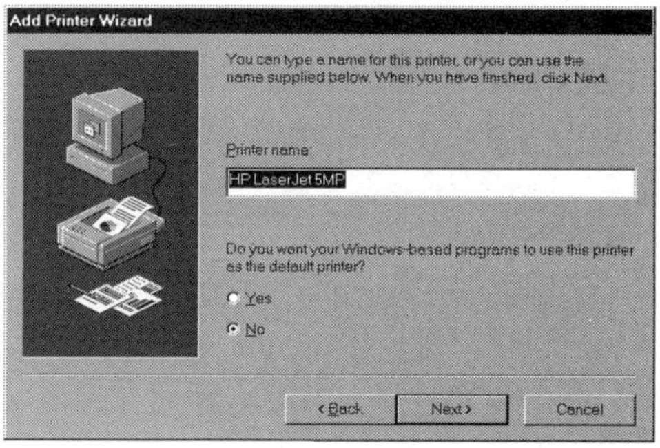

Figure 6.5 *Name the printer and decide whether it will be your default. (Unless you instruct otherwise—via Page Setup, all future print jobs will be directed to the default printer.)*

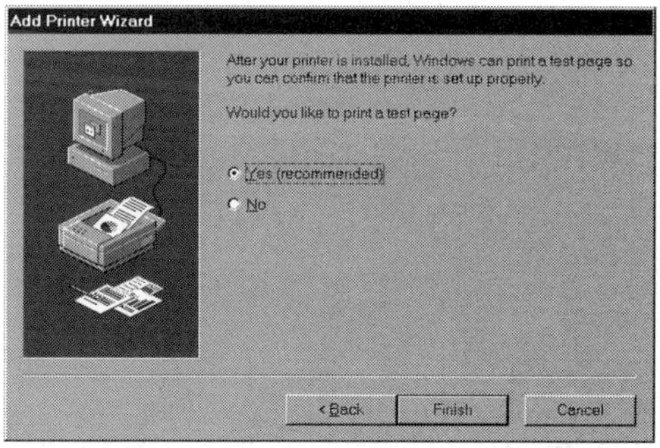

Figure 6.6 *Click Yes to print a test page prior to completing the installation.*

10. If this is your only printer or the one that you will generally use, click Yes to make it the default.
11. Click Next. The dialog box shown in **Figure 6.6** appears.
12. Click Yes to print a test page or No if you want to continue without printing a test page.
13. Click Finish. If asked, insert the requested Windows 95 disk or CD-ROM to complete the installation. After the driver has been copied to your hard disk, the print test commences.

✔ Tips

- If you intent to print documents on a printer that is not at this location (it may be in your home, for example), choose File in Step 6. When you issue the Print command from a Windows program, a print file will be created on disk rather than printing. Bring the print file to the printer's location, and then either download it to the printer with an appropriate utility or use the DOS COPY command to copy it to the printer port, as follows:

  ```
  C:> COPY a:file1.prn lpt1:
  ```

  Note: Substitute the appropriate drive letter, file name, and communications port when using this procedure.
- Any installed printer can be used for any print job. It doesn't matter which printer you've set as your default in Step 10.

Print Settings

Settings for print and paper options—such as the size, orientation, and source of the paper, as well as graphics resolution—can be set globally for all print jobs (to be used as defaults when a given printer is chosen) or individually set for each print job.

- *Default print settings* are established by selecting the printer icon in the Printers control panel and choosing Properties from the File menu (see **Figure 6.7**). These settings are automatically used for each document printed with the printer—except when overridden by document-specific settings.
- *Document-specific print settings* are set by choosing Page Setup (or Print Setup) from the File menu of any Windows program (see **Figure 6.8**). These settings apply only to the current document and—if the document is saved—are stored as part of the document.

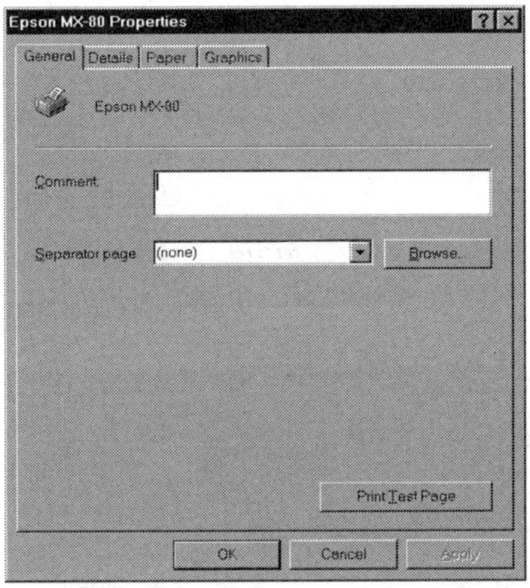

Figure 6.7 *Use the Properties dialog box to specify default options for a printer. Most users will restrict changes to the Paper and Graphics sections of this dialog box.*

✔ Tips

- Most of the Properties and Page Setup options are self-explanatory. Generally, the best way to handle the Properties options is to check them once, make any necessary changes (to reflect the way you usually print), and then forget about them.
- To set header and footer text (to print at the top and bottom of each page, respectively), click Headers/Footers in the Page Setup dialog box and refer to the option codes listed in **Table 6.1**.

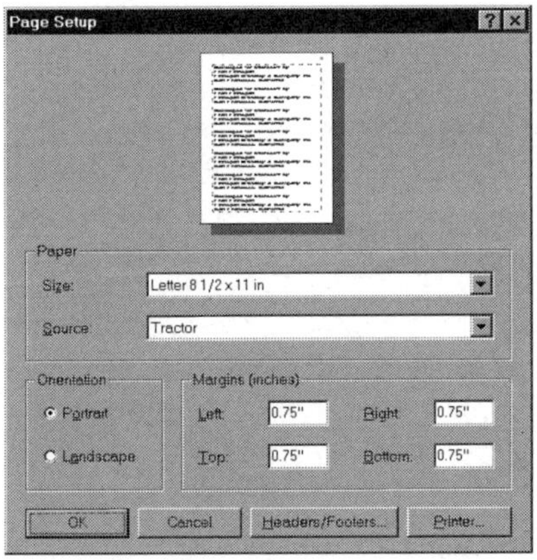

Figure 6.8 *In addition to duplicating most options in the Properties dialog box, use the Page Setup dialog box to set document-specific options, such as header/footer settings and page margins.*

Table 6.1. Header/Footer Codes

Text to Print	Code
Window title	&w
Page address (URL)	&u
Date (short format)*	&d
Date (long format)*	&D
Time[a]	&t
Time (24-hour format)	&T
Current page number	&p
Total pages in document	&P

*The appearance of some date and time formats is determined by settings in the Regional Settings control panel.

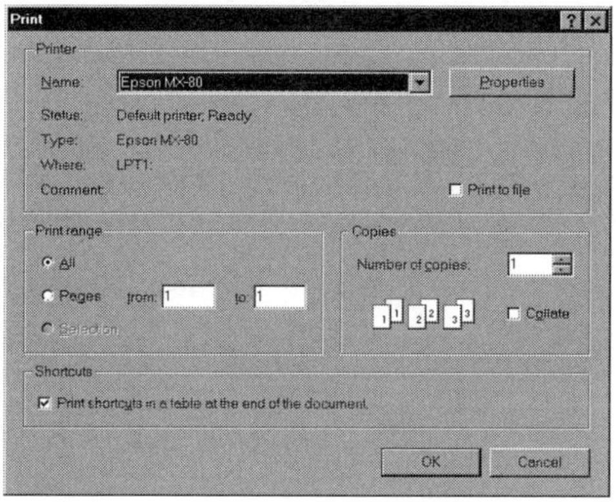

Figure 6.9 *Use the Print dialog box to specify a printer for the current job, whether to print all or only specific pages, and whether to include a table of URLs at the end of the document.*

Printing a Web Page

Following is the procedure for printing the current Web page, as well as a description of options that you can set.

To print a Web page:

1. Display the Web page that you want to print.
2. Click the Print button, choose Print from the File menu, or press Ctrl P. The Print dialog box appears (see **Figure 6.9**).
3. Select a printer to use from the list of currently installed printers.
4. *Optional:* To specify properties for this print job, such as the type and size of paper, graphics quality, and so on, click the Properties button.
5. Set a print range by clicking the All button or by entering numbers in the From and To boxes.

   Note that the From/To range refers to the number of pieces of paper to print rather than to the number of Web pages. "All" prints the entire Web page, regardless of the number of sheets of paper needed.
6. Specify the number of copies to be printed.
7. *Optional:* If you're printing several copies, you can print them in collated order by clicking the Collate check box.
8. *Optional:* To print the addresses of all hypertext and graphic links embedded in the Web page, click the Print Shortcuts check box.
9. Click OK to begin printing.

Figure 6.10 is an example of a Web page printed on a laser printer. Note the URL list at the bottom of the page.

✔ Tips

- If you just want to print a page using your default printer and standard print options, choose Print and press Return.
- To print more pages from the same or another Web site, display each page and issue the Print command for each one.

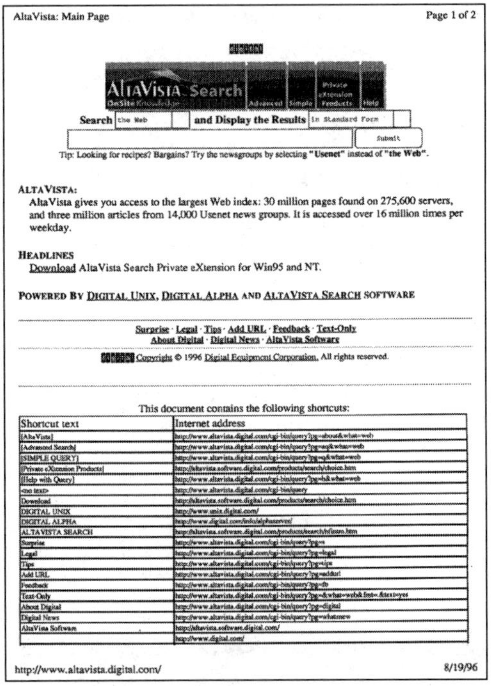

AltaVista: Main Page — Page 1 of 2

Search the Web and Display the Results in Standard Form — Submit

Tip: Looking for recipes? Bargains? Try the newsgroups by selecting **"Usenet"** instead of **"the Web"**.

ALTAVISTA:
AltaVista gives you access to the largest Web index: 30 million pages found on 275,600 servers, and three million articles from 14,000 Usenet news groups. It is accessed over 16 million times per weekday.

HEADLINES
Download AltaVista Search Private eXtension for Win95 and NT.

POWERED BY DIGITAL UNIX, DIGITAL ALPHA AND ALTAVISTA SEARCH SOFTWARE

Surprise · Legal · Tips · Add URL · Feedback · Text-Only
About Digital · Digital News · AltaVista Software

Copyright © 1996 Digital Equipment Corporation. All rights reserved.

This document contains the following shortcuts:

Shortcut text	Internet address
[AltaVista]	http://www.altavista.digital.com/cgi-bin/query?pg=about&what=web
[Advanced Search]	http://www.altavista.digital.com/cgi-bin/query?pg=aq&what=web
[SIMPLE QUERY]	http://www.altavista.digital.com/cgi-bin/query?pg=q&what=web
[Private eXtension Products]	http://altavista.software.digital.com/products/search/choice.htm
[Help with Query]	http://www.altavista.digital.com/cgi-bin/query?pg=h&what=web
<no text>	http://www.altavista.digital.com/cgi-bin/query
Download	http://altavista.software.digital.com/products/search/choice.htm
DIGITAL UNIX	http://www.unix.digital.com/
DIGITAL ALPHA	http://www.digital.com/info/alphaserver/
ALTAVISTA SEARCH	http://altavista.software.digital.com/products/search/nfintro.htm
Surprise	http://www.altavista.digital.com/cgi-bin/query?pg=s
Legal	http://www.altavista.digital.com/cgi-bin/query?pg=legal
Tips	http://www.altavista.digital.com/cgi-bin/query?pg=tips
Add URL	http://www.altavista.digital.com/cgi-bin/query?pg=addurl
Feedback	http://www.altavista.digital.com/cgi-bin/query?pg=fb
Text-Only	http://www.altavista.digital.com/cgi-bin/query?pg=&what=web&fmt=.&text=yes
About Digital	http://www.altavista.digital.com/cgi-bin/query?pg=digital
Digital News	http://www.altavista.digital.com/cgi-bin/query?pg=whatsnew
AltaVista Software	http://altavista.software.digital.com/
	http://www.digital.com/

http://www.altavista.digital.com/ — 8/19/96

Figure 6.10 *With a high-quality printer, you can create a record of the contents of any Web page. Being able to extract the URLs from the page can be a real bonus.*

7

Internet Explorer Options

About Options

You can customize Internet Explorer to work the way that you prefer. You set preferences (called *options*) in the Options dialog box. After setting options, Internet Explorer uses them from that moment on. Of course, you can modify the options if your needs change.

Options are divided into the following categories, each represented by a tab at the top of the Options dialog box:

- *General*. General appearance and multimedia settings.
- *Connection*. Internet connection options.
- *Navigation*. Setting start, search, and Quick Link pages; managing the History folder.
- *Programs*. Choosing e-mail and newsgroup programs to use with Internet Explorer; establishing file associations.
- *Security*. Enabling site ratings (parental controls); personal, site, and publisher certificates; ActiveX and Java support.
- *Advanced*. Warnings; managing and viewing files in the Temporary Internet Files folder; cryptography settings; miscellaneous options.

Use the following procedure to set options for any of the categories:

To set options:

1. Choose Options from the View menu. The Options dialog box appears, as shown in **Figure 7.1**.
2. Choose an options category by clicking its tab at the top of the dialog box.
3. Make the desired changes.
4. To put the changes into effect without closing the dialog box (so you can set other preferences), click Apply.

   or

4. To put the changes into effect and close the dialog box, click OK.

General Options

The General options (see **Figure 7.1**) deal with the browser display. You can hide parts of the window, as well as specify the types of multimedia items that will be shown or ignored when loading pages.

Multimedia

If you have a slow connection or slow modem, you can speed up the display of pages by turning off some of the multimedia options. Because graphics are plentiful on the Web, removing the check mark from Show pictures will have the most pronounced effect on your Internet sessions.

✔ Tip

- If Show Pictures or Play Videos is not checked, you can still view a graphic or video by right-clicking its icon and choosing Show Picture (see **Figure 7.2**).

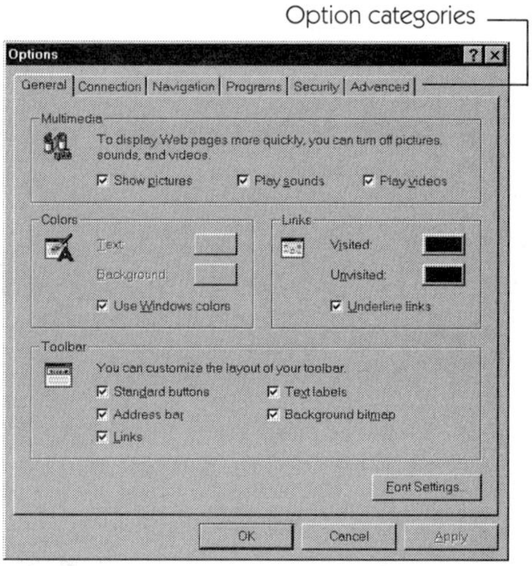

Figure 7.1 *Click a tab at the top of the Options dialog box to select a category.*

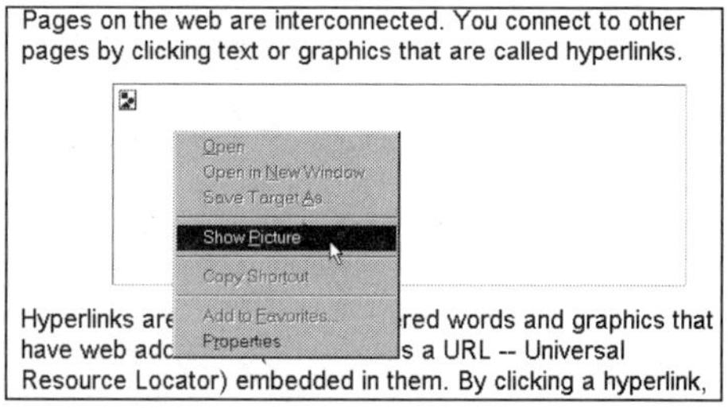

Figure 7.2 *Right-click the blank box or icon for a picture or video, and then choose Show Picture to display the item.*

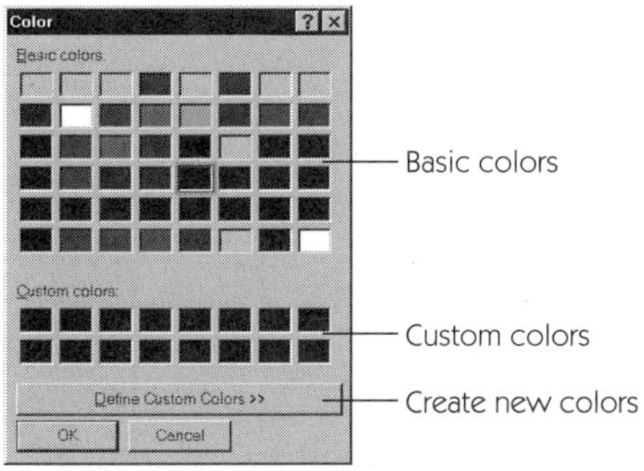

Figure 7.3 *Choose a different color by clicking it. To create a new color, click Define Custom Colors.*

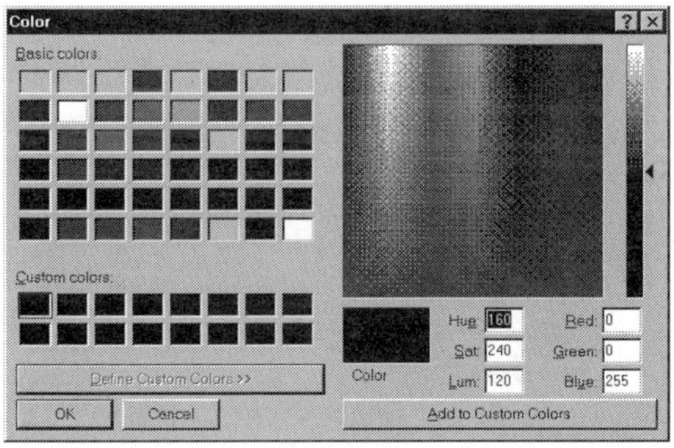

Figure 7.4 *You can create a custom color by dragging the slider, typing numbers directly into the boxes, or clicking in the color panel.*

Colors

You can use the standard Windows colors to display Web page text and backgrounds, or you can choose other colors. Note that your color choices will only be applied to Web pages in which the designer has not specified text or background colors.

To set text or background color:

1. In the General section of the Options dialog box, click to remove the check mark from the Use Windows colors option.
2. Click the box for the color you want to change. The Colors dialog box appears (see **Figure 7.3**).
3. Click a basic or custom color box to select that color.

   or

3. Define a custom color by clicking the color box that you want to replace, and then clicking Define Custom Colors. The Color dialog box expands (see **Figure 7.4**).

   Create a new color by moving the slider, typing numbers into the boxes, or clicking in the color panel. When you are satisfied with the new color, click Add to Custom Colors.
4. Click OK to select the current color, choose another color and click OK, or click Cancel.

✔ Tip

- The custom colors you can create depends on the color palette setting in the Display control panel. When set for 256 or fewer colors, color choices are limited.

Links

You can specify how hypertext links are displayed by choosing options in the General section of the Options dialog box (see **Figure 7.5**).

- To specify whether text links are underlined, add or remove the check mark from Underline links.
- To change the color used to show visited and unvisited links, click the appropriate color box and follow the procedure described previously in "To set text or background color."

If the page designer has set specific colors for showing visited and unvisited links, your color choices are ignored.

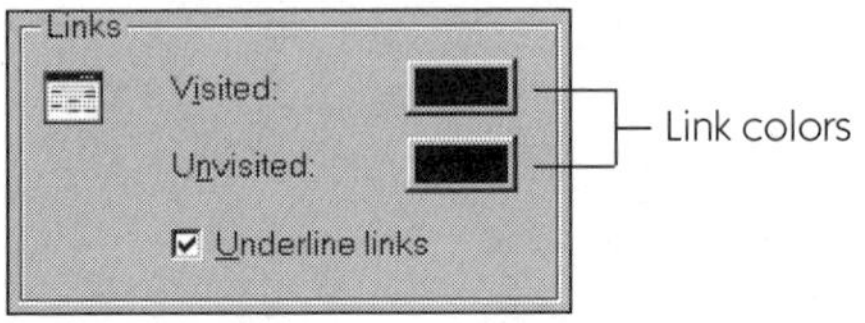

Figure 7.5 *Choose link colors by clicking the colored boxes in the Links section of the dialog box.*

Toolbar

Click check boxes in the Toolbar section of the General options (see **Figure 7.6**) to hide or display toolbar components.

- Click Standard buttons, Address bar, or Links to remove or display these toolbar parts.
- Click Text labels to hide or display the text description beneath the standard buttons.
- Click Background bitmap to hide or display the decorative background pattern in the toolbar.

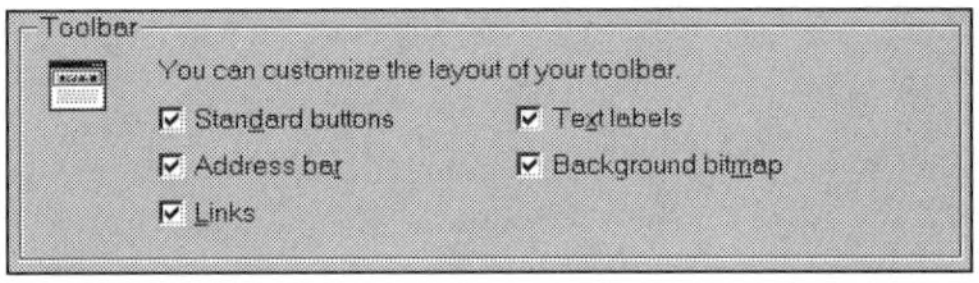

Figure 7.6 *You can customize the browser window by selectively hiding sections of the toolbar.*

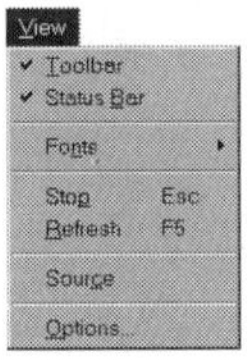

Figure 7.7 *Choose Toolbar or Status Bar from the View menu to hide or show that part of the display. A check mark indicates that the item will be displayed.*

✔ Tip

- You can eliminate or restore the entire toolbar by choosing Toolbar from the View menu, as shown in **Figure 7.7**. You can do the same with the status bar by choosing Status Bar.

Font Settings

If you don't care for the look of the fonts used to display Web page text, click the Font Settings button. You can choose different proportional and fixed-width fonts.

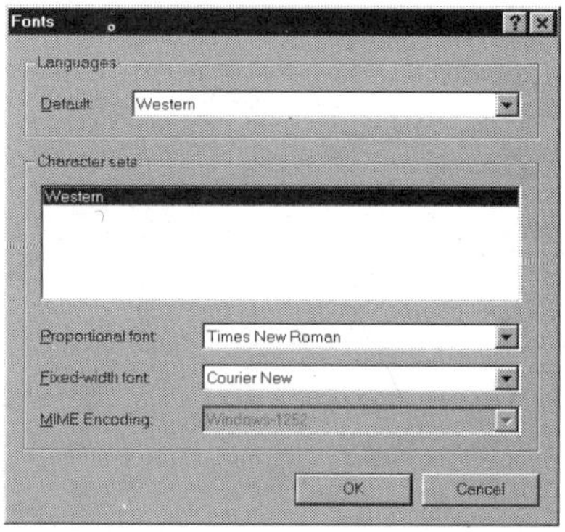

Figure 7.8 *Select new display fonts in the Fonts dialog box.*

To set new display fonts:

1. Click the Font Settings button in the General section of the Options dialog box. The Fonts dialog box appears, as shown in **Figure 7.8**.
2. *Optional*: Select a language from the Default pop-up menu, and choose a character set from the list.
3. Choose a proportional and a fixed-width font from the pop-up menus at the bottom of the dialog box.
4. Click OK to accept the new font choices, or click Cancel to continue using the previous fonts.

✔ Tips

- Before changing fonts or selecting different colors for links and text, make a note of the settings. There is no Use Default button that you can click to restore the original settings.
- As with the other General options, the easiest way to see how your new font choices affect the display is to try them out. Select fonts, and then visit several Web sites.

Connection Options

Settings in Connection options (see **Figure 7.9**) specify when and how you connect to the Internet. The various options are explained below.

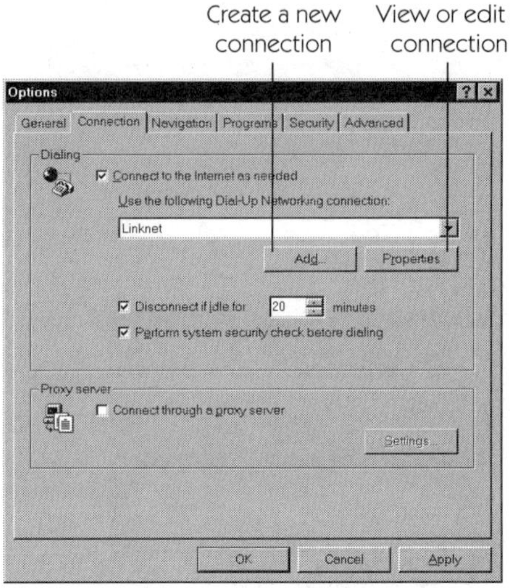

Figure 7.9 *Connection options specify the method for connecting to the Internet.*

Connect to the Internet as Needed

When this option is checked, your computer automatically connects as needed to perform Internet-related activities. For example, launching Internet Explorer and going to a page that isn't in the cache will cause a connection to be made.

✔ **Tips**

- If you use a modem for connections and this option is not checked, you will have to manually connect each time.
- If you have a direct connection to the Internet through a local area network (LAN), remove the check mark from this option.
- Even if this option is checked, you can still work off-line by clicking Cancel when the Connect to dialog box appears (see **Figure 7.10**).

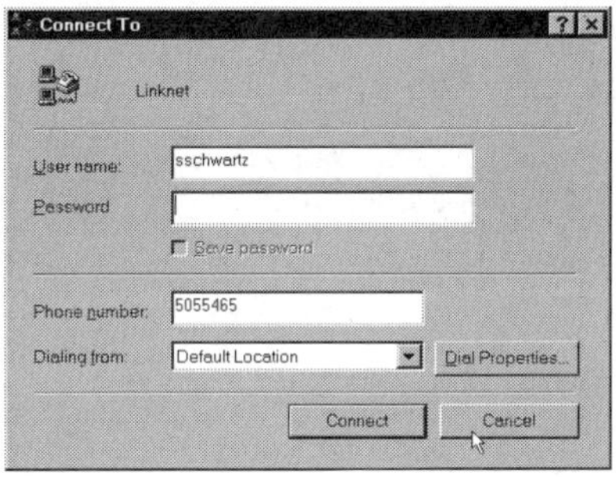

Figure 7.10 *When connecting to the Internet, the Connect To dialog box is presented. Click Connect to dial.*

Use the Following Dial-Up Networking Connection

All connections are stored as icons in the Dial-Up Networking folder (see **Figure 7.11**). The connection specified for this option is used whenever you connect to the Internet. To create a new connection, click the Add button in the Options dialog box. To edit a connection, click Properties.

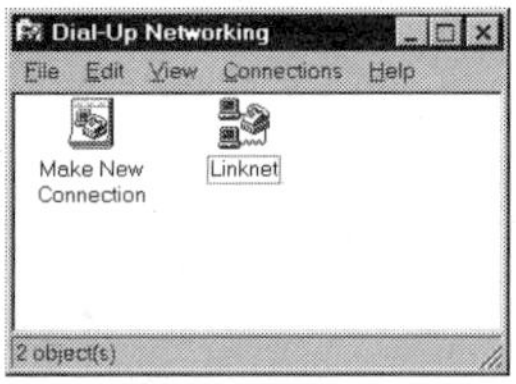

Figure 7.11 *Connections are stored in the Dial-Up Networking folder. You can also add and edit connections by clicking icons or choosing menu commands.*

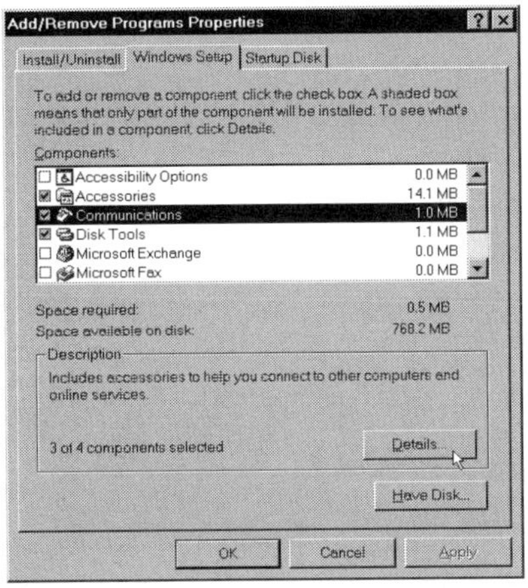

Figure 7.12 *Install Dial-Up Networking using the Add/Remove Programs control panel.*

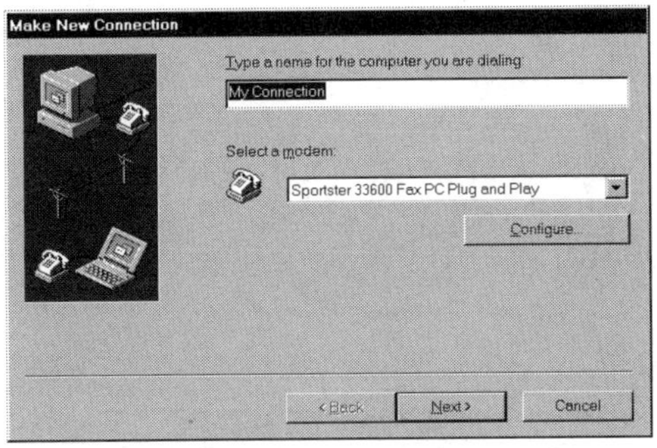

Figure 7.13 *The Make New Connection Wizard makes it simple to set up a new Internet connection.*

Figure 7.14 *Click Disconnect to end an Internet session.*

✔ **Tips**

- If you haven't installed Dial-Up Networking, double-click the Add/Remove Programs control panel (see **Figure 7.12**), and then click these items: Windows Setup tab, Communications, Details button, Dial-Up Networking check box, OK, and OK. Be sure to also install the TCP/IP protocol in the Network control panel.
- You can also create a connection by double-clicking the Make New Connection icon in the Dial-Up Networking folder. An existing connection can be edited by double-clicking its icon.
- The first time you open the Dial-Up Networking folder (and each time you create a new connection), the Make New Connection Wizard helps you set up the connection, as shown in **Figure 7.13**.

Disconnect If Idle for xx Minutes

When checked, this option causes the connection to be broken if there is no line activity for the specified number of minutes. If you pay for Internet use by the hour, you'll probably want to set this to a low number. Then if you forget you're on-line (you're called to a meeting, for instance), the system will automatically disconnect.

If you want to remain constantly connected (so you can instantly receive new e-mail, for example), remove the check mark from this option. You will have to manually end each session by clicking the Disconnect button in the Connected To dialog box (see **Figure 7.14**).

✔ **Tip**

■ You can also avoid disconnects caused by *time outs* by leaving Internet Mail running with instructions to check for new mail every 10 minutes. This ensures that there will be periodic line activity. Then set "Disconnect if idle..." for a longer period, such as 15 minutes.

Perform Security Check Before Dialing

When this option is checked, Internet Explorer will perform a security check before allowing a connection to be made. If your computer is shared by others or is in an open area, this will help prevent unauthorized use of your Internet account.

Connect Through a Proxy Server

Check this option if you connect to the Internet through a proxy server on a local area network (LAN). Otherwise, do not check it.

To set parameters for using a proxy server, click the Settings button. The Proxy Settings dialog box shown in **Figure 7.15** appears. Enter the address and port for each protocol you will use. If you use a single proxy for all Internet activities, check the box at the bottom of the Servers section.

If you intend to make some types of connections using a modem rather than through the LAN, enter the connection types in the Exceptions list, separated by semicolons (;).

If you need help with these settings, see your LAN administrator.

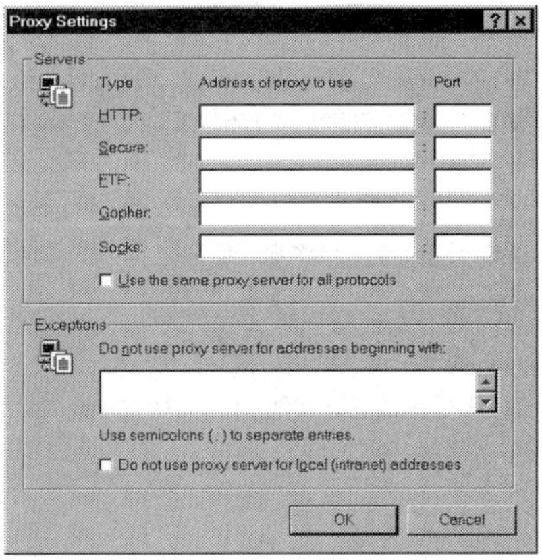

Figure 7.15 *Complete the proxy settings if you connect to the Internet over a LAN.*

Navigation Options

In the top part of the Navigation options (see **Figure 7.16**), you can set a home page, search page, and Quick Links. After setting them, you can go to any of these Web pages by clicking buttons in the toolbar or by choosing menu commands. For help setting these options, refer to:

- "Going to Your Home Page" (Chapter 1)
- "About Quick Links" (Chapter 3)
- "Selecting a Main Search Site" (Chapter 4)

The History section enables you to view and manage the History folder (see **Figure 7.17**), a repository for Web pages you've recently visited. You can view the pages off-line or on-line by opening the History folder and then opening the desired page.

To open the History folder, click View History or choose Open History Folder from the Go menu. Double-click any Web page in the folder to open it in a browser window.

To set the number of days that Web pages are stored in the History folder, type a number in the box or click the small up- and down-arrows. To delete all items in the History folder, click Clear History. (Note that expired items are automatically deleted.)

✔ Tip

- You can go to the most recent pages viewed during the current session by choosing them from the numbered list in the Go menu (see **Figure 7.18**).

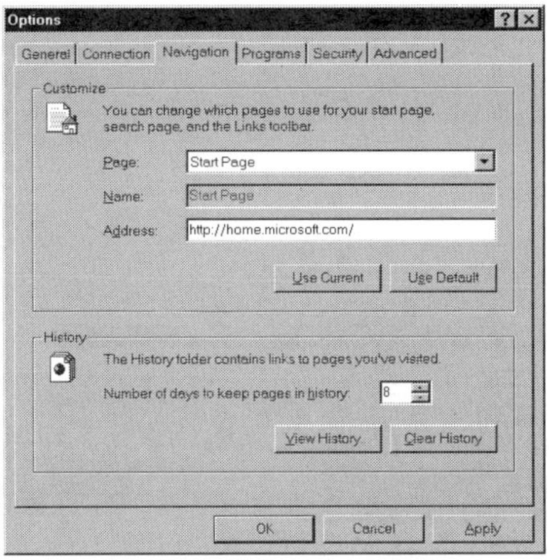

Figure 7.16 *Navigation options enable you to choose new start and search pages, set Quick Links, and manage the History folder.*

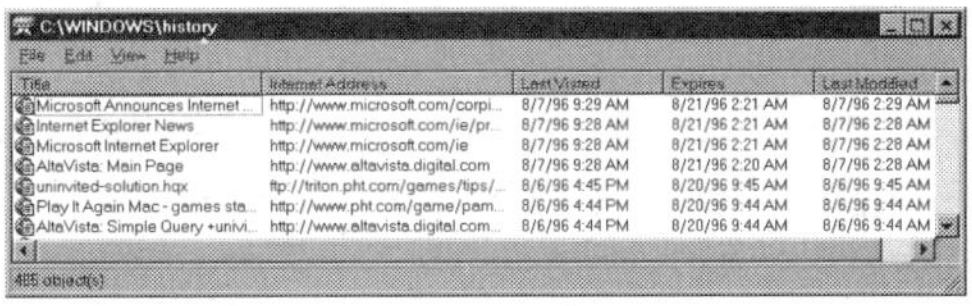

Figure 7.17 *The History folder lists the Web pages you've recently visited.*

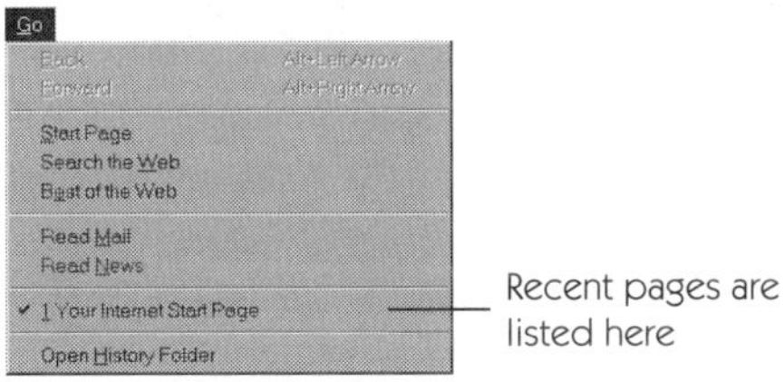

Figure 7.18 *You can go to previously viewed pages by choosing a numbered entry from the Go menu.*

Programs Options

Internet Explorer can be linked to an e-mail program and newsgroup reader. The selected programs are used when you initiate an e-mail or newsgroup-related procedure in Internet Explorer, such as e-mailing a URL to a friend.

If you performed a Full Install, the default choices are Internet Mail and Internet News, as shown in **Figure 7.19**. To select a different program, its name must be listed in the appropriate pop-up menu. (*Note:* At this writing, there are no compatible programs. This will change, of course, as existing programs are updated and new ones are released.)

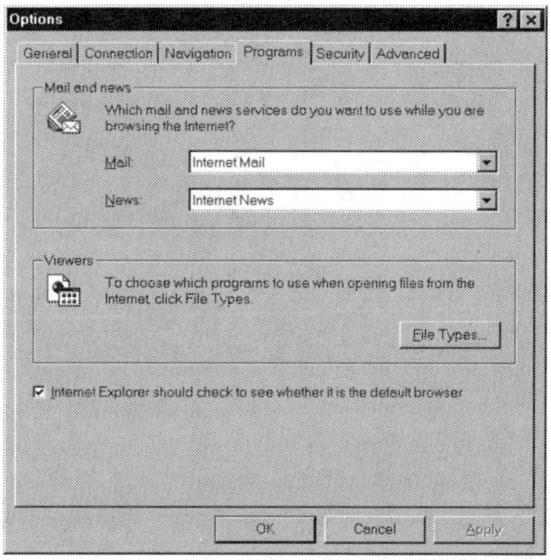

Figure 7.19 *The Programs options enable you to select a default e-mail program and newsgroup reader. You can also create and edit file associations.*

The Viewers section of the dialog box is used to set file associations. When you open a file of a given type, the association setting determines which program on your hard disk will be used to display or handle the file. Many files found on the Internet (GIF and JPEG images, for example) are associated by default with Internet Explorer. Thus, when you double-click such a file, it appears in a browser window. Click the File Types button to examine or change file associations (see **Figure 7.20**).

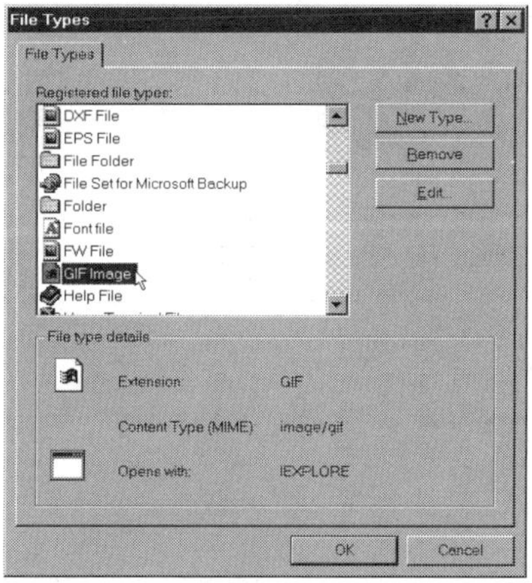

Figure 7.20 *You can view and set file associations in the File Types dialog box.*

Finally, you can have only one *default* browser—although you may have several browser programs installed. The default browser is the one that runs when you double-click a Web page shortcut. If you check "Internet Explorer should check to see…," it will remain your default browser even if another is later installed. When you next run Internet Explorer, it will automatically reset itself as the default browser.

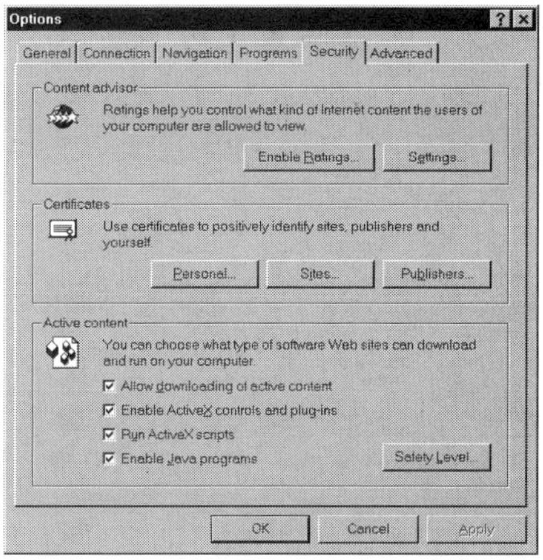

Figure 7.21 *The Security options.*

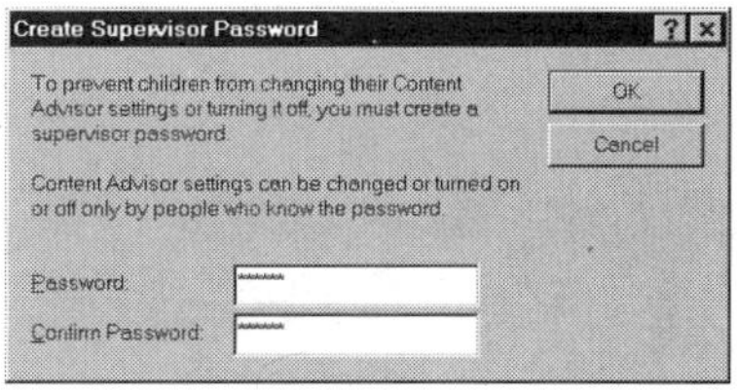

Figure 7.22 *Set and verify the master password in this dialog box. You will need this password to view, modify, or disable the ratings settings.*

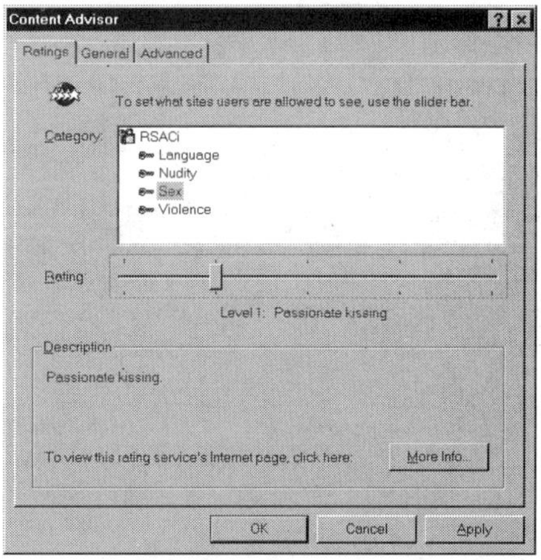

Figure 7.23 *Each rating category has five levels. A description for each level is provided beneath the slider.*

Security Options

By specifying Security options (see **Figure 7.21**), you can control the types of Web pages that can be visited; specify certificates that are used to positively identify yourself, Web sites, and software publishers; and set the types of page-enhancing software that can be downloaded to your computer.

Content Advisor

By clicking Enable Ratings, you can specify the types and amounts of sex, nudity, offensive language, and violence that you want to allow. Internet Explorer includes a ratings file from the Recreational Software Advisory Council (RSAC) covering these content areas. If anyone attempts to view a site whose ratings exceed the levels you've set, admission will be denied.

When you enable ratings, you must create a supervisor password (see **Figure 7.22**). Next, click Settings to set content restrictions. The Content Advisor dialog box appears (see **Figure 7.23**) and is divided into three sections: Ratings, General, and Advanced.

The Ratings Section

Set ratings by selecting a category and then dragging the slider to the desired position. When you're done, click Apply or OK.

To go to RSAC's Web site and learn more about the rating system, click More Info.

The General Section

Set user options and change the supervisor password in this section of the dialog box.

User options (see **Figure 7.24**) are as follows:

- *Users can see sites which have no ratings.* To allow access to unrated sites, check this option. When unchecked, users can visit only rated sites; access is denied to all others.
- *Supervisor can type a password to allow users to view restricted content.* Enabling this option allows persons with the password to view any site.

To change the supervisor password, click Change Password. The Change Supervisor Password dialog box appears (see **Figure 7.25**). Enter the old and new passwords in the appropriate boxes, and then click OK.

Depending on the combination of options chosen, if you try to visit an unrated site, one that is rated by a system you do not have installed, or one that exceeds your rating settings, you will be refused entrance or prompted for the supervisor password, as shown in **Figure 7.26**.

The Advanced Section

Use this section of the Content Advisor dialog box (see **Figure 7.27**) to add or remove rating systems and bureaus. To view or modify your installed rating systems, click Rating Systems. The Rating Systems dialog box appears, as shown in **Figure 7.28**.

To remove a rating system, select it and click Remove. To add a new system (one that is on your hard disk), click Add, select the rating (.RAT) file from the file list, and click Open.

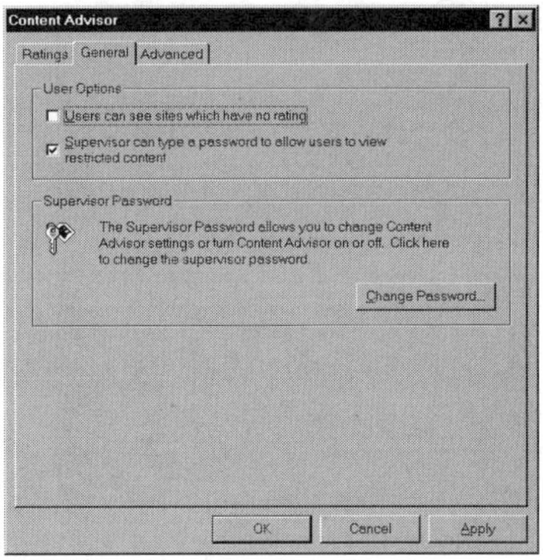

Figure 7.24 *Use the General section of the Content Advisor dialog box to set user options and the supervisor password.*

Figure 7.25 *To change the supervisor password, type the old and new passwords in this dialog box.*

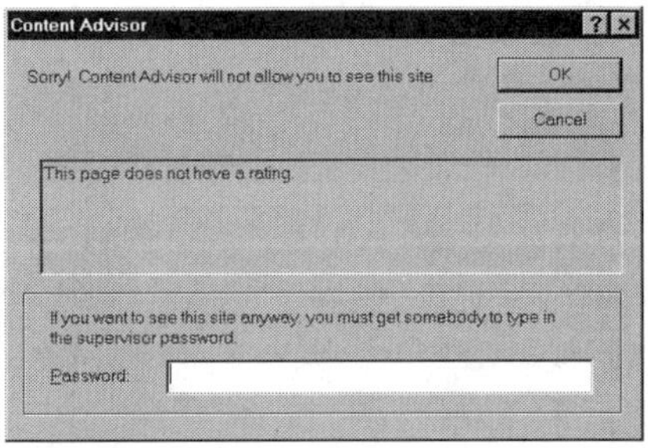

Figure 7.26 *Whenever you are refused entry to a site, a dialog box such as this one appears. It lists the reason(s) for the refusal.*

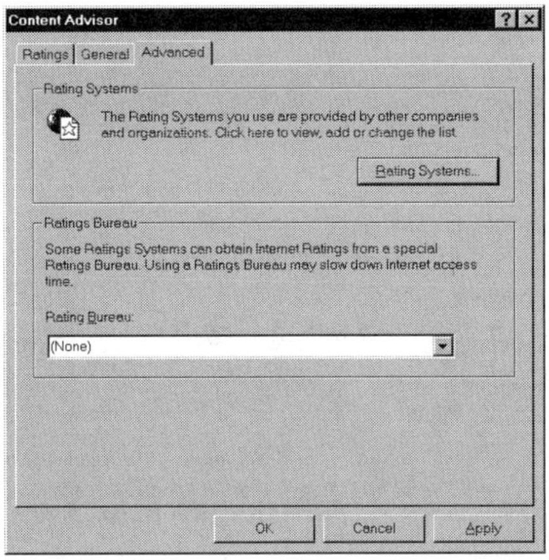

Figure 7.27 *Use the Advanced section of the Content Advisor dialog box to manage rating systems and bureaus.*

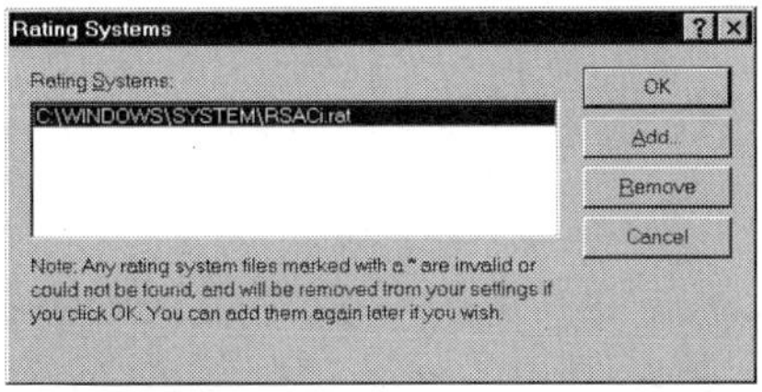

Figure 7.28 *New rating systems can be added or removed in the Rating Systems dialog box.*

If you subscribe to or have access to a rating bureau, type its name in the Rating Bureau box.

✔ Tips

- Ratings are not done "on the fly." Internet Explorer does not examine the content of pages before displaying them. Either a given page or site is *already* rated—and is included in one of the installed rating databases—or it isn't.
- Only a tiny fraction of all sites are rated by RSAC. If you restrict all viewing to only rated sites, you will find yourself blocked from viewing many pages—even those of innocuous sites. On the other hand, if you allow access to unrated sites, you relinquish all content control.

  One compromise is to check "Supervisor can type a password to allow users to view restricted content." Your children will have to ask permission to enter unrated sites. During *your* surfing sessions, however, you may find it more convenient to disable the ratings, and enable them again when you quit. Otherwise, you will spend an inordinate amount of time typing the password—over and over.
- New rating system (.RAT) files are stored in the Windows\System directory of your hard disk. You can learn about other rating systems, rating bureaus, and available rating files at the following site:

  `http://www.w3.org/pub/WWW/PICS/`

Certificates

In many ways, exploring the Internet is like using a telephone on an open party line. You never know who may be "listening in," so to speak. Certificates provide security for your on-line transactions. There are three types:

- *Personal*. These certificates can be used to identify yourself to certain sites, such as ones that conduct financial transactions or are meant to be viewed only by subscribers. Several companies offer personal certificates—usually for a fee (see **Figure 7.29**). Click Personal to see the certificates that are installed.
- *Sites*. Some sites have their own certificates, uniquely identifying them as the site to which you are connected. To examine certificates of which your system is aware, click Sites. The Site Certificates dialog box appears, as shown in **Figure 7.30**.
- *Publishers*. When displayed by a software publisher, a certificate (see **Figure 7.31**) helps insure that the file you are about to download actually comes from that vendor and that it has not been altered.

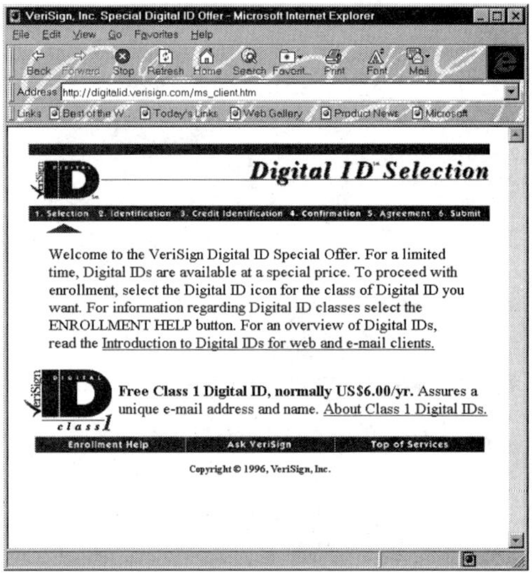

Figure 7.29 *VeriSign is one of several Internet companies that offers personal certificates.*

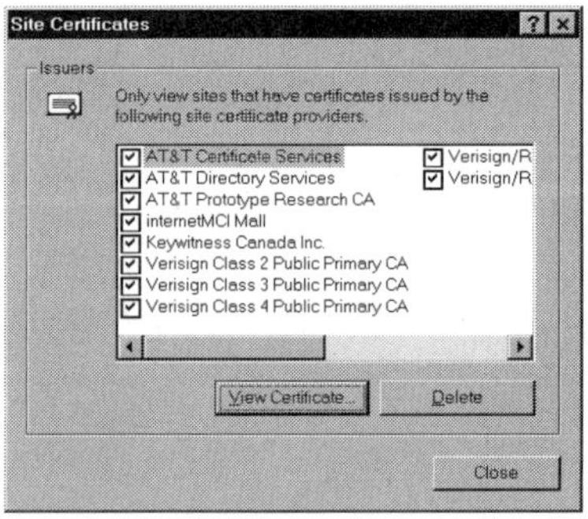

Figure 7.30 *To view information about a site certificate, such as the issuing company and the effective dates, select the certificate from the list and click View Certificate.*

✔ Tip

- For a limited time, you can obtain a free Class 1 personal certificate from VeriSign (refer to **Figure 7.29**). For details, visit this Web page:

```
http://digitalid.verisign.com
/ms_client.htm
```

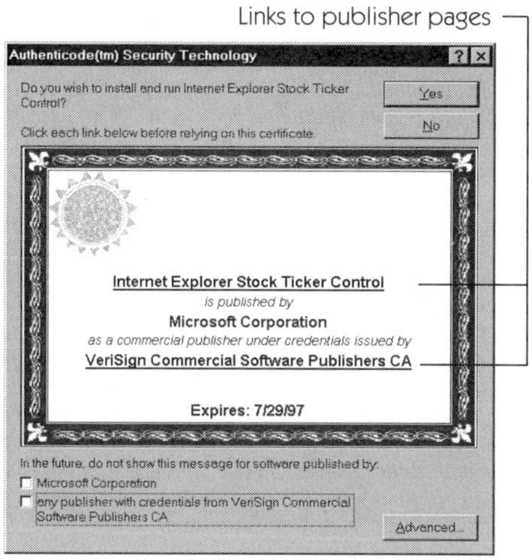

Figure 7.31 *When downloading active content from some sites, a certificate may appear. Click the links to learn about the software and certificate companies. Click the publisher check box to automatically accept all future downloads from the same company.*

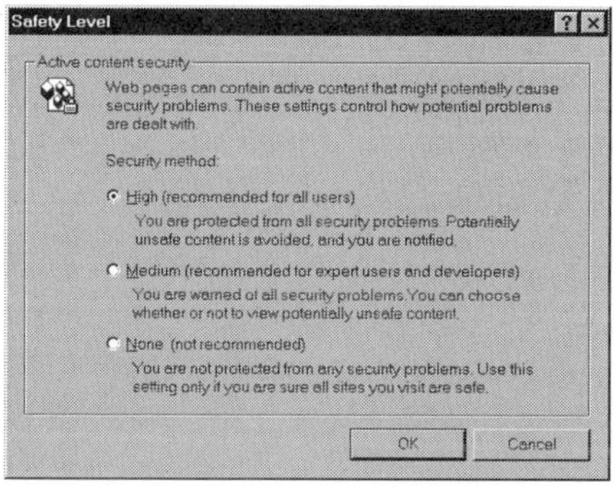

Figure 7.32 *Click the radio button in the Safety Level dialog box that best reflects your active content security needs.*

Active Content

Active content options (refer to **Figure 7.21**) determine the types of page-enhancement software that can be automatically downloaded to your computer by Web sites. Options are:

- *Allow downloading of active content.* When checked, active content in Web pages (such as animations) is automatically downloaded to your computer.
- *Enable ActiveX controls and plug-ins.* Some Web sites use ActiveX controls and plug-ins to present special features, such as control pads or pop-up menus. When checked, these features are automatically available to you. Remove the check mark to ignore items that require ActiveX.
- *Run ActiveX scripts.* When checked, you can view Web sites that perform ActiveX scripts.
- *Enable Java programs.* When checked, you can view Web sites that perform Java scripts.

You can also set a general safety level for handling active content by clicking the Safety Level button. Safety options are displayed in **Figure 7.32**.

- *High.* You are warned of potential security problems; active content is not downloaded.
- *Medium.* You are warned when there is a potential security problem and given the option to decide what you want to do.
- *None.* No protection; active content is automatically downloaded to your computer.

Security Options

Advanced Options

Click the Advanced options tab (see **Figure 7.33**) to specify the types of warnings that Internet Explorer will present, view and manage the cache, and set other special options.

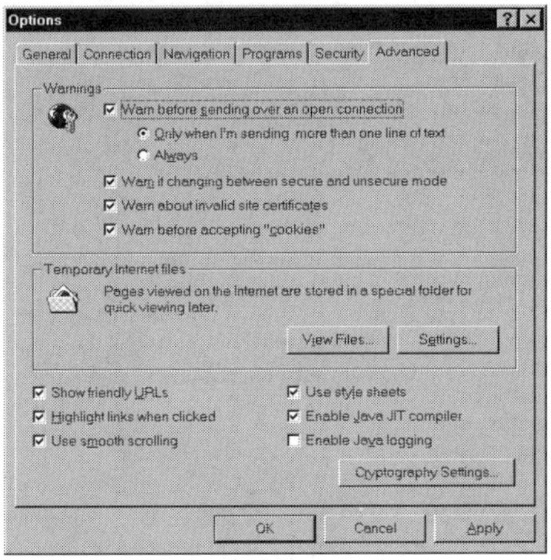

Figure 7.33 *The Advanced Options dialog box.*

Warnings

When you perform an unsecure action, Internet Explorer can present a warning dialog box (see **Figure 7.34**). By themselves, however, warnings do not protect you. It is up to you to decide how to respond to each warning.

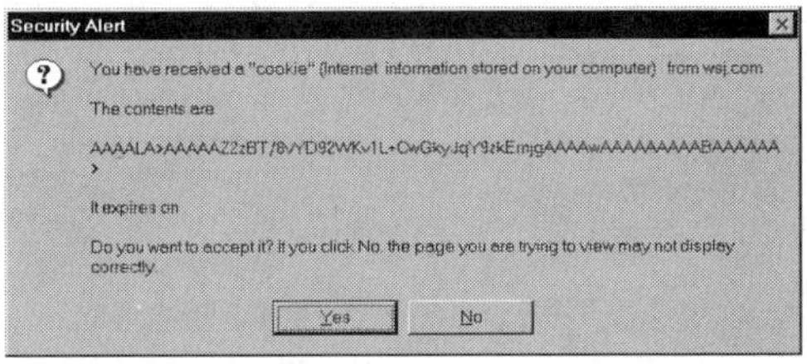

Figure 7.34 *Whenever a "cookie" is sent to your computer by a Web site, you have the option of accepting or refusing it.*

- *Warn before sending over an open connection*. Information you send over the Internet has the potential for being intercepted by others. Enable this option to provide a warning/reminder.
- *Warn if changing between secure and unsecure mode*. Some Web sites are secure; some are not. This option presents a warning when switching from one type of site to the other.
- *Warn about invalid site certificates*. A site certificate specifies a URL that is associated with the certificate, as well as an expiration date. If the URL does not match the one on the certificate or the certificate has expired, a warning appears.
- *Warn before accepting "cookies."* Some Web sites send information (called a *cookie*) that is stored on your hard disk. When subscribing to an on-line service, for example, cookie data may be used to identify you to the site on later visits. A cookie warning gives you the

option of refusing unwanted data of this kind.

Note that some Web sites send multiple cookies—one per page, in some cases. When this warning option is enabled, you will have to respond to *every* cookie that is transmitted to you.

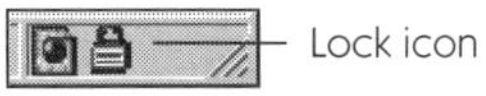

Figure 7.35 *When visiting a secure site, this padlock icon appears at the right end of the status bar.*

✔ **Tip**

- You can always tell if you're in a secure site. Check the status bar for the presence of a lock icon (see **Figure 7.35**). Examine the URL in the address box, too. Secure Web sites show *https://* as the prefix rather than *http://*.

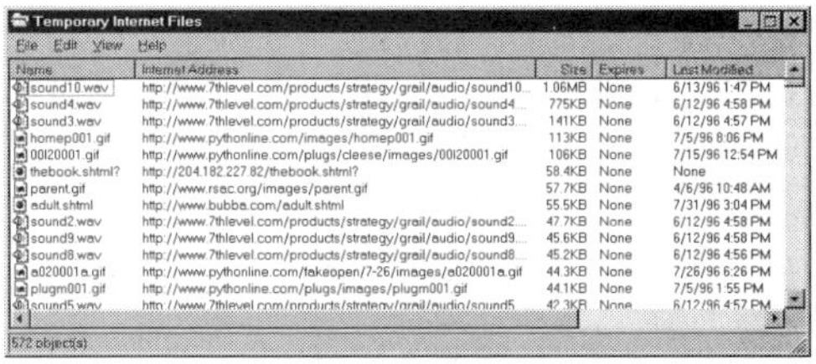

Figure 7.36 *To speed up subsequent visits to Web pages, Internet Explorer stores copies of pages and other elements in the Temporary Internet Files folder. On later visits, the pages can be drawn from your hard disk rather than being downloaded again.*

Temporary Internet Files

Internet Explorer's cache is stored in the Temporary Internet Files folder. The cache contains the Web pages you have recently visited, as well as any graphic and multimedia files you have seen and heard.

To view or open files from the cache, click View Files. The folder opens, as shown in **Figure 7.36**. Double-click any file to display it in a browser window.

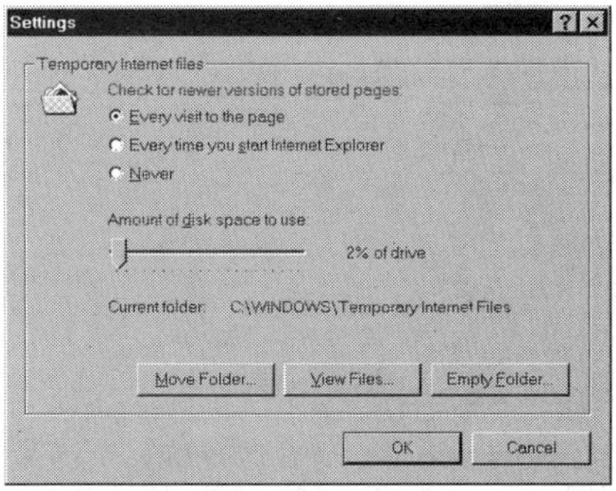

Figure 7.37 *Use the Settings dialog box to manage the cache.*

To manage the cache, click the Settings button. The Settings dialog box appears (see **Figure 7.37**). Options include the following:

- The setting for "Check for newer versions of stored pages" determines how often Internet Explorer checks to see if the current Web page has changed; i.e., whether it is different from the copy in the cache.

Never is the fastest option. If the page you're visiting is in the cache, the cached version is automatically displayed. However, if the page has changed, you'll still be viewing the older version from the cache.

Every time you start Internet Explorer causes the program to check for a changed page once each session. This is a compromise. If you visit a page more than once in a session, you run a risk—in most cases, a small one—that the page will have changed.

Every visit to the page is the safest—but slowest—choice. If you visit the same page five times in a session, it is checked for changes every time.

- Move the slider (see **Figure 7.38**) to allocate a percentage of your hard drive to be used for the cache. As the cache fills, the oldest items are automatically deleted to make room for new ones.
- To change the drive or folder where the cache is stored, click Move Folder and choose a location from the Browse for Folder dialog box (see **Figure 7.39**).
- Click View Files to view the contents of the cache. (This is the same as clicking View Files in the dialog box shown in **Figure 7.33**).
- Click Empty Folder to delete all files in the cache.

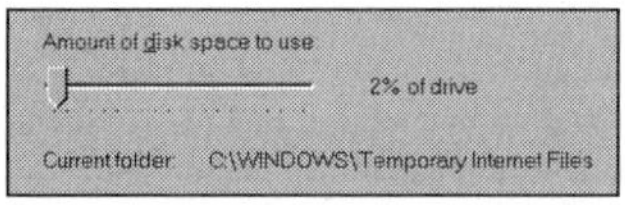

Figure 7.38 *Because you can't specify an amount in megabytes, you may have to dig out a calculator to determine the amount of disk space that the percentage represents.*

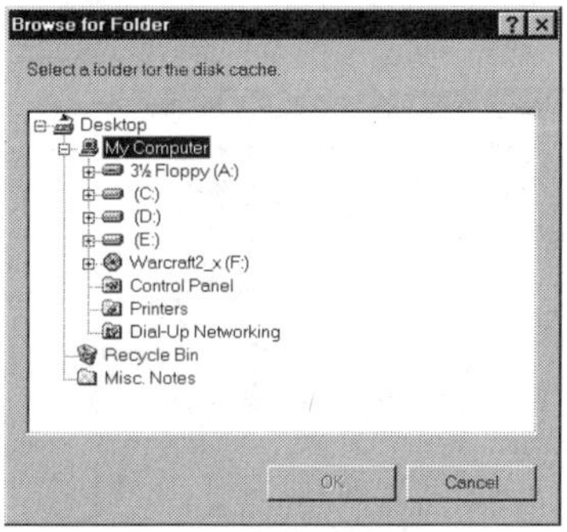

Figure 7.39 *To choose a different folder for the cache, select the folder and click OK.*

Figure 7.40 *Click Refresh to force the current Web page to be reloaded from the Web site.*

✔ **Tip**

- Regardless of how often Internet Explorer has been set to check pages for changes, you can force it to display the most current version of a page by clicking the Refresh button (see **Figure 7.40**).

Miscellaneous Options

There are also several miscellaneous options that you can set (refer to the bottom of the dialog box shown in **Figure 7.33**).

- *Show friendly URLs*. When friendly URLs are enabled, the program attempts to show complete addresses in the status bar. Rather than identify a page by a numerical address (e.g., Connecting to: 206.34.56.1), text URLs are used whenever they are available.
- *Highlight links when clicked*. When this option is enabled, a dotted box surrounds the currently chosen link.
- *Use smooth scrolling*. When enabled, page scrolling is fluid.
- *Use style sheets*. Internet Explorer supports style sheets, allowing designers to specify fonts and point sizes, margins, and leading in their Web pages. Enable this option to view such pages the way that the designer intended.

  To learn about using style sheets in your own pages, refer to:

  `www.microsoft.com/workshop/author/other/htmlfaq1-f.htm`
- *Enable Java JIT compiler*. When the JIT (Just-In-Time) compiler is enabled, Java scripts are compiled

as they are encountered in Web pages. (Compiled scripts run faster.)

- *Enable Java logging*. Setting this option causes all Java-related Web activity to be logged.
- *Cryptography*. To view the current options, click the Cryptography Settings button. The Cryptography Protocols dialog box appears, as shown in **Figure 7.41**.

  Select the cryptography protocols that you will accept. Note that the second and third options are proprietary and will not be accepted by all Web sites.

  If you are concerned about security problems in your office, you can enable the option marked "Do not save secure pages to disk."

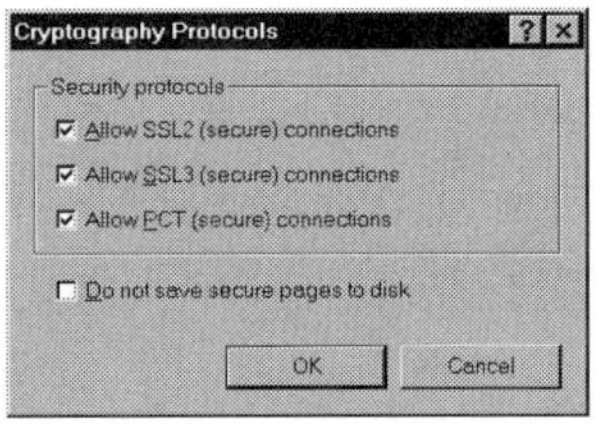

Figure 7.41 *Specify acceptable cryptography protocols in the Cryptography Protocols dialog box.*

Part II: Internet Mail

8

E-Mail Essentials

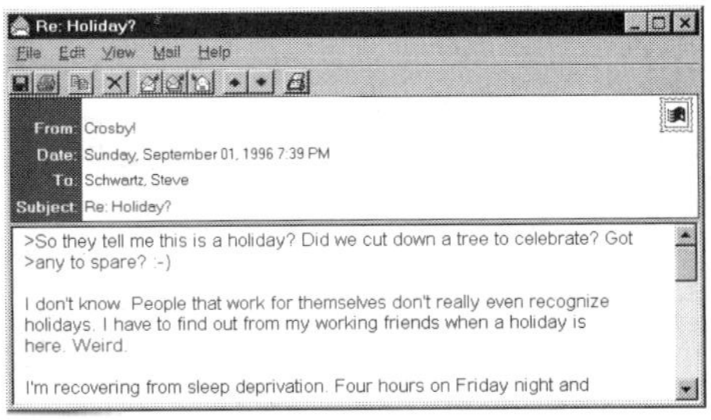

Figure 8.1 *E-mail messages are like any other computer documents. They can be read on-screen, printed, or saved to disk.*

About E-Mail

An e-mail message is an electronic note sent from one person to another (see **Figure 8.1**). E-mail can be transmitted within a company (over a LAN) and between BBS or information service subscribers (e.g., America Online and CompuServe). And if you have Internet access, you can send e-mail to anyone on the Internet. It doesn't matter where in the world they are or whether they work through an *ISP* (Internet Service Provider) or an information service. As long as you know a person's *e-mail address* (discussed later in this chapter), you can send e-mail to him or her.

In many businesses and homes, e-mail is replacing internal memos, telephone calls, and letters. (I send dozens of e-mail messages each month, but seldom write more than three letters.)

E-Mail Advantages

E-mail has several advantages over traditional communication mediums:

- *Immediacy*. Although not as immediate as a phone call or fax, e-mail is often delivered within minutes.
- *Low cost*. If you have an unlimited use Internet account, there is usually no additional fee for sending or receiving e-mail. There are no per message, long-distance, postage, or delivery charges.

- *Complex content.* You can attach other files to e-mail, such as word processing documents, spreadsheets, graphics, and programs. Such files are called *attachments* (see **Figure 8.2**).
- *No length or weight limit.* Mail messages can be very long; attachments can consist of megabytes of data.
- *Multiple recipients.* It takes no more effort to send a message to a dozen recipients than it does to send it to one (see **Figure 8.3**).
- *Convenience.* Because all e-mail is sent and received from your computer, you can quickly reply to incoming messages. And you can forward received messages with a button click.

E-Mail Disadvantages

Like other communication mediums, e-mail also has some disadvantages:

- *Confirmation.* Unless your mail program can request receipts, you may not know if a message was delivered. And if the recipient does not regularly check for new mail, it may never be read.
- *Reliability.* If your ISP's mail server malfunctions, your outgoing or incoming messages can sometimes disappear into the ether.
- *Paper shuffling.* If the document you want to send wasn't composed on a computer, you must scan or retype it.

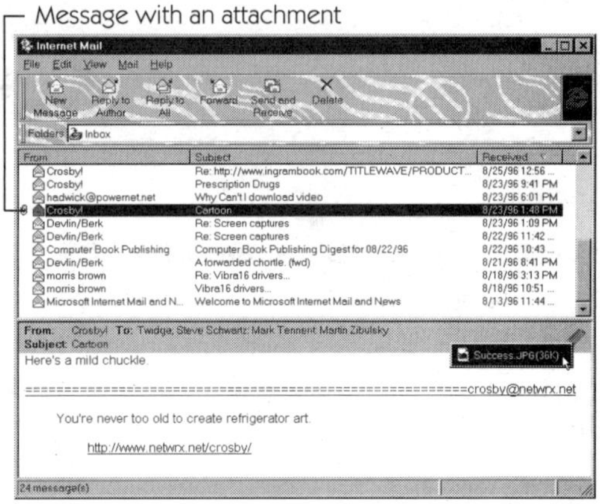

Figure 8.2 *In Internet Mail, messages that contain attachments are marked with paper-clip icons.*

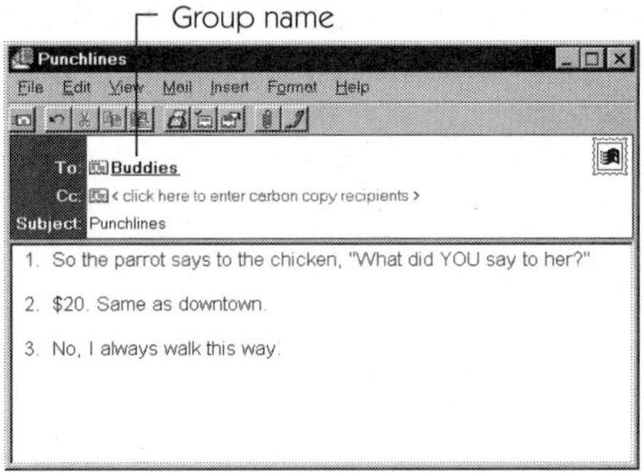

Figure 8.3 *Any message can be addressed to multiple recipients. If there is a group of people with whom you routinely correspond (magazine editors, for example), you can either create a group for them (shown here) or send the same message to everyone by including their names in the To: or Cc: lines.*

About E-Mail Addresses

Every person with Internet access has a unique address that identifies him or her. When you send a message, you indicate the intended recipient by specifying an *e-mail address*.

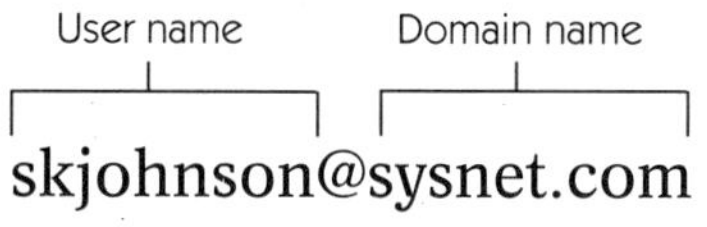

Figure 8.4 *E-mail addresses consist of two parts, separated by an @ symbol.*

Every e-mail address has two parts (see **Figure 8.4**): a *user name* and a *domain name* (the service on which the person has an account). The service might be an ISP (netwrx.net), an information service (aol.com), an educational institution (hnrc.tufts.edu), or a company (globalvillage.com).

Every domain name has a suffix that indicates what type of institution it is. Common suffixes include:

- com (commercial)
- net (network)
- org (organization)
- edu (educational)
- gov (government)

User names are either created by the individual or assigned by their service or institution. User names can include letters, numbers, and special characters, such as underscores and periods. Spaces are not allowed. Although hundreds of people on the Internet may have the same user name, there can be only one person with a given user name in a domain.

The user and domain names are separated by an @ character. Here are some typical e-mail addresses:

- spatterson@aol.com
  [America Online address]
- johnadams@postoffice.ptd.net
  [ISP address]

- dave73@eng.uchicago.edu [educational address]
- 74664.1402@compuserve.com [CompuServe address]

As you can see, you may or may not be able to determine a person's name from an e-mail address.

To make it easy to deal with complex, lengthy addresses, most mail programs provide an *address book* in which to record addresses. Every address is linked to the person's full name, company, and other identifying data (see **Figure 8.5**). When addressing e-mail, you can choose the recipient's name from the address book (see **Figure 8.6**). Thus, after recording an address, you will never have to type it again!

✔ Tips

- If you are allowed to choose your user name, create one that readily identifies you. Unless you want to remain anonymous, sschwartz, saschwartz, and steve_schwartz are all better choices than zippie, roadrunner, or duke_of_earl.
- Although letter case does not matter, the convention is to enter addresses in all lowercase letters.
- Include your e-mail address on letterhead, business cards, and fax forms. When making new business contacts, it's important to provide as many convenient ways to contact you as possible.
- If you change ISPs, inform everyone in your address book of your new e-mail address. (It changes when you switch providers.)

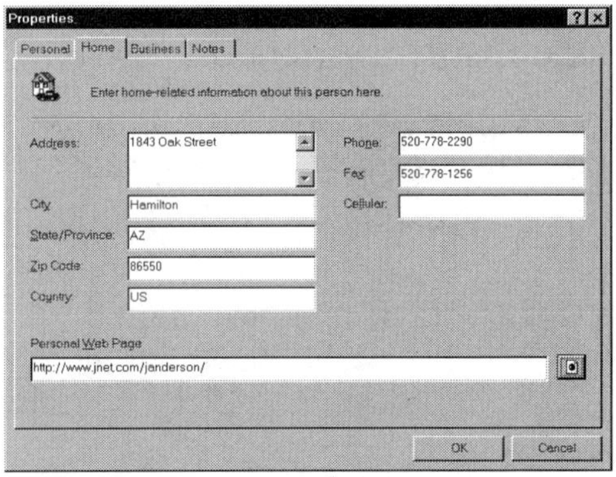

Figure 8.5 *In addition to each person's name, you can enter other useful information in an address record, such as work and home phone numbers, mailing address, and notes.*

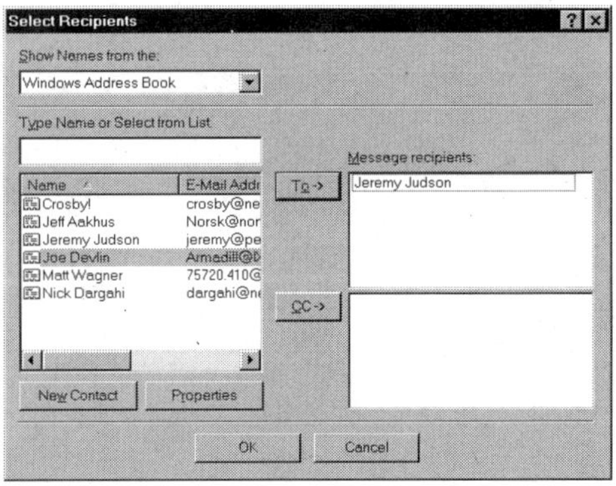

Figure 8.6 *In Internet Mail, you can select mail recipients from the address book.*

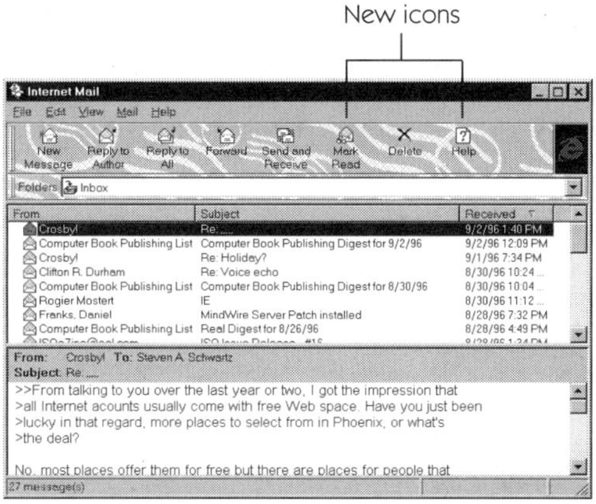

Figure 8.7 *You can customize the toolbar by adding new icons for common mail actions.*

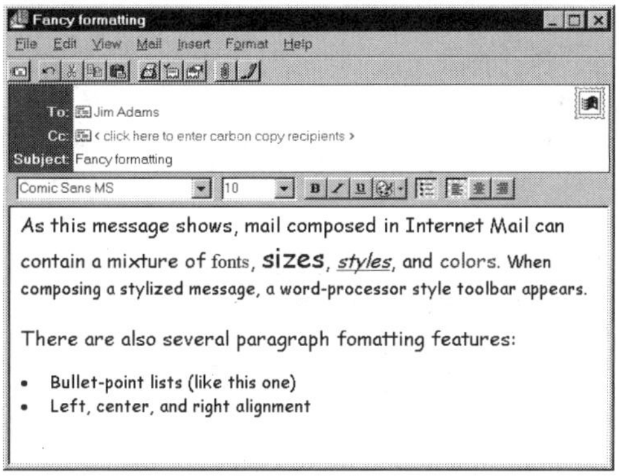

Figure 8.8 *Messages created in Internet Mail don't have to be plain text.*

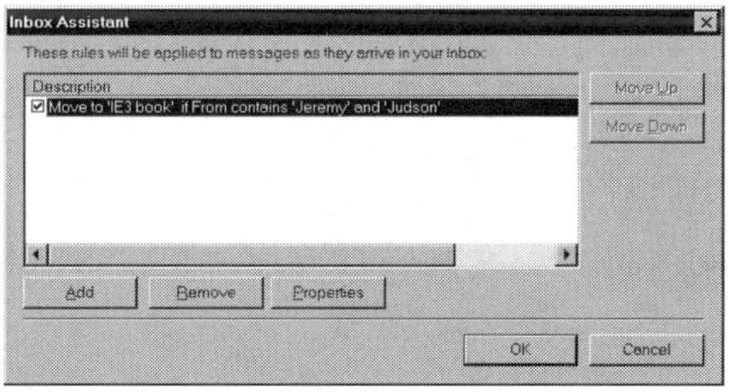

Figure 8.9 *You can use Inbox Assistant to specify how different types of incoming mail will be handled.*

About Internet Mail

Internet Mail is a full-featured e-mail program that is integrated with both Internet Explorer and Internet News. In addition to making it easy to send and receive e-mail, Internet Mail has the following special features:

- You can customize the interface and toolbar (see **Figure 8.7**).
- The address book can be used to record detailed background information about each person.
- You can address mail by typing any part of the recipient's name.
- You can send and receive formatted messages that contain fonts and styles (see **Figure 8.8**).
- You can create new folders to store different classes of mail, such as Budget Project, Business, and Sales Leads.
- Mail handling can be automated (see **Figure 8.9**).
- Mail can also be composed and sent from Internet Explorer and Internet News.
- If an e-mail message contains an address for a Web page, you can click the address to launch Internet Explorer and visit the page.

In the remainder of this chapter, I'll briefly explain the functions of the parts of the mail window.

Parts of the Mail Window

The mail window is divided into three parts, as shown in **Figure 8.10**:

- *Toolbar*. Contains buttons for common functions and a folder pop-up menu from which to pick a class of mail to view.
- *Message list*. Displays basic information for each message.
- *Preview pane*. Shows the text of the message that is selected in the message list.

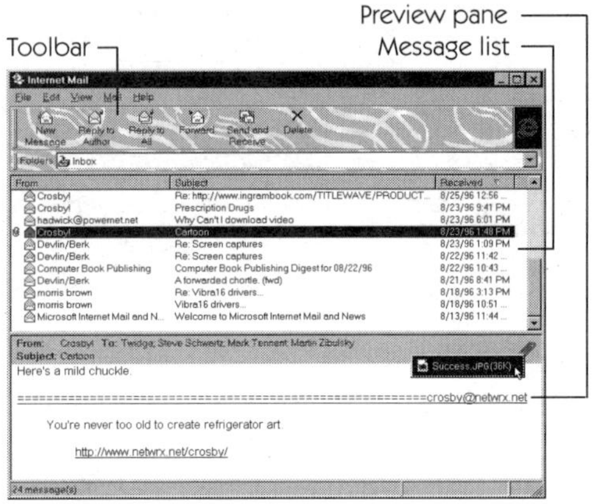

Figure 8.10 *The parts of the Internet Mail window.*

Using the Toolbar

Many mail functions can be performed by clicking toolbar buttons (see **Figure 8.11**). The buttons perform the following functions:

Figure 8.11 *This toolbar is displayed at the top of the Internet Mail window. It can be customized by adding or removing icons.*

- *New Message*. Opens a New Message window in which to create a new letter.
- *Reply to Author*. Opens a message window in which to reply to the author of the current message.
- *Reply to All*. If you receive a message from a group (such as a mailing list), choose this option to reply to the group or list.
- *Forward*. Send a copy of a received message to another individual.
- *Send and Receive*. Connect with your mail server, send all outgoing mail, and check for new messages.
- *Delete*. Move the selected message to the Deleted Items folder.

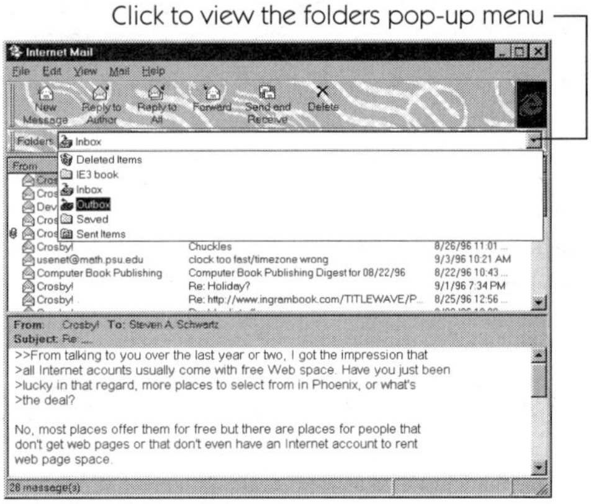

Figure 8.12 *Select a mail folder to view by clicking the folders pop-up menu.*

At the bottom of the toolbar is the folders pop-up menu (see **Figure 8.12**). Messages are organized in folders by type. To view a message class, select a folder from the Folders pop-up menu. The default folders are:

- *Inbox*. Contains incoming messages.
- *Outbox*. Contains new outgoing messages, forwarded messages, and replies. After they have been sent, the messages move to the Sent Items folder.
- *Sent Items*. Contains messages that you previously sent.
- *Deleted Items*. Contains messages that you have marked for deletion.

✔ Tip

- You can create additional folders as needed. Refer to Chapter 12.

Using the Message List

The message list contains the to/from, subject, and date information for each message. As mentioned previously, however, you can view only one mail folder at a time.

To read, reply to, forward, or delete a message, you begin by selecting it in the message list. You can open any message in its own window by double-clicking its line in the message list.

You can also select messages with the mouse or use any of the following keys to move through the message list: [Home], [End], [Pg Up], [Pg Dn], [↑], and [↓].

Using the Preview Pane

The preview pane displays the text of the selected message. You can read any message in the preview pane, regardless of which folder it is in.

Message Windows

In addition to reading messages in the preview pane, you can open a message in its own window (see **Figure 8.13**). Messages that you create—including new messages, replies, and forwarded messages—are automatically displayed in a new window.

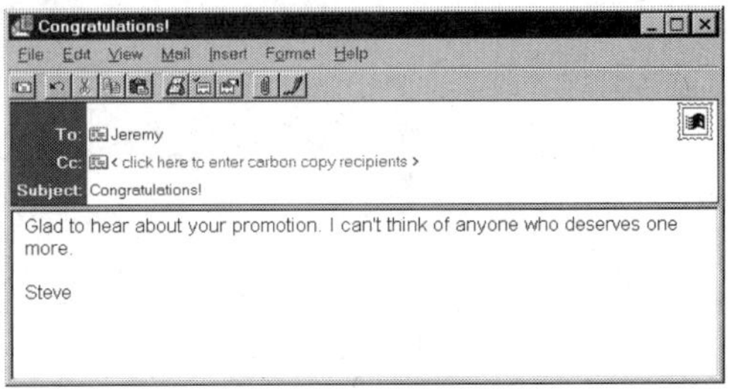

Figure 8.13 *All outgoing messages are created in a new window. You may find it easier to read incoming messages by opening windows for them, too.*

The message toolbar (see **Figure 8.14)** is slightly different from the normal toolbar. The functions—from left to right—are as follows:

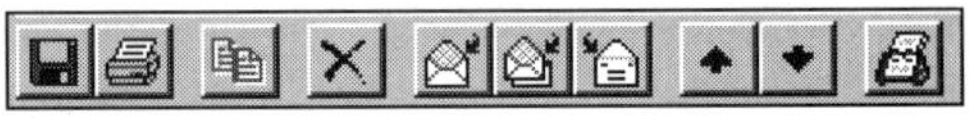

Figure 8.14 *This mini-toolbar appears atop individual message windows.*

- *Save*. Save the message to disk (in a location of your choice).
- *Print*. Print the current message.
- *Copy*. Copy the selected text.
- *Delete*. Delete the current message, moving it to the Deleted Items folder.
- *Reply to author*. Send a reply to the author of the message.
- *Reply to all*. Reply to a message from a group. (This option enables you to post a response to a message read in an Internet list or newsgroup.)
- *Forward*. Send a copy of the current message to another person.
- *Previous message*. Display the previous message from the message list (according to the current sort order).
- *Next message*. Display the next message from the message list (according to the sort order).
- *Address book*. Open the address book.

Using the Address Book

About the Address Book

Internet Mail's address book is the repository for the e-mail addresses of business associates, family, friends, and acquaintances. After you have entered addresses in the address book, any message can be addressed by simply pointing and clicking.

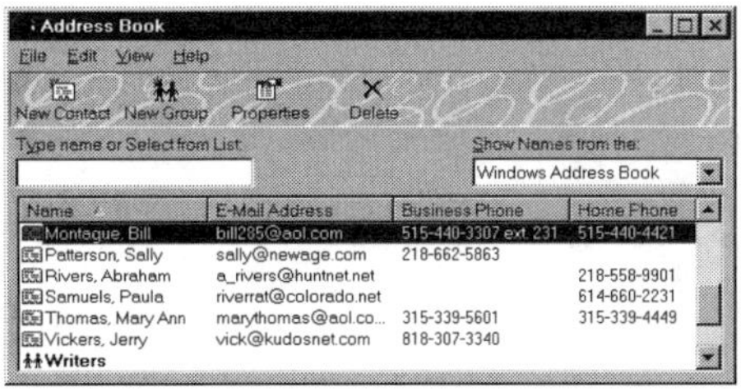

Figure 9.1 *Although the main purpose of the address book is to store e-mail addresses, it also has many features found in stand-alone address book programs.*

Address Book Features

You may notice that the address book is similar in design and function to many stand-alone address book programs. In addition to storing e-mail addresses, it can hold other information, such as a company name, street address, phone numbers, Web site address, and notes (see **Figure 9.1**).

Other features of the address book include the following:

- You can record multiple e-mail addresses for each contact, and select one as the default.
- You can create groups to organize contacts according to some common element.
- The address list can be displayed in a variety of formats and sort orders.
- You can quickly find names in the list by typing part of a name.
- You can import address data from Microsoft Exchange and Windows Messaging address books.

Address Book Limitations

Before you decide to use the Internet Mail address book as your sole repository for contact information, you should be aware of several important limitations:

- Information in the address book cannot be printed. Thus, although you can enter volumes of data for each contact, you cannot print phone directories or mailing labels, for example.
- Address book data cannot be exported for use in other programs.
- Although you can enter several phone numbers for each person, the address book has no dialing capabilities.

Opening the Address Book

To view, create, edit, or delete contact records, you must open the address book. Choose Address Book from the File menu (see **Figure 9.2**) or click the Address Book icon in a message window (see **Figure 9.3**). The address book opens (refer to **Figure 9.1**).

To find a particular contact, you can either scroll through the list or type part of the person's name in the Type name or Select from List box.

✔ Tip

- Address Book is a *modal* window. Thus, while it is open, you are in address book mode; you cannot work in any other Internet Mail window. If you need to use another part of the program, you must first close the Address Book.

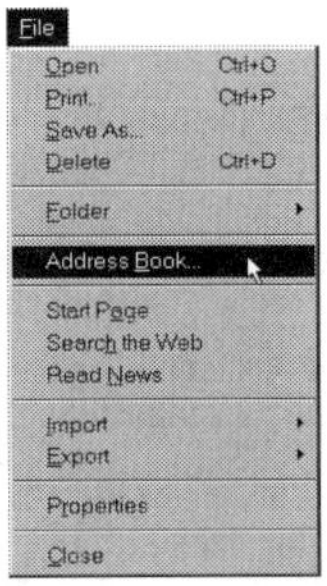

Figure 9.2 *To open the address book, choose Address Book from the File menu.*

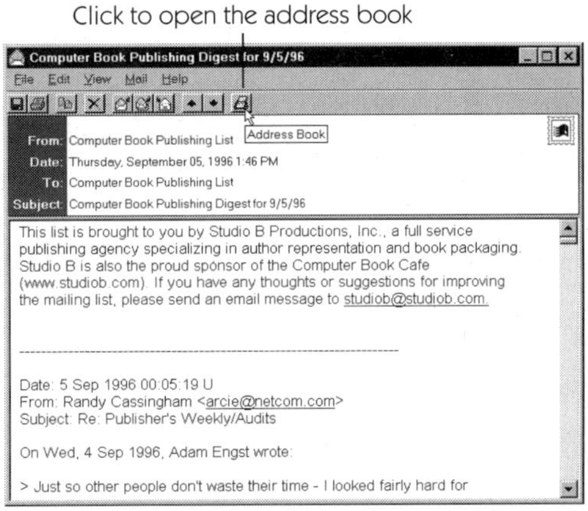

Figure 9.3 *You also can open the address book by clicking the Address Book icon in any message window.*

Section tabs

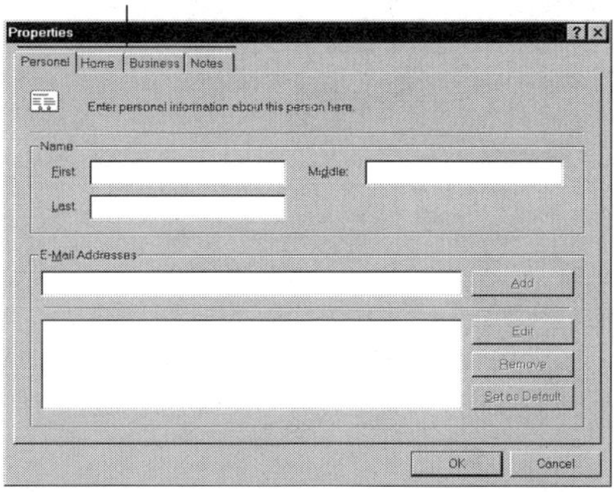

Figure 9.4 *Each address record has four sections, indicated by the tabs at the top of the Properties dialog box.*

Click this icon to go to the Web site

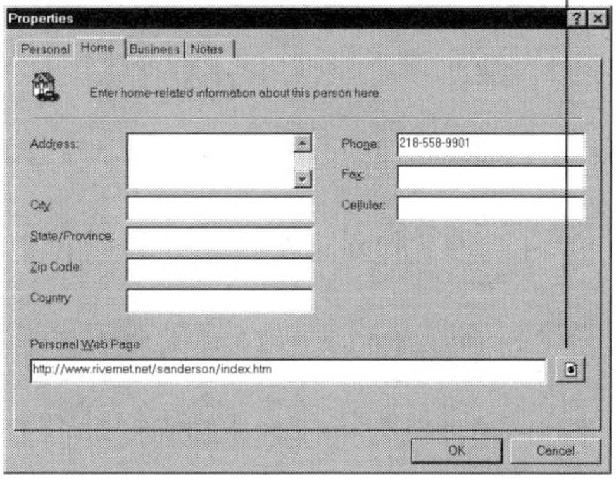

Figure 9.5 *If a URL is present, you can visit a contact's Web site by clicking.*

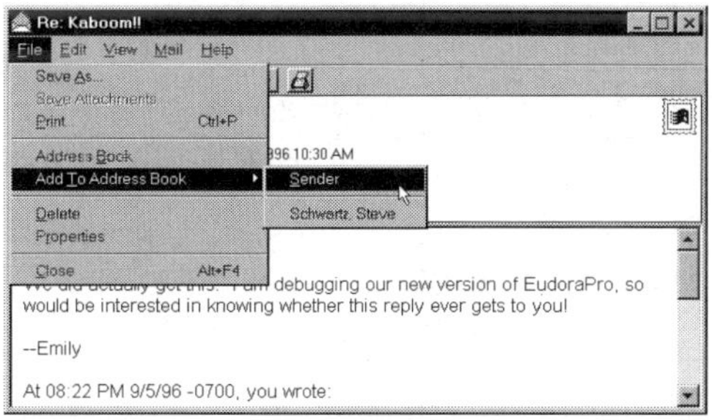

Figure 9.6 *Perhaps the easiest way to create a new record is to choose the Add To Address Book command.*

Creating New Records

When the address book is open, you can create new contacts, as well as edit or delete existing contact records. Data for a new record can be entered manually, or it can be extracted from a received message.

To manually create a new record:

1. Choose New Contact from the File menu, or click the New Contact button. A blank Properties dialog box appears, as shown in **Figure 9.4**.
2. Fill in the fields. To move from one field to the next, press [Tab].
3. Type the person's e-mail address, and then click Add. The first e-mail address that you enter is set as the person's default address.

   If the person has other e-mail addresses, enter each one and click Add. To specify a new default address, select it in the bottom window and click Set as Default.
4. *Optional*: Enter information in other sections of the dialog box by clicking the tabs (see **Figure 9.5**).
5. Click OK to save the record.

To create a new record from a received message:

1. Open the received message in its own window. (Double-click the message in the message list, or select the message and choose Open from the File menu.)
2. Choose Add To Address Book from the File menu, as shown in **Figure 9.6**.

Choose Sender or a recipient's name to indicate which person is to be added to the address book.

or

2. Right-click the sender's name in the From line, and then choose Add To Address Book from the pop-up menu (see **Figure 9.7**).

or

2. In a message with several recipients, right-click a person's name in the To line, and then choose Add To Address Book from the pop-up menu (see **Figure 9.8**).

   The Properties dialog box appears (see **Figure 9.9**). The contact's name and e-mail address are already filled in.

3. Complete other fields as desired, and click OK.

✔ Tips

- At a minimum, you must enter a contact name (first name, last name, or both) and an e-mail address for each record. Without this information, the record is considered incomplete.
- The address book list (refer to **Figure 9.1**) only displays the name, e-mail address, business phone, and home phone fields. Unless you intend to use it as your main address program, you may want to restrict entries to these fields.

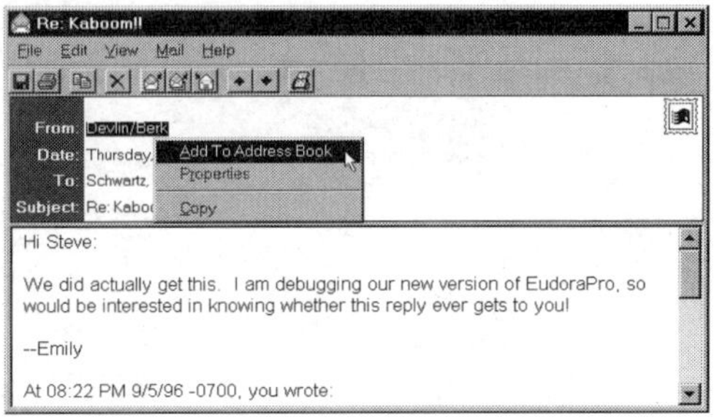

Figure 9.7 *Right-click the From line to add that person to the address book.*

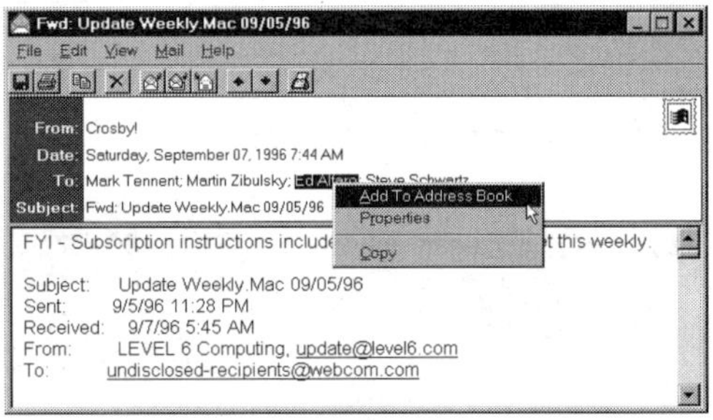

Figure 9.8 *Right-click a name in the To line to add it to your address book.*

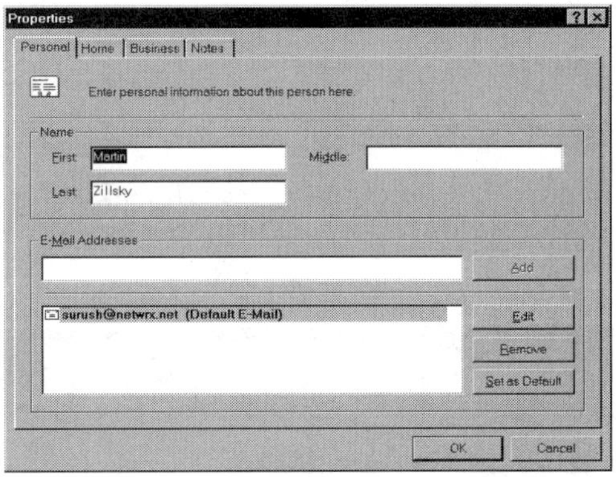

Figure 9.9 *The basic contact information is automatically entered in the record.*

Editing Records

Whether you need to correct a mistake or update a person's address information, you can modify address records whenever you wish.

To edit a record:

1. Open the address book by choosing Address Book from the File menu or by clicking the Address Book icon in a message window.
2. In the address list, highlight the record you want to edit.
3. Open the record by doing one of the following:
   - Choose Properties from the File menu.
   - Click the Properties button.
   - Double-click the record line.
   - Press Enter or Return.
4. Make the necessary changes. You can click the tabs at the top of the dialog box to view other sections of the record.
5. Click OK to save the changes.

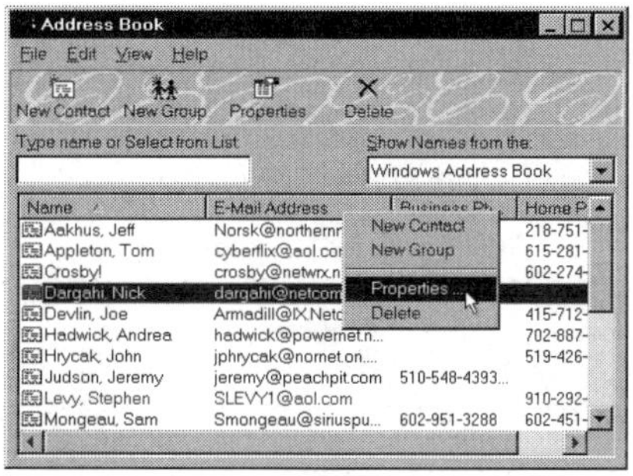

Figure 9.10 *Right-click in the column headings to display the File menu.*

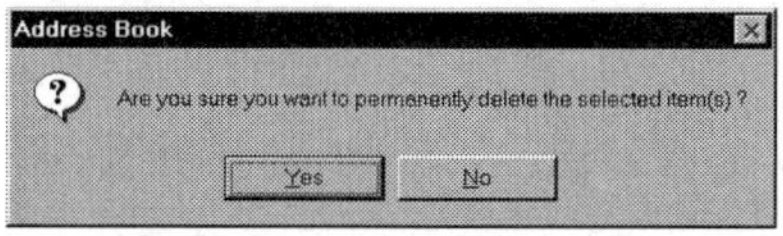

Figure 9.11 *Click Yes to confirm a record deletion.*

✔ Tips

- There is another way to open a record. Right-click in the column headings for the address list. A copy of the File menu appears, as shown in **Figure 9.10**. Choose the Properties command.
- To delete a contact record, select it in the address list and click the Delete button, choose Delete from the File menu, or press Del. Then confirm the deletion by clicking Yes (see **Figure 9.11**).

Creating Groups

If you sometimes send the same message to several contacts, you may find it helpful to define them as a *group*. The next time you need to send them all a message, you can simply address it to the group.

To create a group:

1. Open the address book by choosing Address Book from the File menu or by clicking the Address Book icon in a message window.
2. Do one of the following:
   - Choose New Group from the File menu.
   - Click the New group button.
   - Right-click in the column headings for the address list, and choose New Group from the File pop-up menu.

   The Properties dialog box appears, as shown in **Figure 9.12**.
3. Enter a name for the group in the Group Name box.
4. Click Add to add a group member. The Select Group Members dialog box appears (see **Figure 9.13**).
5. Select a contact from the address list. Click Add or double-click the contact's line to add the person to the group. Repeat this step to add other members to the group.
6. Click OK in both dialog boxes to save the new group. (See **Figure 9.14** for an example of a complete group.)

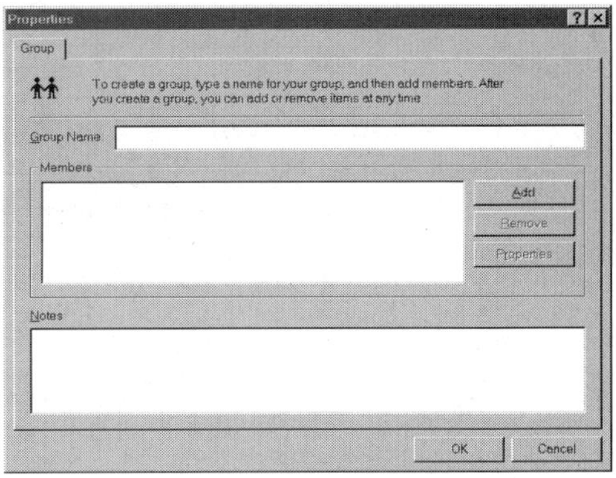

Figure 9.12 *Groups are defined in this version of the Properties dialog box.*

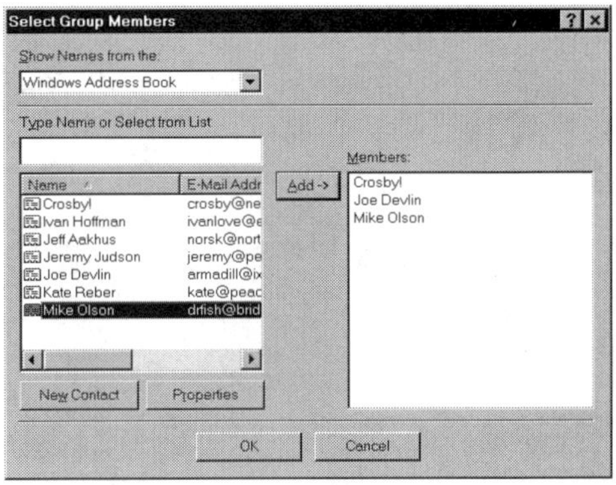

Figure 9.13 *You add group members in the Select Group Members dialog box.*

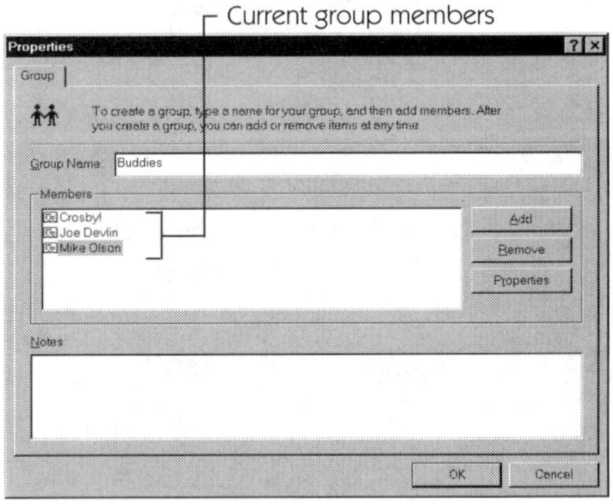

Figure 9.14 *These three people make up a group named Buddies.*

Modifying a Group

You can modify any existing group by deleting the group, changing the group name, or changing the members.

To delete a group:

1. Open the address book by choosing Address Book from the File menu or by clicking the Address Book icon in a message window.
2. Select the group name in the address list, and do one of the following:
   - Click the Delete button.
   - Choose Delete from the File menu.
   - Press [Del].
   - Right-click in the column headings, and choose Delete from the pop-up menu that appears.
3. Confirm the deletion by clicking Yes in the dialog box that appears.

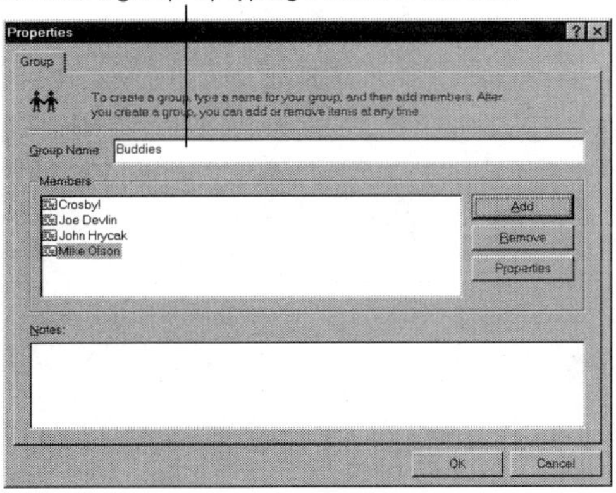

Figure 9.15 *The group name and members are shown in the Properties dialog box.*

To rename a group:

1. Open the address book by choosing Address Book from the File menu or by clicking the Address Book icon in a message window.
2. Select the group name in the address list, and then either choose Properties from the File menu, click the Properties button, double-click the group record, or press [Enter] or [Return].
3. Type a new name in the Group Name box (see **Figure 9.15**).
4. Click OK.

To change a group's members:

1. Open the address book by choosing Address Book from the File menu or by clicking the Address Book icon in a message window.
2. To open the Properties dialog box for the group (refer to **Figure 9.15)**, select the group name in the address list, and do one of the following:
   - Choose Properties from the File menu.
   - Click the Properties button.
   - Double-click the record line.
   - Press Enter or Return.
3. To delete a member, select the member's name, and do one of the following:
   - Click Remove.
   - Right-click the member's name, and choose Remove from the pop-up menu that appears.

   Note that deletions are immediate; there is no opportunity for you to confirm or cancel the member's removal.
4. To add a member, click Add. The Select Group Members dialog box appears (see **Figure 9.16**). Select a name in the contact list, and click Add. Repeat for all other members you wish to add.
5. Close the dialog box (or boxes) by clicking OK.

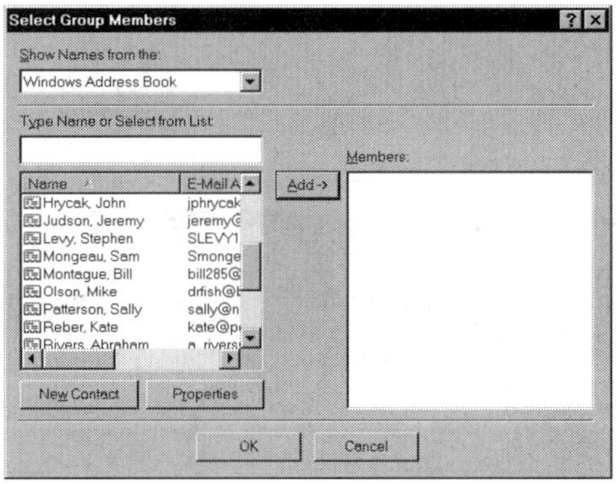

Figure 9.16 *Choose new group members in the Select Group Members dialog box.*

Organizing the Address List

You can't change the address book's toolbar or column headings, but you can set a display format and a sort order for the list.

Setting Display Format Options

The standard display format is Details, which shows all four fields for each contact. In other views, only the contact name is shown.

Figure 9.17 *Use the View menu to set a display format and sort order for the address list.*

To set a display format for the address list, choose Large Icons, Small Icons, List, or Details from the View menu, as shown in **Figure 9.17**.

✔ Tips

- If you only use the address list to choose e-mail recipients, you may prefer the uncluttered look of Large Icons, Small Icons, or List view. You can still sort the list by first or last name.
- You can hide the toolbar by choosing Toolbar from the View menu. (This command works as a toggle. When the toolbar is visible, the command is preceded by a check mark.)
- You can widen, shrink, or hide column headings in Details view. Move the pointer between any pair of columns until it changes to a double arrow. Then drag to widen or shrink the column on the left.

Setting a Sort Order

Regardless of the view you have chosen, you can specify a sort order for the address list, as follows:

- Select a sort order from the Sort By submenu of the View menu, as shown in **Figure 9.18**. To choose between ascending and descending sorts, choose the appropriate option from the bottom of the Sort By submenu.
- In Details view, click a column heading to sort the list by that field. To change between ascending and descending sorts, click the same column heading again.

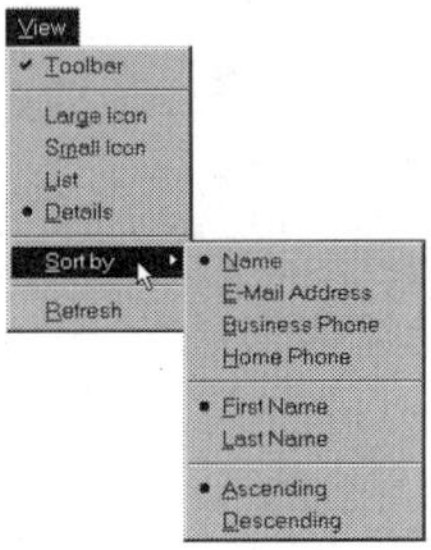

Figure 9.18 *Select a sort order from the Sort By submenu of the View menu. The listed options vary depending on the view mode that is currently selected.*

✔ **Tip**

- In Details view, you can make a name sort display as either last name/first name or first name/last name by repeatedly clicking the Name heading.

Importing Address Data

If you use Microsoft Exchange or Windows Messaging, you can import address data into the Internet Mail address book. Choose Address Book from the Import submenu of the File menu (see **Figure 9.19**) and follow the on-screen instructions.

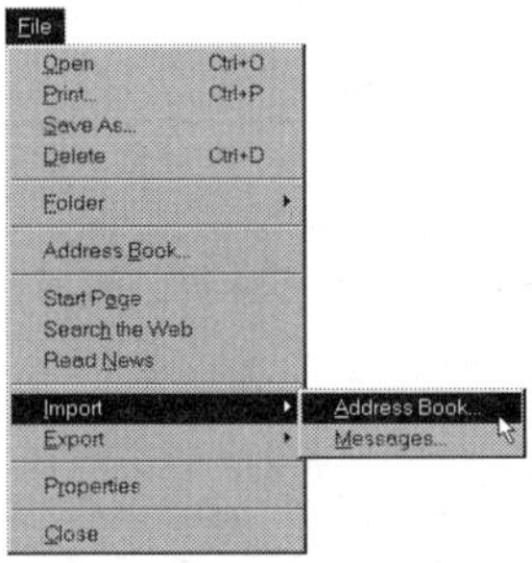

Figure 9.19 *To import an existing address book, choose Address Book from the Import submenu of the File menu.*

If you use another e-mail program or address book utility, however, there is no simple way to move addresses into Internet Mail. For now, the best you can do is copy and paste address data into Internet Mail—one field at a time.

And, as mentioned earlier in this chapter, Internet Mail cannot export its address book. If you want to use the address book in another program, the program must be able to read or import the file.

Composing and Sending Mail

10

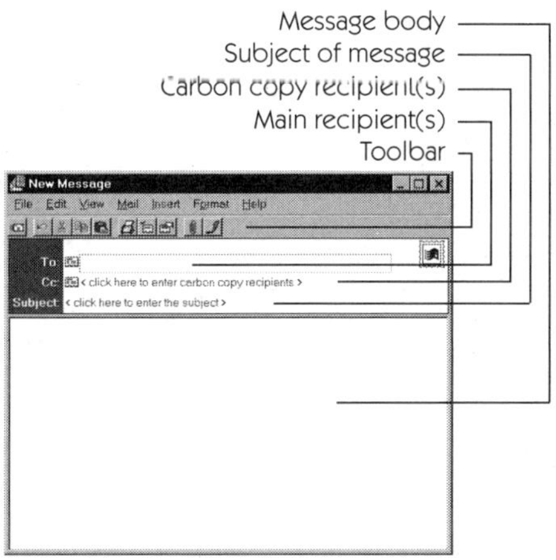

Figure 10.1 *The parts of the New Message window.*

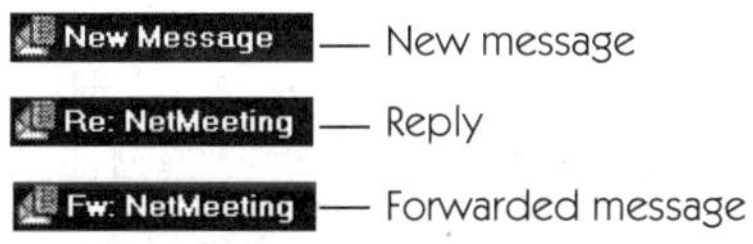

Figure 10.2 *Different types of messages have different window titles.*

Figure 10.3 *One convenient way to open a New Message window is to click the New Message button.*

About Composing Mail

There are three types of messages that you can create in Internet Mail:

- *New messages*. Messages that you compose from scratch.
- *Replies*. Received messages to which you are responding.
- *Forwarded messages*. Received messages that you are forwarding to someone else.

All messages—whether new, replies, or forwarded—are composed in a New Message window (see **Figure 10.1**).

The New Message Window contains two main parts: the message header (the To, Cc, and Subject lines) and the message body (the text of the message). Note that the window title differs for each message type, showing *New Message* for an original message, *Re:* for a reply, and *Fw:* for a forwarded message (see **Figure 10.2**).

The first step in creating a message is to open a New Message window. The procedure differs slightly depending on the type of message being created.

To open a New Message window for a new message:

- Click the New Message button in the toolbar (see **Figure 10.3**), choose New Message from the Mail menu, or press Ctrl N.

  or

- Click a *mail-to* link (a link to an e-mail address) in a Web page.

  or

- Click an e-mail address in the body of a received message.

To open a New Message window for a reply:

- If the message is selected in the message list, click the Reply to Author or Reply to All button, or choose Reply to Author (Ctrl R) or Reply to All (Ctrl Shift R) from the Mail menu.
- If the message to which you want to reply is already open in its own window, click the Reply to Author or Reply to All button (as shown in **Figure 10.4**), or choose Reply to Author (Ctrl R) or Reply to All (Ctrl Shift R) from the Mail menu.

It is customary to quote relevant parts of the message to which you are replying (see **Figure 10.5**). To automatically insert a copy of the original message into your reply, choose "Include message in reply" in the Send section of the Options dialog box. You can edit the quoted text as necessary.

To open a New Message window for a forwarded message:

- If the message is selected in the message list, click the Forward button, choose Forward from the Mail menu, or press Ctrl F.
- If the message is already open in its own window, click the Forward button, choose Forward from the Mail menu, or press Ctrl F.

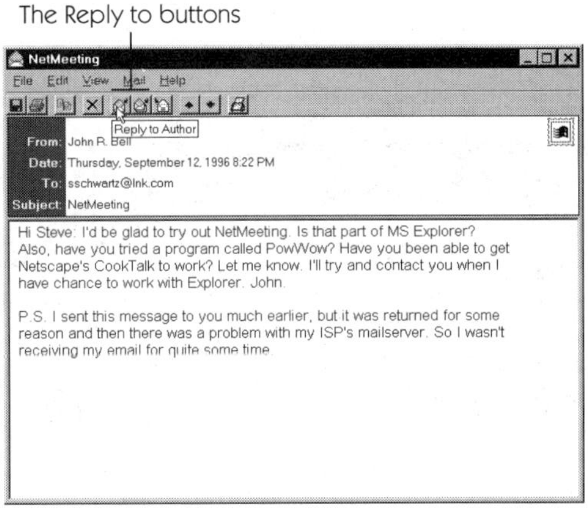

Figure 10.4 *The Reply to Author and Reply to All buttons are displayed in received message windows (shown here) and in the mail window.*

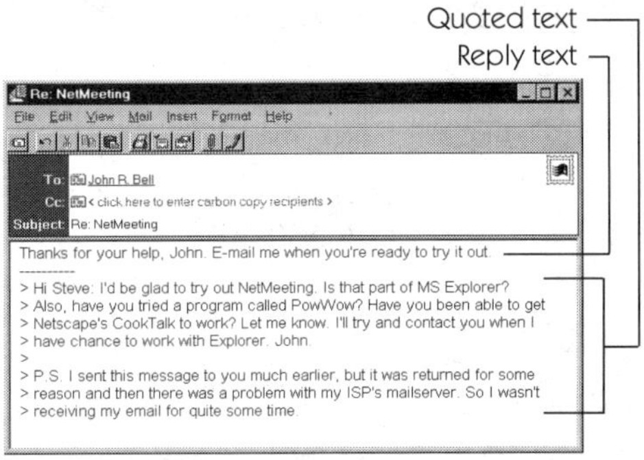

Figure 10.5 *Replies often quote text from the original message.*

Writing a Message

When you're writing messages, Internet Mail works like a typical word processing program or text editor. Words automatically wrap from one line to the next. You only have to press Return when you want to start a new paragraph.

Similarly, the standard editing commands are available. You can choose the following commands from the Edit menu (see **Figure 10.6**), or you can use the keyboard shortcuts:

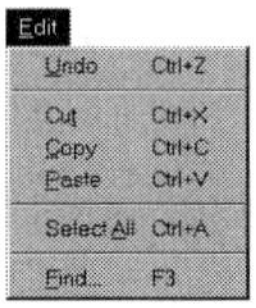

Figure 10.6 *The Edit menu.*

- *Undo* (Ctrl Z). Undo the most recent edit or command.
- *Cut* (Ctrl X). Delete the selected text, and place a copy of it on the clipboard (making it available for pasting).
- *Copy* (Ctrl C). Copy the selected text to the clipboard (making it available for pasting).
- *Paste* (Ctrl V). Paste text from the clipboard at the cursor location.
- *Select All* (Ctrl A). Select all text in the document.
- *Find* (F3). Find a text string in the message body (see **Figure 10.7**).

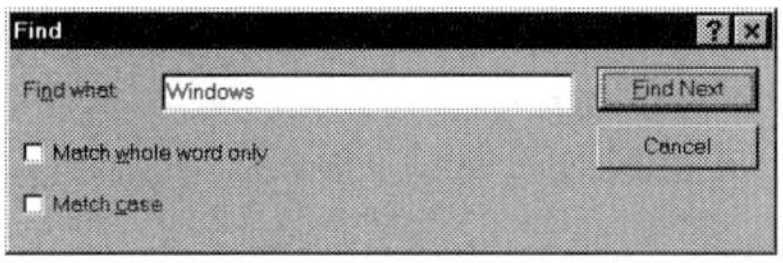

Figure 10.7 *Use Find to locate a text string in the message. If it is found, the window scrolls to display the string. Click Find Next to search for additional instances.*

✔ **Tips**

- You can select a word by double-clicking anywhere within the word. Triple-click to select an entire line.
- If Microsoft Office is installed, the Check Spelling (F7) command is enabled.

Writing a Message

Formatting a Message

Internet Mail can create plain text and HTML-formatted messages. Options available for the two formats differ significantly.

You can set a default message format in the Send section of the Options dialog box (see **Figure 10.8**). Regardless of the default setting, you can select a format for each outgoing message from the Format menu (see **Figure 10.9**).

Plain Text Formatting

Plain Text messages are formatted with a single font and point size. There is no style support (such as boldface or italic) and no paragraph alignment commands. Tabs can be included, but are treated as a string of eight spaces. To ensure compatibility with other mail programs and computer systems, most messages are Plain Text.

HTML Formatting

HTML messages can contain multiple fonts, sizes, styles, and colors. You can sct paragraph alignments (left, right, and centered) and create bullet lists.

To set formatting for selected text or the current paragraph, you can choose options from the format toolbar (see **Figure 10.10**) or from the Format menu.

✔ **Tip**

■ HTML formatting is visible only in HTML-capable mail programs and browsers. At the moment, few mail programs can display HTML. To save yourself some unnecessary work, you may want to reserve such messages for other users of Internet Mail.

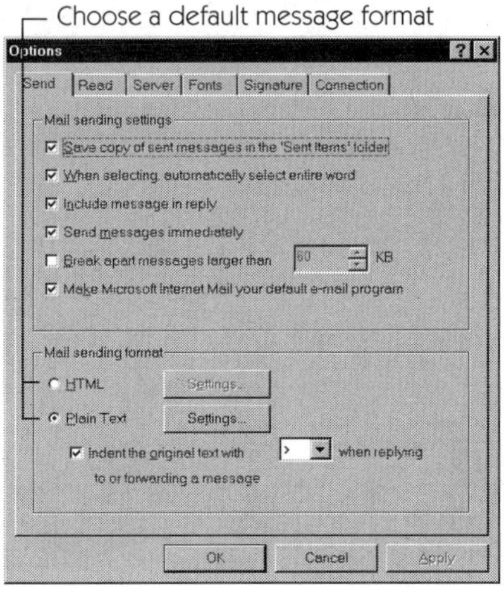

Figure 10.8 *Click a radio button to set the default message format.*

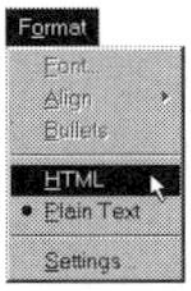

Figure 10.9 *You can choose Plain Text or HTML format. The chosen format is marked with a bullet.*

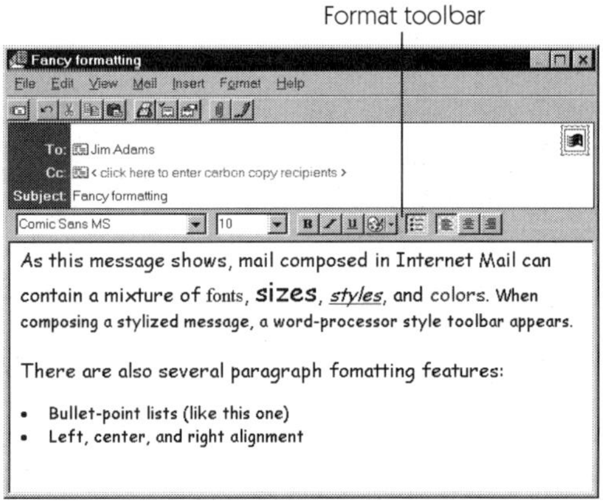

Figure 10.10 *When creating an HTML message, a format toolbar (similar to the ones found in many word processing programs) can be used to apply text and paragraph formatting.*

Inserting a Text File

There are two ways to insert text from other documents into a message. One way is to copy the text in the other document (Ctrl C), and then paste it into the message (Ctrl V). The second method is to insert a text file from disk.

To insert a text file into the current message:

1. Position the cursor where you want to insert the text file.
2. Choose Text File from the Insert menu (see **Figure 10.11**). The Insert Text File dialog box appears (see **Figure 10.12**).
3. Select a text (.TXT) file to insert, and click Open.

Figure 10.11 *To insert a text file from disk into the message, choose Text File from the Insert menu.*

Figure 10.12 *Select a file to insert from the Insert Text File dialog box. Only .TXT files can be inserted.*

✔ **Tip**

- Only text files can be inserted. To insert a word processing file, you must first save a copy of it in ASCII, Plain Text, or a similar format. (Note that the file's extension must be .TXT.)

Adding a Signature

Optionally, a message can end with a *signature* (one or more lines that provide your name and postal address, Web site URL, or a brief message).

To add a signature to the current message, do one of the following:

- Choose Signature from the Insert menu (refer to **Figure 10.11**).
- Click the Insert Signature button in the toolbar.
- In the Signature section of the Options dialog box, check "Add signature to end of all outgoing

messages” (see **Figure 10.13**). In that case, a signature is automatically added to *every* message.

Signature text is specified in the Signature section of the Options dialog box. To learn more about signatures, see “Signature Options” in Chapter 13.

Adding Attachments

One popular use of e-mail is to transfer formatted documents, graphic images, and programs along with a message. Such files are *attachments*.

To add an attachment:

1. Choose File Attachment from the Insert menu.

   or

1. Click the Insert File button on the message toolbar.

   The Insert Attachment dialog box appears (see **Figure 10.14**).

2. Select a file, and click Attach. An icon for the file is added to the bottom of the message window (see **Figure 10.15**).

   You can select additional attachments by repeating these steps. To remove an attachment, click its icon in the message window and press Del.

✔ Tip

- Attachments are encoded using MIME (Multipurpose Internet Mail Extensions). To decode them, the recipient must have an e-mail program or utility that can handle this task.

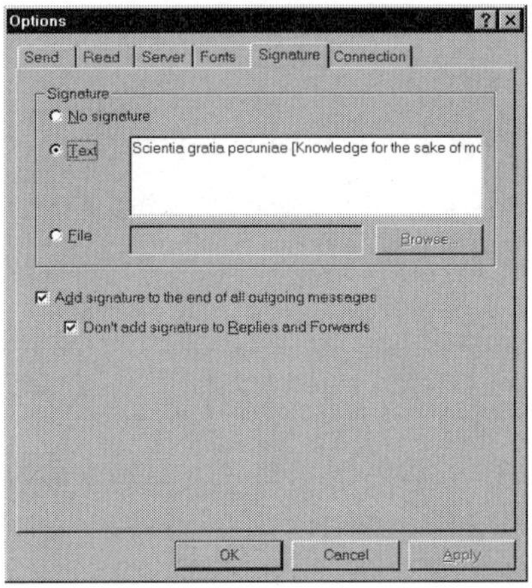

Figure 10.13 *You can specify a signature to include in messages in the Options dialog box.*

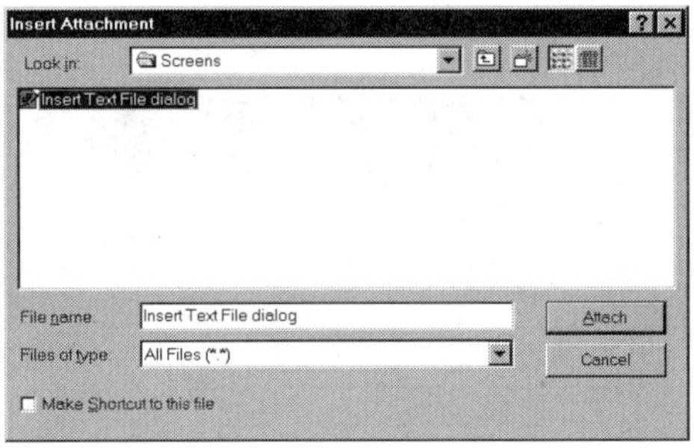

Figure 10.14 *Choose attachment files in this dialog box. Any type of file can be an attachment, such as a movie or sound.*

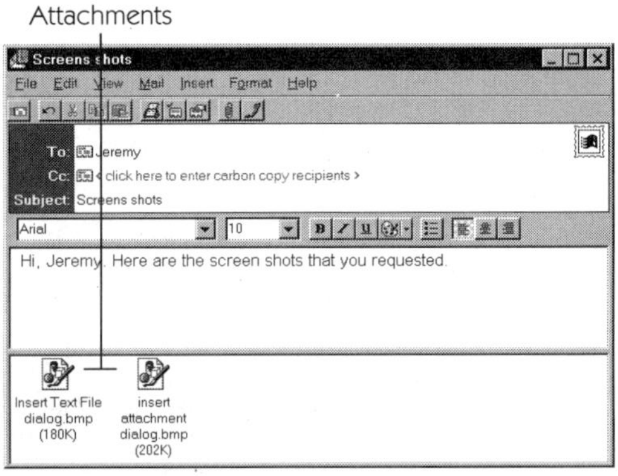

Figure 10.15 *Attachments are displayed at the bottom of the message window.*

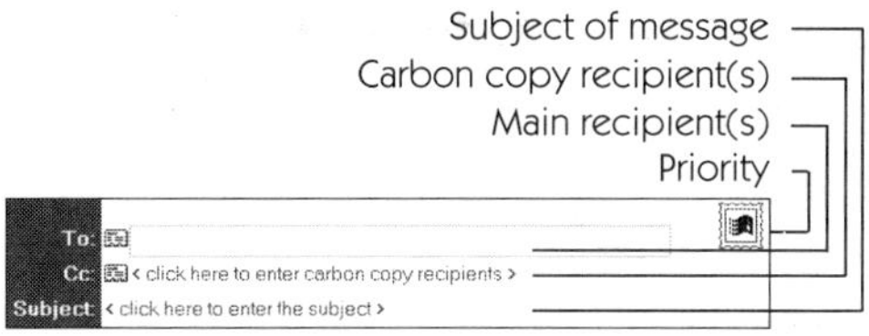

Figure 10.16 *The components of the message header.*

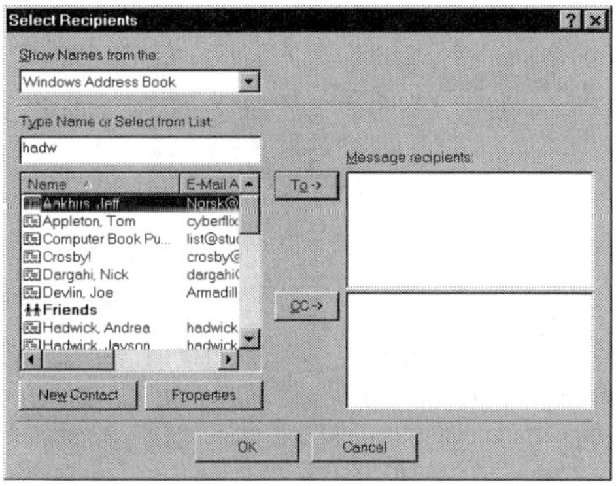

Figure 10.17 *One way to address an outgoing message is by picking one or more names from the address book.*

The Message Header

Before sending a message, you must enter information in the header (see **Figure 10.16**). Every message header contains three lines: To, Cc, and Subject. The postage stamp is used to set an optional priority for the message.

Addressing a Message

The names or addresses of the primary recipients are entered in the To line. Use the Cc line to specify recipients of a carbon copy of the message. A short title or explanation of the subject matter is entered in the Subject line. At a minimum, there must always be an entry in the To line.

Internet Mail provides several ways for you to select message recipients, as described below.

To select an address from the address book:

1. To open the address book, click the icon beside To or Cc in the header.

   or

   Click the Pick Recipients button in the message window toolbar.

   or

   Choose the Choose Recipients command from the Mail menu.

   The address book opens, as shown in **Figure 10.17**.

2. Select a name from the contact list, and click the To or CC button to add it to the appropriate recipient list.

   or

Double-click a name in the contact list to automatically add it to the To message recipients.

or

Type a full or partial name in the Type Name or Select from List box. As you type, the closest matching contact is highlighted. Click To or CC to add it to the appropriate recipient list.

3. Click OK to close the address book, accepting the recipient list. The chosen name or names appear in the message header (see **Figure 10.18**).

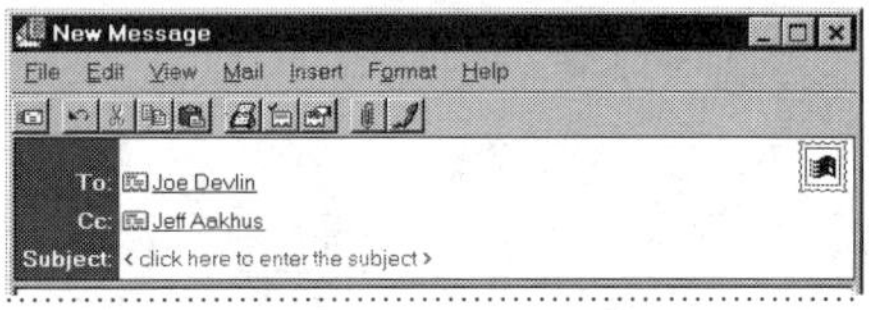

Figure 10.18 *This message and a copy of the message will be sent to Joe Devlin and Jeff Aakhus, respectively.*

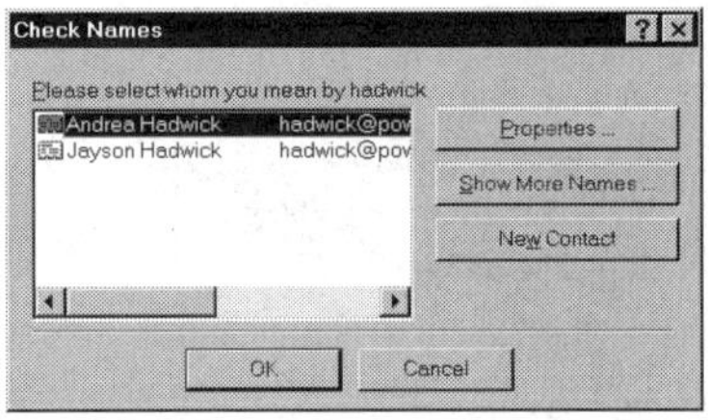

Figure 10.19 *When Internet Mail is not sure of the intended recipient, the Check Names dialog box is presented. You can also instruct the program to examine recipient names by choosing Check Names from the Mail menu.*

Manually Entering a Recipient

You can also type or paste a name or an e-mail address into the To or Cc lines of the message header.

- If the contact is not in the address book, type or paste the person's full e-mail address in the To or Cc line (e.g., tsjones@logon.net).
- If the contact is in your address book, type all or part of his or her name in the To or Cc line (e.g., Steve, Simms, or Steve Simms). When you send the message, Internet Mail prompts for the correct recipient, if necessary (see **Figure 10.19**).

✔ **Tip**

- Web pages often contain mail-to links that when clicked instruct your default mail program to address a letter to that person or company (see **Figure 10.20**).

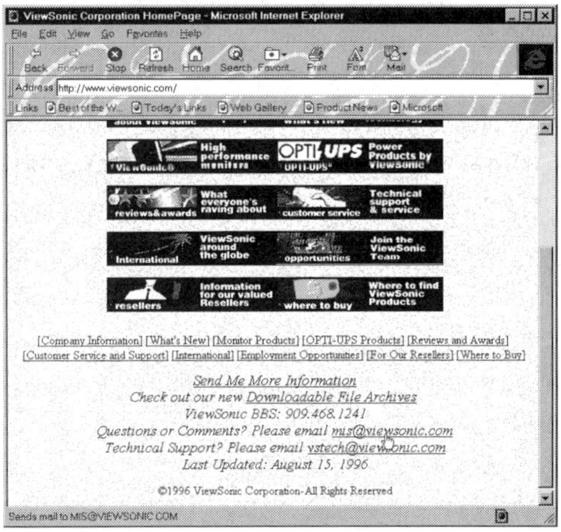

Figure 10.20 *You can click an e-mail link in a Web page to launch Internet Mail and open a New Message window that is addressed to the person or company.*

Other Message Options

There are several other message options that you may sometimes want to use, as described below.

Sending to a Group

Messages—as well as attachments—can be sent to a group (see **Figure 10.21**). Rather than picking individual recipient names from the address book, select the name of their group. See Chapter 9 for information on defining a group.

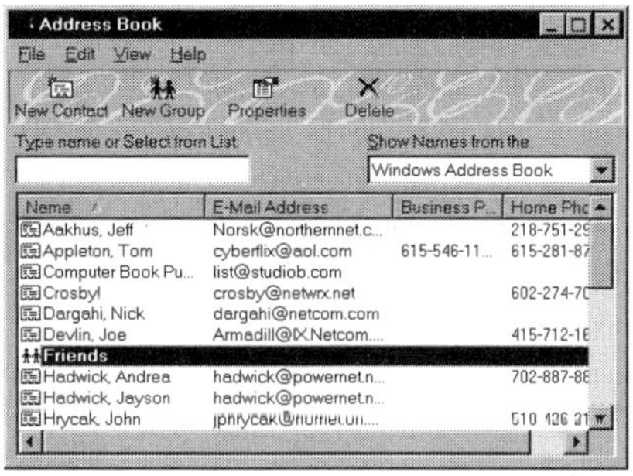

Figure 10.21 *To send a message to a group, select the group name in the Address book or type it in the To line.*

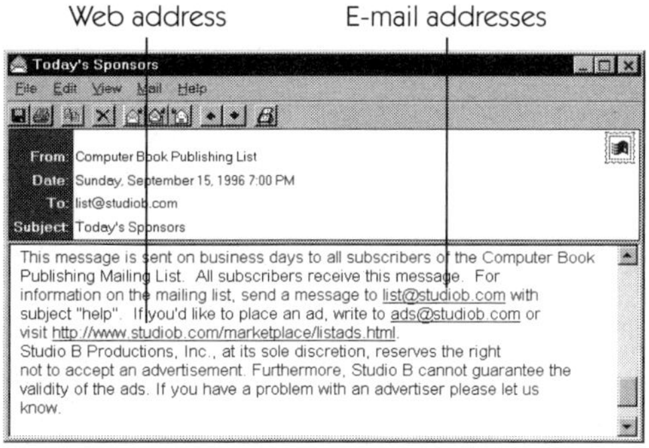

Figure 10.22 *Any URL or e-mail address in a message is automatically treated as a link by Internet Mail.*

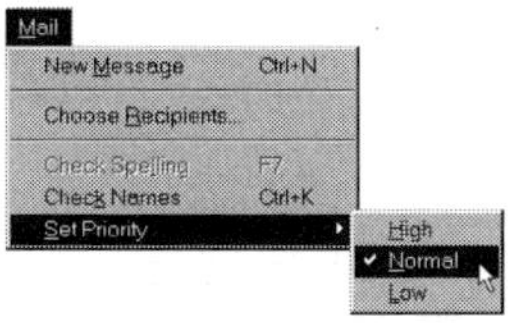

Figure 10.23 *A priority can be assigned by choosing a command from the Set Priority submenu of the Mail menu.*

Including URLs in Messages

Any Web page address that you type in the body of a message can be clicked by the recipient to open that page in Internet Explorer (see **Figure 10.22**). Similarly, clicking an e-mail address in the body opens a New Message window addressed to the person. (This feature is available only to users of Internet Mail.)

Setting a Message Priority

You can set a priority for an outgoing message to indicate its level of importance. Setting a priority, however, has no impact on the manner in which it is delivered, and many mail programs do not recognize or use priorities.

To set a priority for a message:

1. Open the message in its own window.
2. Click the postage stamp icon to reveal the Set Priority pop-up menu, or choose Set Priority from the Mail menu (see **Figure 10.23**).
3. Choose a priority: High, Normal, or Low.

Sending Messages

There are several methods you can use to send messages, as described below.

To send an individual message:

- Click the Send button in the New Message window, as shown in **Figure 10.24**).

  or

- Choose Send Message from the File menu, or press Alt S.

If the option to "Send messages immediately" has been checked in the Send section of the Options dialog box, the message is immediately transmitted to your mail server. Otherwise, it is held in the Outbox and will be sent the next time that mail is exchanged with the server.

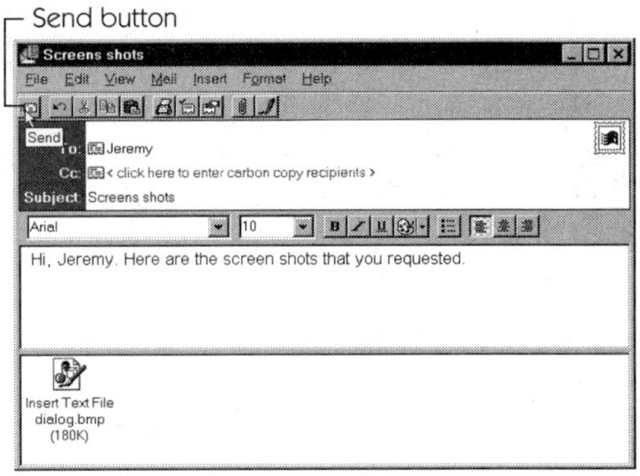

Figure 10.24 *When you are done writing a message, click Send.*

To send and receive all waiting messages:

- In the main mail window, click the Send and Receive button.

  or

- Choose Send and Receive from the Mail menu, or press Ctrl M.

Receiving Mail

There's more to receiving mail than simply opening and reading it. In this chapter, you'll learn how to manage incoming mail, print messages, handle attachments, and import and export messages.

Checking for New Mail

You can check for new mail manually or automatically. (This is a two-way process. Whenever you check for mail, any messages in the Outbox are sent.)

Send and Receive button

Figure 11.1 *To manually send mail and check for new messages, click Send and Receive.*

To manually check for new mail:

1. Switch to the mail window.
2. Click the Send and Receive button in the toolbar (see **Figure 11.1**).

   or

3. Choose Send and Receive from the Mail menu, or press Ctrl M.

Set this option to automate mail delivery

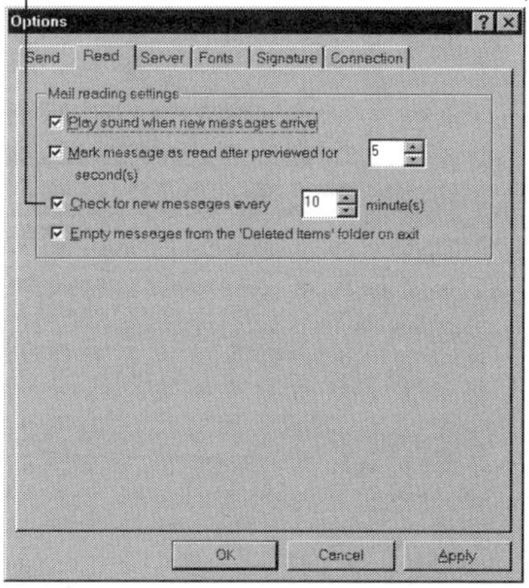

Figure 11.2 *To automatically send and receive at regular intervals, check this option in the Read section of the Options dialog box.*

To automatically check for mail:

1. Choose Options from the Mail menu. The Options dialog box appears.
2. Click the Read tab at the top of the dialog box (see **Figure 11.2**).
3. Set the option for "Check for new messages every *xx* minutes," and set the number of minutes you want to wait between mail checks.

Whenever Internet Mail is running and you are connected to the Internet, the program will now send and receive at the designated intervals.

Reading Messages

When mail arrives, it is announced by a sound effect and an icon in the Taskbar (see **Figure 11.3**). You can read mail in the preview pane or in individual message windows.

To read a message:

1. Switch to the mail window.
2. From the Folders pop-up menu, select the folder in which the message is stored (see **Figure 11.4**).
3. Select the message in the message list. The message text appears in the preview pane at the bottom of the mail window.
4. Read the message in the preview pane. Scroll the pane as required.

   or

4. To read a message in its own window (see **Figure 11.5**), double-click it in the message list or choose Open from the File menu.

✔ **Tip**

- As long as a message is stored in one of the mail folders, it can be read—regardless of whether the message is new or old. This includes mail in Deleted Items.

Read and Unread Messages

When a message arrives, its name is displayed in boldface in the message list (indicating that it has not been read). After reading it or letting the cursor rest over it in the message list, the boldface is removed (indicating that the message has been read).

Figure 11.3 *The new mail notifier is a tiny envelope icon that appears in the taskbar.*

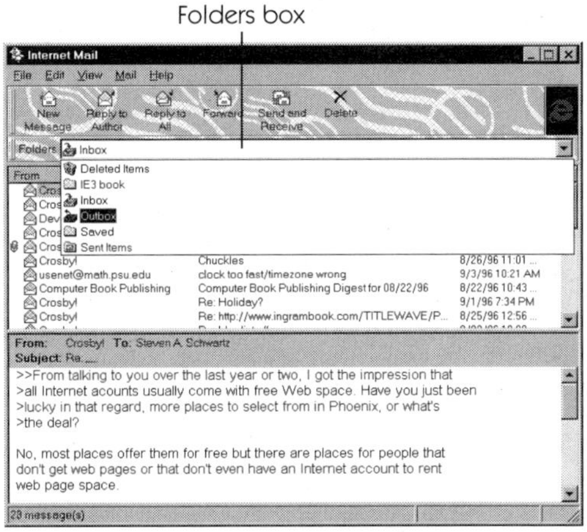

Figure 11.4 *You can click anywhere in the Folders box to display the folder list.*

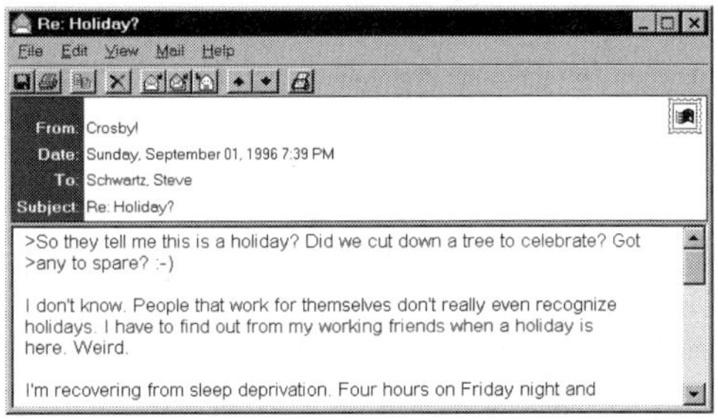

Figure 11.5 *You can view any message in its own window.*

To manually change the status of a message:

1. Select one or more messages from the message list. (To choose additional messages, Ctrl-click them.)
2. Choose Mark as Read from the Edit menu, or press Ctrl Enter.

   or

2. Choose Mark as Unread from the Edit menu, or press Ctrl Shift Enter.

✔ Tips

- Marking messages as read or unread is a convenience option. It does not affect the handling of the messages in any way. Read messages are not automatically moved to the Deleted Items folder, for example.
- One reason to mark an unread message as having been read is so you can ignore the message. This procedure, as well as deleting the message, is handy for dealing with unwanted or junk e-mail.

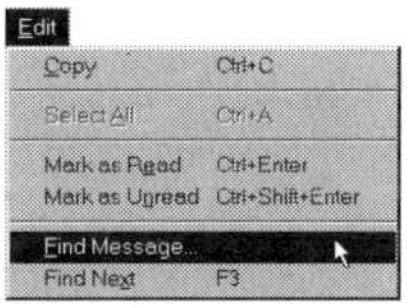

Figure 11.6 *To search for a message, choose Find Message from the Edit menu.*

Figure 11.7 *Enter search criteria in the Find Message dialog box.*

Finding Messages

If a folder contains many messages, you can use the Find command to help locate the one(s) of interest.

To find a message:

1. Switch to the mail window.
2. Select a folder from the Folders pop-up menu. (The Find command only searches the current folder.)
3. Choose Find Message from the Edit menu (see **Figure 11.6**). The Find Message dialog box appears (see **Figure 11.7**).

4. Enter the search criteria.
5. Click Find. If a matching message is found, it is highlighted in the message list.
6. To look for additional matches, choose Find Next from the Edit menu or press F3.

✔ Tips

- The initial Find begins its search at the top of the message list, based on the current sort order. You may sometimes find it helpful to specify a different sort order before issuing the Find command.
- The Find command identifies only those messages that match *all* of the criteria specified. Specifying fewer criteria will result in more potential matches.
- A Find only searches the current folder. To search other folders, you must change to each folder and then choose the Find command. Find automatically retains the last criteria specified.
- Date-based searches can be facilitated with a pop-up calendar that you can use to specify dates (see **Figure 11.8**). To use the calendar, click the pop-up indicator to the right of either the After or Before date box.
- To search for a message between two dates, enter date criteria for both Received After and Received Before.

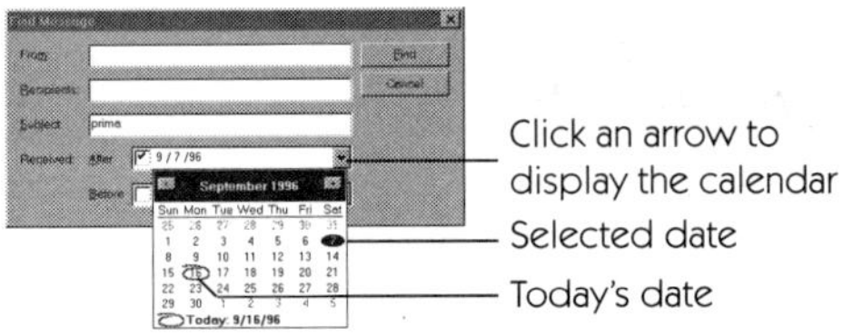

Figure 11.8 *The pop-up calendar makes it easy to choose search dates.*

Managing the Mail

Internet Mail offers many features to help you organize and manage your messages.

Deleting Messages

Perhaps the simplest way to manage received mail is by deleting unwanted messages; that is, any messages you do not want to save.

To delete messages, select one or more messages in the message list, and do one of the following:

- Click the Delete button in the toolbar (see **Figure 11.9**).
- Choose Delete from the File menu, or press Ctrl D.
- Press Del.

Figure 11.9 *The standard toolbar has a Delete button.*

The selected messages are moved to the Deleted Items folder. To permanently delete these items, you can do either of the following:

- Open the Deleted Items folder, select the message(s) to delete, and press Del. Click Yes in response to the dialog box that appears (see **Figure 11.10**).
- In the Read section of the Options dialog box, click the option to "Empty messages from the 'Deleted Items' folder on exit." Each time you quit Internet Mail, the deleted messages are removed.

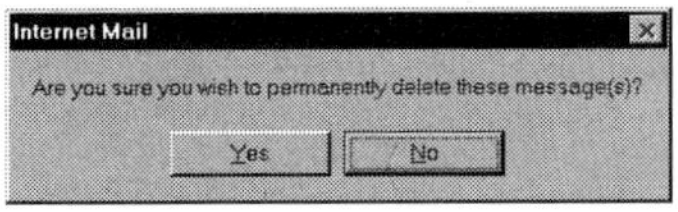

Figure 11.10 *Click Yes to permanently delete the selected messages, or click No to cancel.*

✔ **Tip**

- Until a message has been permanently deleted from the Deleted Items folder, it can be read or moved to another folder.

Using Folders

Internet Mail has four default folders: *Inbox* (received messages), *Outbox* (outgoing messages), *Deleted Items* (messages marked for deletion), and *Sent Items* (messages moved to this folder after having been sent).

To help further organize your mail, you can create new folders, move or copy messages between folders, compact folders, and delete folders.

Creating Folders

You can create as many message folders as you like. With separate folders, you can organize messages by project or subject, for example.

To create a new message folder:

1. Choose Create from the Folder submenu of the File menu (see **Figure 11.11**). The Create New Folder dialog box appears, as shown in **Figure 11.12**.
2. Name the folder, and click OK.

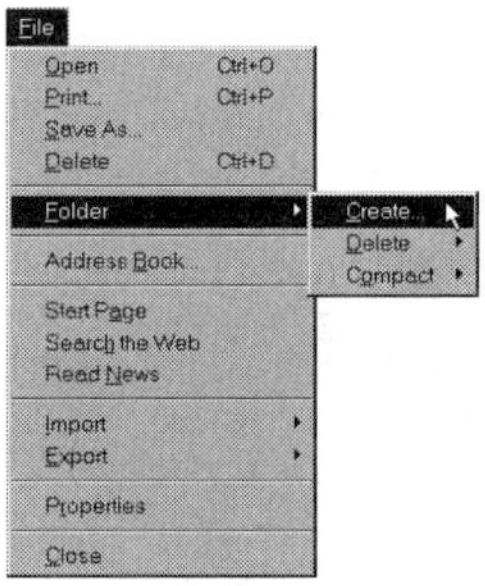

Figure 11.11 *Select a command from the Folder submenu to create or manage folders.*

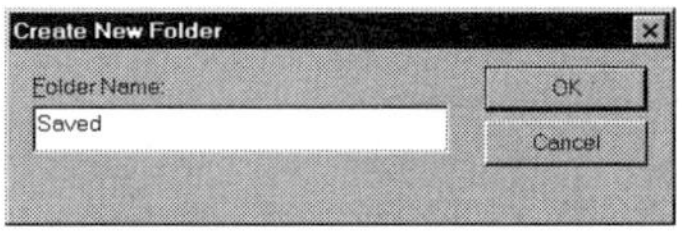

Figure 11.12 *To create a new folder, simply name it in the Create New Folder dialog box and click OK.*

Moving, Copying, and Saving

Messages can be moved between folders, copied to new folders, or saved on disk as new files.

To move or copy a message:

1. Open the folder where the messages are stored. To select multiple messages, Ctrl-click each one. (You can only select messages in one folder at a time.)
2. Choose a destination folder from the Move to or Copy to submenu of the Mail menu, as shown in **Figure 11.13**. The selected messages are moved or copied, as directed.

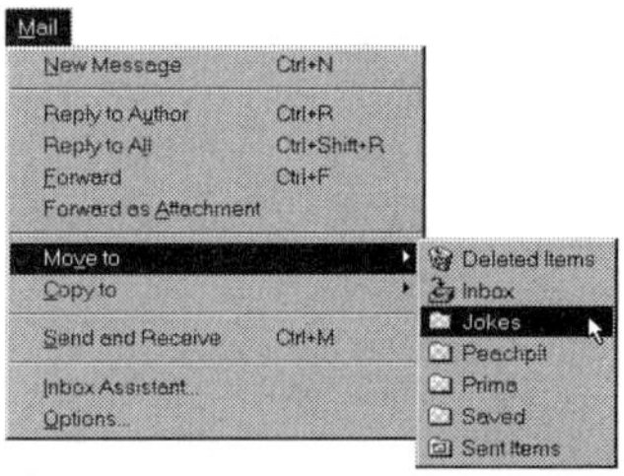

Figure 11.13 *Select a destination folder from the Move to or Copy to submenu of the Mail menu.*

✔ **Tip**

- You can automatically move various types of incoming messages to specific folders by setting rules in the Inbox Assistant. For information about using this feature, see "Mail-Handling Automation" in Chapter 12.

To save a message as a file:

1. Select the message in the message list, and choose Save As from the File menu.

   or

1. If the message is already open in its own window, choose Save As from the File menu or click the Save This Message button on the message toolbar (the disk icon).

   The Save Message As dialog box appears (see **Figure 11.14**).

2. *Optional*: Rename the message.
3. Select a format for the message. Choose Mail (.EML) to save it as an Internet Mail file. Choose Text (.TXT) to save it as an ordinary text file.
4. Click Save.

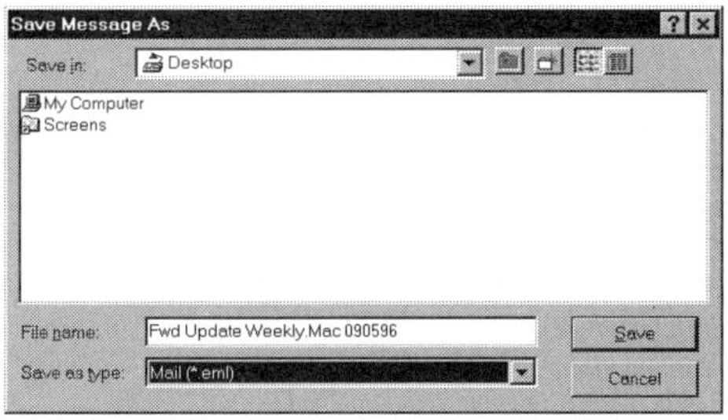

Figure 11.14 *To save a message as a separate file, select a location and click Save.*

✔ **Tip**

- The file type you should select when saving depends on what you intend to do with the message. To save the message in a form that can be read by any text editor or word processing program, choose Text. To move the message to another computer with Internet Mail, choose Mail.

Compacting Folders

Compacting folders is an easy way to reclaim wasted disk space without deleting messages. All messages are retained, but they take up less space.

To compact a folder:

1. Choose Compact from the Folder submenu of the File menu.
2. Choose the name of the folder you want to compact, or choose All Folders.

Deleting Folders

Any folder that you create for storing messages can be deleted. (You cannot delete the default folders.) Deleting an entire folder is one of the fastest ways to delete many messages at once. You can then recreate the folder, if desired.

To delete a folder, choose Delete from the Folders submenu of the File menu, and highlight the folder's name. You must then click Yes in the confirmation dialog box that appears.

Printing Messages

You can print any message. Select the message in the mail window, or open it in its own window. Then choose Print from the File menu, or press Ctrl P. Individual message windows also have a Print button that you can click (see **Figure 11.15**).

Figure 11.15 *Individual message windows have a Print button in the toolbar.*

✔ **Tip**

- You cannot print a message that you are still writing. After you have marked it for sending, however, you can select it in the Outbox or Sent Items folder, and then print it.

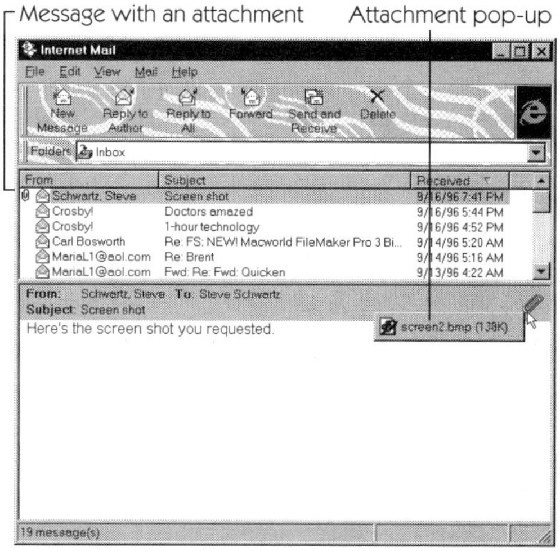

Figure 11.16 *In the message window, a message with an attachment is marked with a paper clip icon. Click the paper clip icon above the preview pane to show the name of the attached file.*

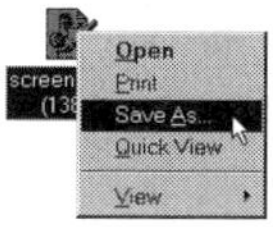

Figure 11.17 *Right-click the file icon at the bottom of the message window to display this pop-up menu.*

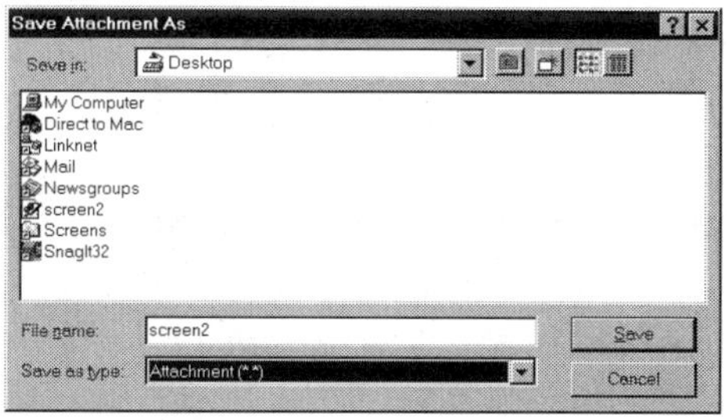

Figure 11.18 *Save the attachment in the Save Attachment As dialog box.*

Working with Attachments

When you receive a message with an attachment, you can open the attachment and/or save it to disk.

To open an attachment:

1. In the message list, select the message with the attachment.
2. Click the paper click icon above the preview pane. The name of the attached file appears, as shown in **Figure 11.16**.
3. Click the file name. If you have a program that is associated with the file, the file opens.

✔ **Tip**

■ If no program on your hard disk is associated with the attachment's file type, you will not be able to open the attachment by clicking it. Obtain the necessary program, and use it to open the attachment.

To save an attachment:

1. Open the message, right-click the attachment icon at the bottom of the message window, and choose Save As from the pop-up menu that appears (see **Figure 11.17**). Or you can choose Save Attachments from the File menu.

or

1. Select the message in the message list, click the paper clip icon above the preview pane, and [Ctrl]-click the attachment's file name.
2. The Save Attachment As dialog box appears (see **Figure 11.18**). Select a location for the file, and click Save.

Odds and Ends

This section offers several additional tips and tricks for handling messages. You'll learn how to:

- Determine a sender's e-mail address.
- Forward an e-mail message as an attachment.
- Import and export messages.

Determining a Sender's E-Mail Address

Most mail programs display the sender's e-mail address in the message header. But Internet Mail doesn't. Although you can store the address in your address book (see "To create a new record from a received message" in Chapter 9), there's another way to learn the sender's address.

To determine a sender's address:

1. Right-click the message in the message list.
2. Choose Properties from the pop-up menu that appears.
3. Click the Details tab at the top of the dialog box that appears (see **Figure 11.19**). The sender's e-mail address will be listed in the "From" line.

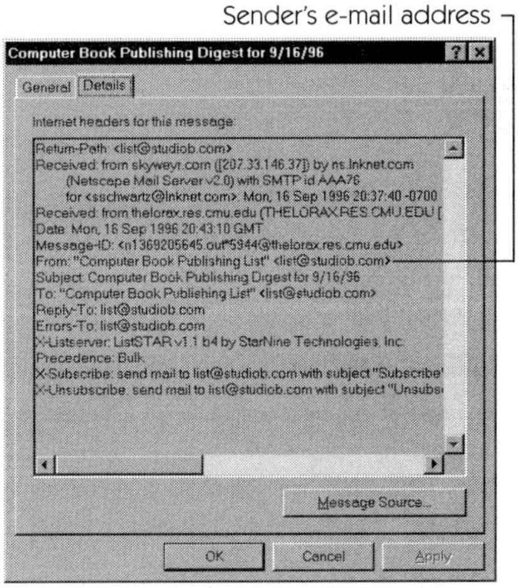

Figure 11.19 *Click the Details tab, and look for the "From" line to see a sender's e-mail address.*

Forwarding an E-Mail Message as an Attachment

You can forward a message as an attachment to a new message, rather than forwarding it as quoted text (as is done when you use the Forward command).

Figure 11.20 *A message forwarded as an attachment appears as an icon at the bottom of the message window.*

To forward a message as an attachment:

1. Select the message to forward from the message list.
2. Choose Forward as Attachment from the Mail menu. A New Message window opens, and the selected message is shown as an icon at the bottom of the window (see **Figure 11.20**).
3. Compose and address the message, and then click the Send button.

Importing and Exporting Messages

If you previously used or also use Microsoft Exchange, messages can be moved between the programs. Choose Messages from the Import or Export submenu of the File menu, and then follow the prompts. (Exchange must currently be installed in order for the import or export to proceed.)

12

Customizing Internet Mail

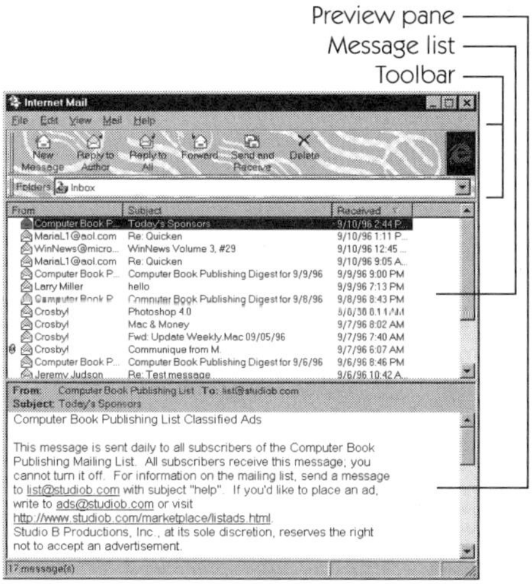

Figure 12.1 *The mail window has three sections: toolbar, message list, and preview pane.*

About Internet Mail Customization Options

Although the standard display and features of Internet Mail will suffice for many users, there are also several ways that you can customize the program. You can make any of the following changes to the standard mail window, as shown in **Figure 12.1**:

- *Customize the display.* Change the size and orientation of the message list and preview panes; rearrange, resize, and change the column headings; and establish a sort order for the message list.
- *Customize the toolbar.* Add or remove buttons, display buttons with or without labels, change the placement of the toolbar, and hide sections or the entire toolbar.
- *Automate the handling of incoming mail.* Depending on the criteria that you set, different types of received mail can automatically be placed in particular folders.

Additional customization options are discussed in Chapter 13, “Internet Mail Options.”

Customizing the Display

The message list and preview pane can be changed in several ways by dragging, clicking, and choosing commands.

Modifying the Message List and Preview Pane

The message list and preview panes can be modified in the following ways:

- To change the size of the message list and preview pane, move the pointer between the two sections. The pointer changes to a double arrow. Drag up and down or left and right, depending on whether the areas are split horizontally or vertically. One area increases in size as the other decreases.
- You can remove the header information that separates the message list from the preview pane (see **Figure 12.2**). Choose Header Information from the Preview Pane submenu of the View menu. Choose the same command again to restore the header text.
- To change the orientation of the message list and preview pane, choose Split Horizontally or Split Vertically from the Preview Pane submenu of the View menu (see **Figure 12.3**).
- To eliminate the preview pane, choose None from the Preview Pane submenu. After doing so, you will have to read messages by opening them in their own windows. (Double-click a message line, or select the message and choose Open from the File menu.)

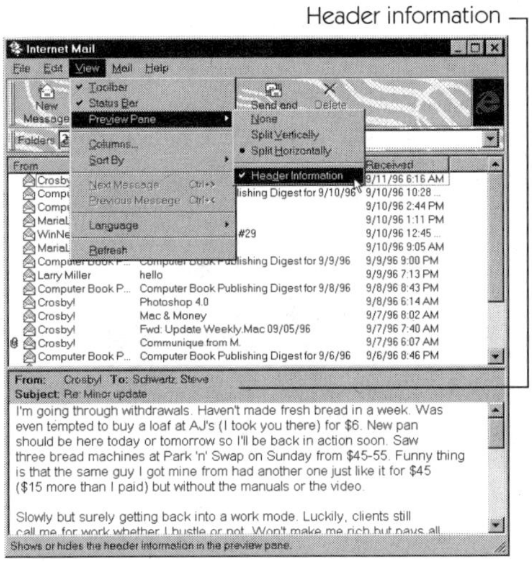

Figure 12.2 *The Header Information command is responsible for displaying or hiding the header information above the preview pane.*

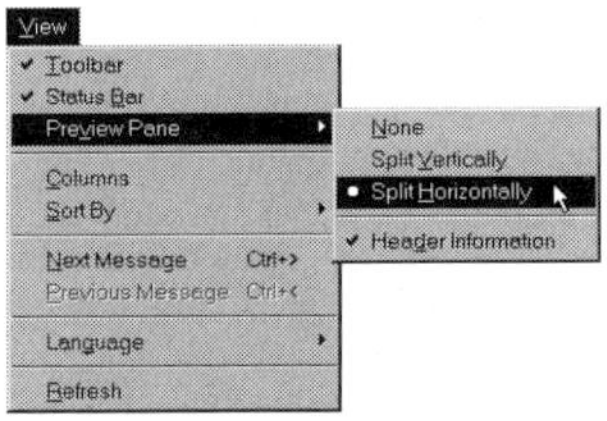

Figure 12.3 *To set a different orientation for the message list and preview pane, choose a command from the Preview Pane submenu of the View menu.*

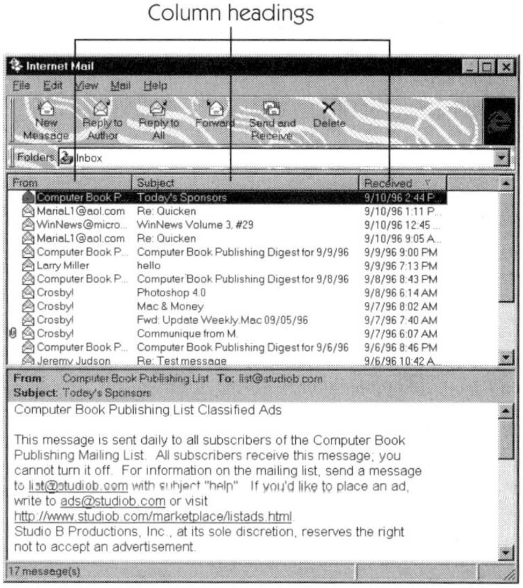

Figure 12.4 *The column headings determine the information shown for each message in the message list.*

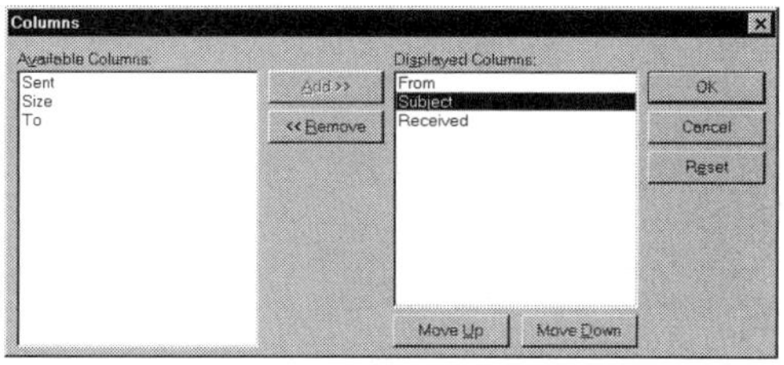

Figure 12.5 *Use the Columns dialog box to rearrange, add, or remove column headings in the message list.*

Modifying Column Headings

You can resize, rearrange, or change the column headings for the message list (see **Figure 12.4**).

To resize column headings:

1. Move the pointer over the right edge of a column heading. The pointer changes to a double arrow.
2. Drag to the left or right to reduce or widen the column.
3. Release the mouse button when the column is the desired width.

To rearrange column headings by dragging:

1. Click to select a column heading.
2. Drag the heading to its new position, and then release the mouse button.

To rearrange column headings using the Columns command:

1. Choose the Columns command from the View menu. The Columns dialog box appears (see **Figure 12.5**).
2. In the Displayed Columns list, select a column to move.
3. Click Move Up or Move Down to change the column's position.
4. When all columns are arranged correctly, click OK.

✔ Tip

- To return the columns to their default positions, click Reset. Note, however, that if you have added or removed columns, those changes will also be reset.

To change the column headings:

1. Choose the Columns command from the View menu. The Columns dialog box appears (see **Figure 12.5**).
2. To add a column, select a column heading in the Available Columns list and click Add.
3. To remove a column, select a column heading in the Displayed Columns list and click Remove.
4. To change the order in which the columns are displayed in the message list, select a heading in the Displayed Columns list and click Move Up or Move Down.
5. Click OK to save your changes.

✔ **Tip**

■ To restore the default set of columns and their original positions, click Reset.

Setting a Sort Order for the Message List

You can set a sort order for the message list. The order you set remains until it is next modified.

■ Select a sort column from the Sort By submenu of the View menu, as shown in **Figure 12.6**. To toggle between ascending and descending sorts, choose the Ascending command.

or

■ Click a column heading to sort the message list by the contents of that column. To change between ascending and descending sorts, click the same heading again.

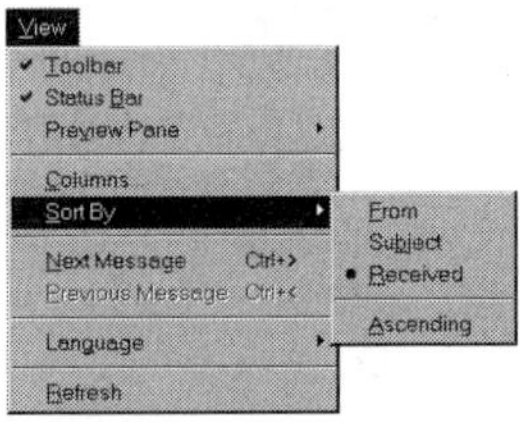

Figure 12.6 *You can sort the message list by the contents of any single column heading. The list of headings in the Sort By submenu will be different if you have customized the message list by adding or removing columns.*

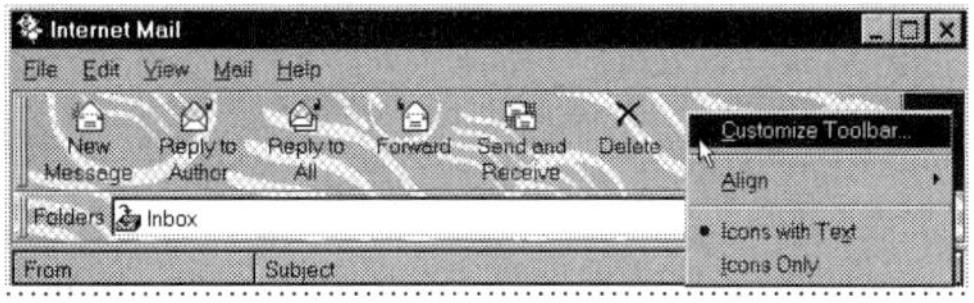

Figure 12.7 *Right-click in the toolbar to make the toolbar customization menu appear.*

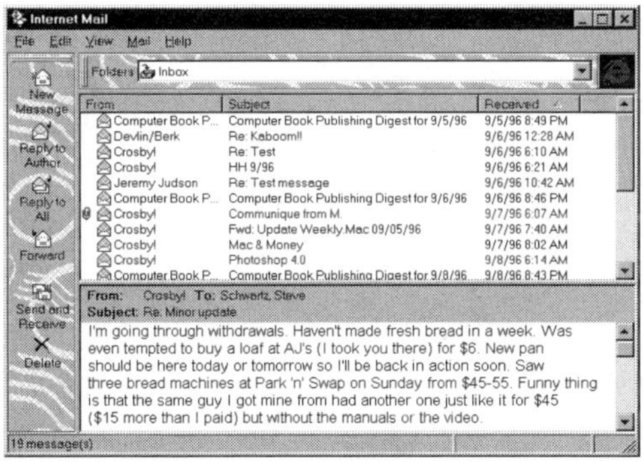

Figure 12.8 *You can display the buttons on the left side of the mail window, if you prefer.*

Customizing the Toolbar

Customization options for the toolbar include rearranging and hiding the toolbar, changing its placement in the mail window, displaying small or large buttons, and adding and removing buttons.

Rearranging the Toolbar or Hiding a Section

You can rearrange the Mail toolbar in the same way you rearrange the Internet Explorer toolbar. Click any vertical bar in the toolbar, and drag up, down, left, or right. (Not all directions are possible at all times.)

Hiding the Entire Toolbar

To hide the toolbar, choose Toolbar from the View menu. To remove the status bar from the bottom of the mail window, choose Status Bar from the View menu. Both commands work as toggles.

Changing the Toolbar Placement

When you right-click in a blank area of the toolbar, a pop-up menu appears (see **Figure 12.7**). To specify a new placement for the toolbar, choose Top or Left from the Align menu. **Figure 12.8** shows a mail window with the toolbar on the left side.

Setting Button Sizes and Labels

To set the button size for the toolbar, right-click in a blank area of the toolbar and choose Icons with Text or Icons Only. The latter command displays small, unlabeled buttons.

Adding and Removing Buttons

In addition to altering the appearance of the toolbar, you can add functionality to it.

To add or remove buttons:

1. Right-click in a blank area of the toolbar. A pop-up menu appears (refer to **Figure 12.7**).
2. Choose Customize Toolbar from the pop-up menu. The Customize Toolbar dialog box appears, as shown in **Figure 12.9**.
3. To add a button to the toolbar, select a function in the Available Buttons section of the dialog box, and click Add.
4. To remove a button from the toolbar, select a function in the Toolbar Buttons section of the dialog box, and click Remove.
5. To change the order in which the buttons appear in the toolbar, select a function in the Toolbar Buttons section of the dialog box, and click Move Up or Move Down.
6. To save the new toolbar, click Close.

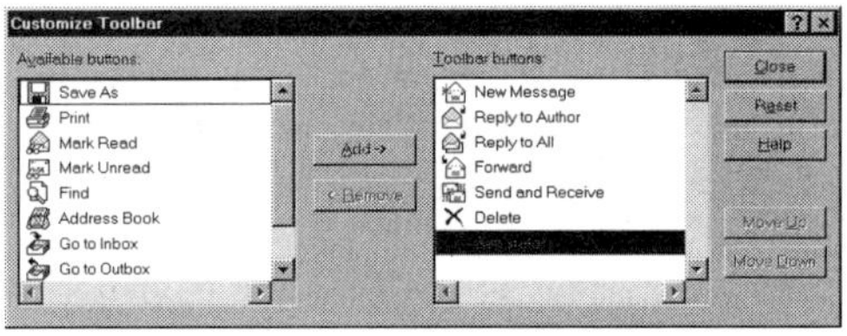

Figure 12.9 *You can add or remove toolbar buttons—as well as change their order—in this dialog box.*

✔ Tips

- You can also open the Customize Toolbar dialog box by double-clicking in a blank area of the toolbar.
- To restore the default set of buttons and reset the standard button order, click Reset.

Mail-Handling Automation

You can automate the handling of certain classes of incoming mail using Inbox Assistant rules. Messages that meet your criteria are automatically routed to the folder of your choice.

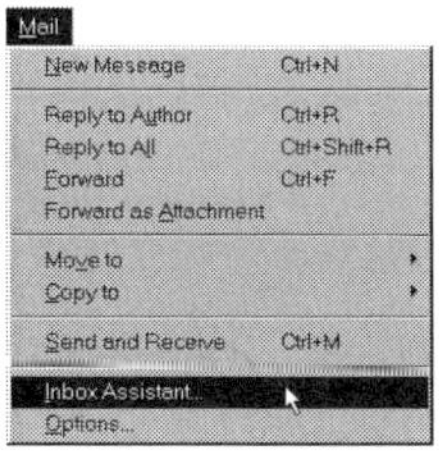

Figure 12.10 *Choose Inbox Assistant from the Mail menu.*

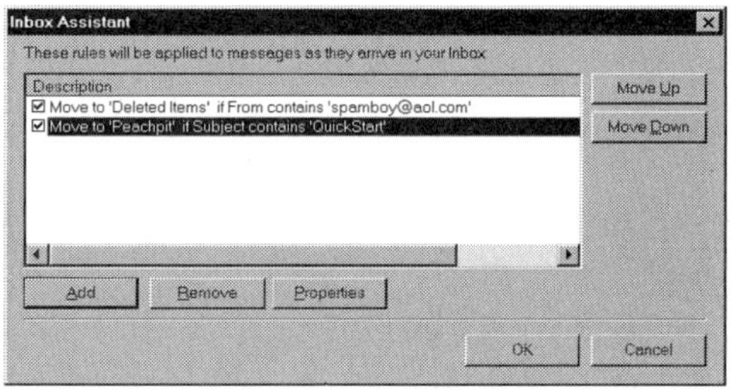

Figure 12.11 *You can review, modify, delete, or rearrange mail-handling rules.*

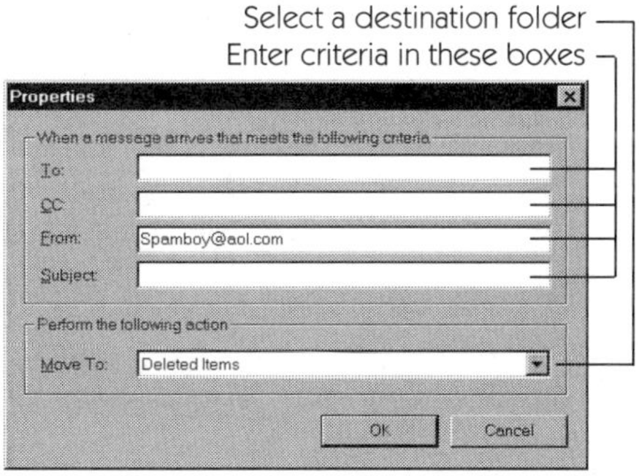

Figure 12.12 *To create an Inbox Assistant rule for a class of mail, enter criteria and specify a destination folder.*

To set an Inbox Assistant rule:

1. Choose Inbox Assistant from the Mail menu, as shown in **Figure 12.10**. The Inbox Assistant dialog box appears (see **Figure 12.11**).
2. To create a new mail rule, click Add. The Properties dialog box appears (see **Figure 12.12**).
3. Type criteria in the To, From, CC, and/or Subject boxes.
4. Select a folder into which the mail will be routed by clicking the pop-up menu at the end of the Move To box.
5. Click OK. The Inbox Assistant dialog box appears again.
6. Create additional mail rules, as desired. When you are ready to save the new rules, click OK.

✔ Tips

- To edit a rule, select it in the Inbox Assistant dialog box, and click Properties. To delete a rule, select it and click Remove.
- Some classes of mail aren't worth reading. For example, you can route all messages from a particular person into the Deleted Items folder.
- The only folders into which you can route mail are Deleted Items and new folders that you have

created. To create other folders, choose Create from the Folder submenu of the File menu.

- If you specify multiple rules, they are evaluated from the top down. Thus, if a given message meets the criteria of two or more rules, it is handled by the rule that is highest in the list. You can change the order of rules by selecting a rule in the Inbox Assistant dialog box and clicking Move Up or Move Down.
- There is an important consequence of using Inbox Assistant. You may not realize that a folder contains new mail. You must remember to periodically check the folders.

13

Internet Mail Options

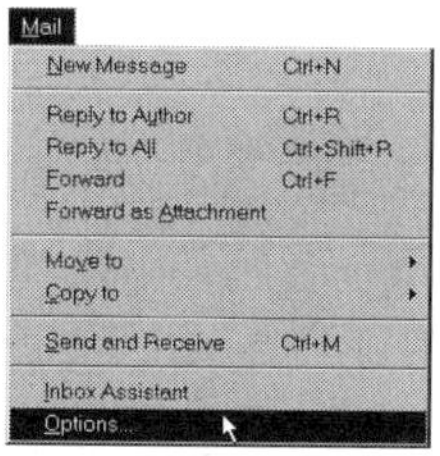

Figure 13.1 *To set preferences for Internet Mail, choose Options from the Mail menu.*

About Internet Mail Options

Like Explorer and News, Internet Mail can be customized by setting preferences in the Options dialog box. Although the default settings will suffice for most users, you should glance through this chapter to learn about options that can make your computing sessions more productive.

To set options, choose Options from the Mail menu, as shown in **Figure 13.1**. The Options dialog box appears. There are six option categories that correspond to the tabs at the top of the dialog box:

- *Send*. Settings used for composing and sending e-mail messages.
- *Read*. Checking for new mail and announcing its arrival.
- *Server*. Specifying e-mail account information.
- *Fonts*. Selecting a language, default font, and text color for messages.
- *Signature*. Specifying a signature line or file to be appended to outgoing messages.
- *Connection*. Specifying the connection method used for sending and retrieving mail.

Send Options

Send options are set in the Send section of the Options dialog box, as shown in **Figure 13.2**.

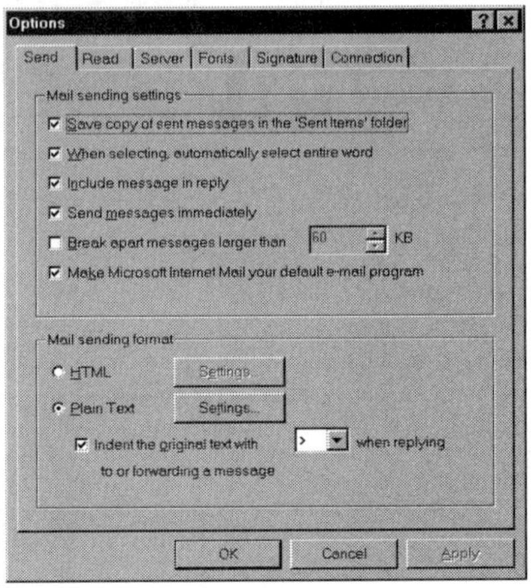

Figure 13.2 *Send options for Internet Mail.*

Mail Sending Settings

- *Save copy of sent messages in the 'Sent Items' folder*. Check this option to store copies of outgoing messages.
- *When selecting, automatically select entire word*. When composing or editing messages, this setting makes it easy to select full words—for copying, cutting, or overwriting. If you often need to select *parts* of words, on the other hand, turn this option off.
- *Include message in reply*. When checked, a copy of the message to which you are replying is automatically inserted at the bottom of the message (see **Figure 13.3**).
- *Send messages immediately*. When checked, outgoing messages are sent the moment you issue the Send Message command. Otherwise, they are held until the next scheduled send or until you issue the Send and Receive command.
- *Break apart messages larger than...* Some older systems cannot handle large messages. When this option is checked and a message exceeds the specified size, it is sent as a series of smaller messages. The recipient must have a mail program or a utility that can combine the message pieces.

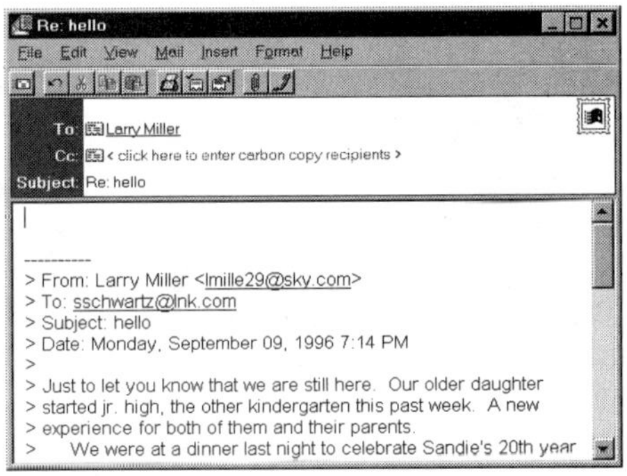

Figure 13.3 *You can automatically quote a message when writing a reply. Like all other text in the message, you can edit the quoted material (by eliminating unnecessary passages, for example).*

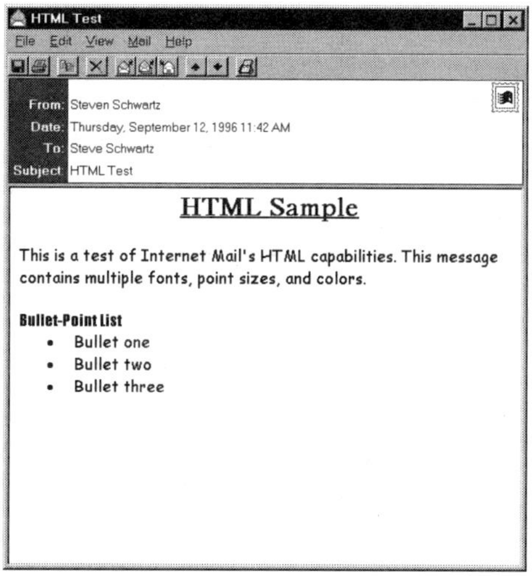

Figure 13.4 *HTML-formatted messages can contain an array of fonts, styles, colors, and paragraph formatting. However, these features disappear when such a message is viewed in most current mail programs.*

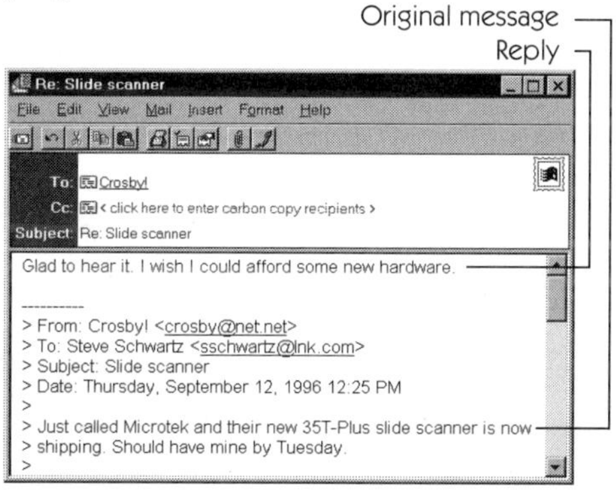

Figure 13.5 *Internet Mail automatically places quoted text at the end of a message, separated from the new text by a dashed line. You can edit or move the quoted material, if you like.*

- *Make Microsoft Internet Mail your default e-mail program.* When you perform an e-mail activity in another program (such as sending a message from your browser), the default mail program is invoked.

✔ **Tip**

- You can also create copies of outgoing messages by including your mail address in the To or CC lines.

Mail Sending Format

- *HTML.* Messages formatted with HTML (Hypertext Markup Language) can contain paragraph alignments, fonts, sizes, styles, and colors (see **Figure 13.4**). Such formatting, however, is visible only to users who have HTML-capable mail programs or when the message is viewed in a browser.
- *Plain Text.* Currently, most messages are plain, unformatted text. Choosing this option assures you of compatibility with all mail systems and computer platforms.
- *Indent the original text with > when replying to or forwarding a message.* This is the standard way to quote a message when replying to or forwarding a message (see **Figure 13.5**). If you prefer, you can pick a different character or no character to mark the quoted text.

✔ **Tip**

- If the "Include message in reply" option is not checked, the setting for "Indent the original text..." is irrelevant.

HTML and Plain Text Settings

To specify settings for HTML or text messages, click the associated Settings button and pick options from the dialog box that appears (see **Figures 13.6** and **13.7**).

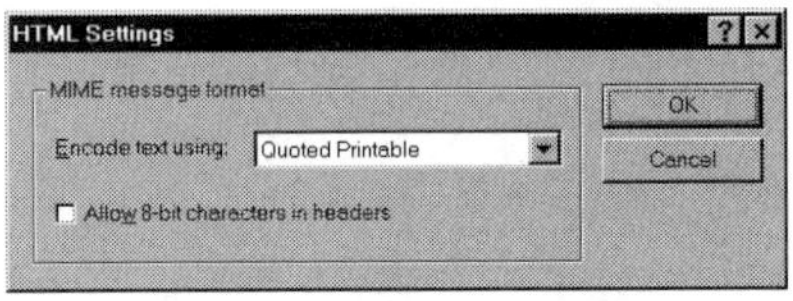

Figure 13.6 *HTML settings.*

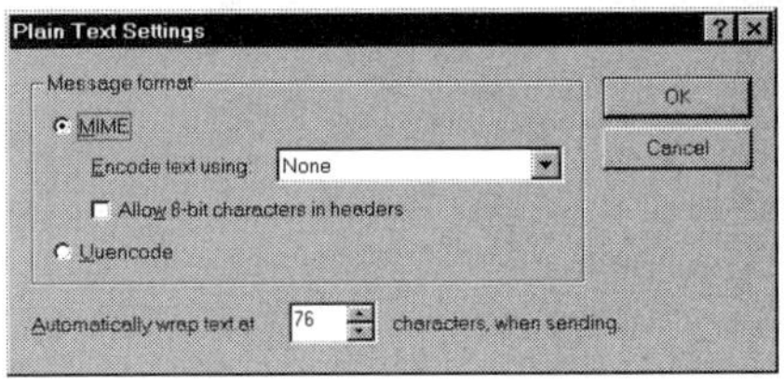

Figure 13.7 *Plain Text settings.*

HTML Settings

- *Encode text using.* All HTML messages are sent as MIME (Multipurpose Internet Mail Extensions) files. Choose Quoted Printable to send text files that optionally can contain upper ASCII characters. Choose Base64 to send binary files as text.
- *Allow 8-bit characters in headers.* These are upper ASCII characters, such as foreign language letters, bullets, and so on. Some mail readers may not be able to interpret these characters.

Plain Text Settings

- *MIME format: Encode text using.* When sending ordinary text, choose None. For a discussion of the other options, refer to "HTML Settings," above.
- *MIME format: Allow 8-bit characters in headers.* Refer to the discussion of this option in "HTML Settings," above.
- *Uuencode formatting.* Uuencode is a common format for sending binary files, such as graphic images and programs, as ordinary text within the body of a message.
- *Automatically wrap text at xx characters when sending.* Some mail systems limit the length of message lines. It is best to wrap lines at fewer than 80 characters.

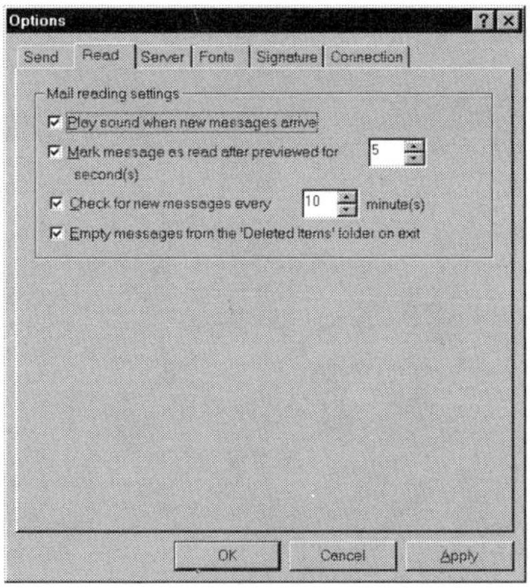

Figure 13.8 *Read options for Internet Mail.*

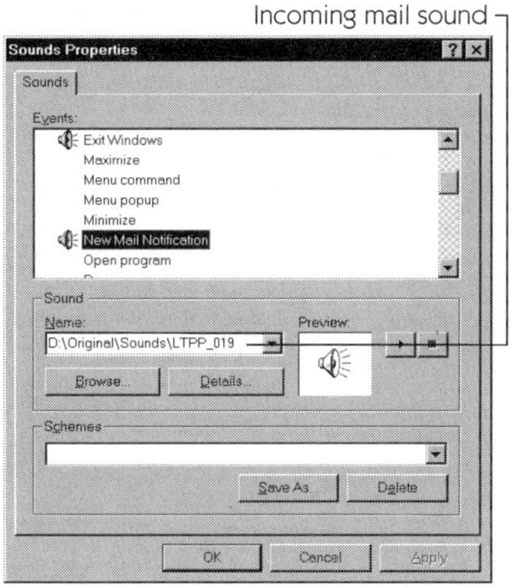

Figure 13.9 *You can set a different sound in New Mail Notification.*

Read Options

These options (see **Figure 13.8**) apply primarily to incoming mail.

- *Play sound when new messages arrive.* Many users find an audible notification of new mail helpful.
- *Mark message as read after previewed for xx seconds.* Unread messages are shown in boldface, so they can easily be identified. If a message is selected in the message list for longer than the specified time, it is marked as read; i.e., the boldface is removed.

  If you remove the check mark, a message is only marked as read if you open it, scroll the preview pane while the message is selected, or issue the Mark as Read command.
- *Check for new messages every xx minutes.* When this option is set, Internet Mail automatically sends and receives mail at the designated intervals.
- *Empty messages from the 'Deleted Items' folder on exit.* When this option is checked, all messages marked for deletion are removed from the Deleted Items folder when you quit the program.

  If you do not check this option, you must manually delete the messages in the Deleted Items folder.

✔ **Tip**

- You can change the sound that announces the arrival of new mail. Open the Sounds control panel, and select a sound for New Mail Notification (see **Figure 13.9**).

Server Options

Information entered in the Server section of the Options dialog box (see **Figure 13.10**) is used when connecting with your ISP or on-line service to exchange e-mail.

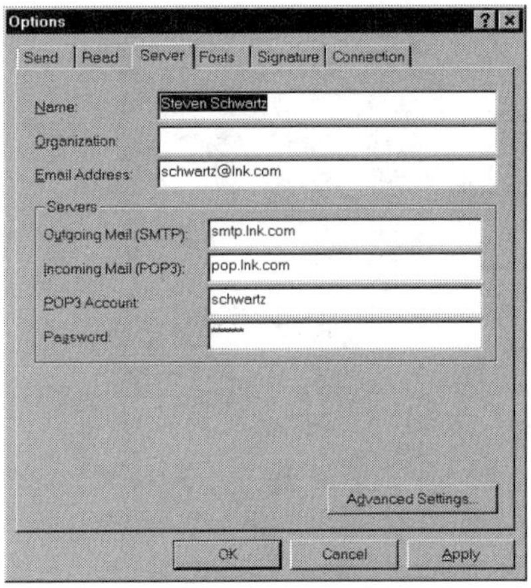

Figure 13.10 *Basic server options for Internet Mail.*

Basic Server Settings

- *Name*. Enter the "friendly" name that you want to appear in the From line of all outgoing messages, such as Alice Sanders.
- *Organization*. Enter a group, company, or organization name, if desired.
- *E-mail Address*. Enter your complete e-mail address, such as jonas_smith@aol.com.
- *Outgoing Mail (SMTP)*. Enter the address of the mail server that handles your outgoing mail, such as mail.lnk.com.
- *Incoming Mail (POP3)*. Enter the address of the mail server that handles your incoming mail, such as pop.lnk.com.
- *POP3 Account*. Enter the user name assigned to you by your ISP or information service, such as bobpaul or sally247.
- *Password*. Enter the password that you use to log onto the mail server.

✔ **Tip**

- The settings for Server options are critical. If you have trouble sending or receiving mail, one or more settings may be wrong. Contact your ISP, information service, or network administrator for help.

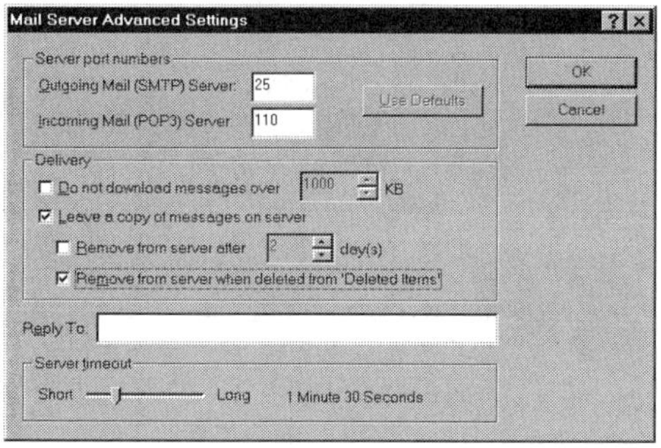

Figure 13.11 *Advanced server options for Internet Mail.*

Advanced Server Settings

To view or change additional server options, click Advanced Settings. The dialog box shown in **Figure 13.11** appears.

Server Port Numbers

Most users can leave these settings alone. Change them only if told to do so by your service provider.

Delivery

- *Do not download messages over...* Check this option to avoid automatically receiving large messages. (Such messages will be left on the server. You can uncheck this setting to download the files.)
- *Leave a copy of messages on server*. After a message has been transmitted, it is normally deleted from the server. If an error occurs, there is no way to retrieve the message again. Select this option to temporarily store copies of messages on the server. (Not all ISPs offer this service.)

Other Options

- *Reply to*. Enter an e-mail address if you want replies to your mail to be sent to a different account.
- *Server timeout*. Set a *timeout interval* (the length of time that Mail will attempt to connect with the server before giving up).

✔ Tip

- If you save messages on the server, you may want to set a very short storage period. Until they are deleted from the server, all stored messages will be repeatedly sent to you each time you connect.

Fonts Options

Use the Fonts options (see **Figure 13.12**) to select a default language and font for composing and displaying messages.

- *Language*. Select a language to be used when composing messages.
- *Default font*. Click Change to select a default font, size, style, and color for displaying messages. The Font dialog box appears (see **Figure 13.13**). You can choose any currently installed font.
- *Use this color for composing messages*. Click the color box to display a pop-up list of available colors (see **Figure 13.14**). All typed text will be displayed in the chosen color. Text quoted from messages (when writing a reply, for example) will appear in the default font and color.

✔ Tips

- The various font options are for displaying messages on *your* screen. When you create a Plain Text message, it doesn't matter which font or color you've chosen—the message is delivered as a one-font, uncolored text file.

  On the other hand, when you compose an HTML message, the default font *is* used to format the message (unless you override it by choosing other fonts, sizes, styles, and colors).

- To make it easy to distinguish new text from quoted text, you may want to choose contrasting colors for the two font settings.

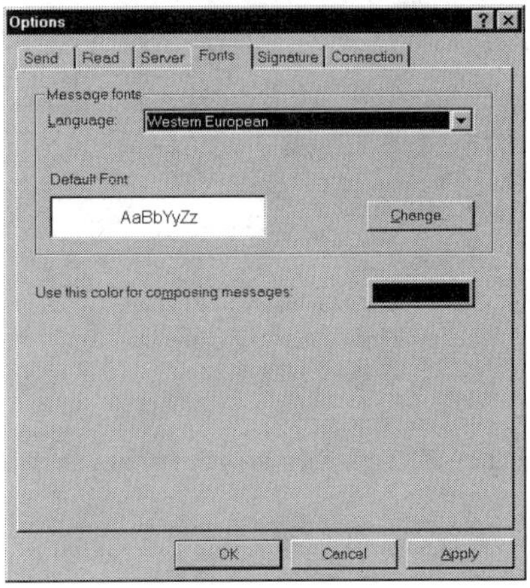

Figure 13.12 *Fonts options for Internet Mail.*

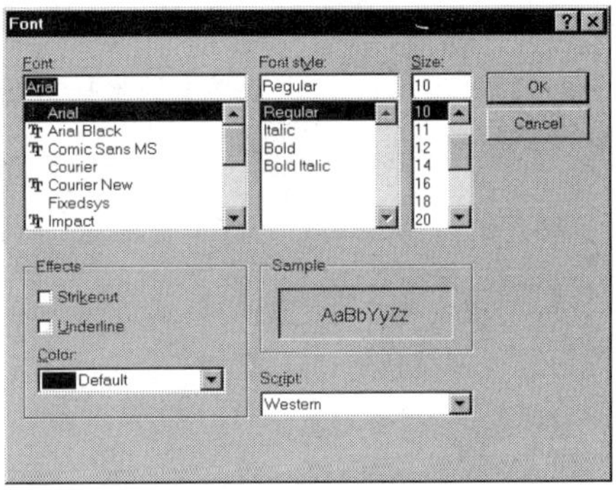

Figure 13.13 *Select a display font and options from the Font dialog box.*

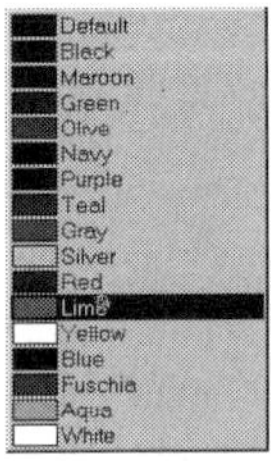

Figure 13.14 *The color chosen from this menu is used to display all message text that you type.*

Signature Options

A *signature* is an optional tag line that is used to conclude messages. A signature can convey a personal message, offer a bit of humor, or explain your philosophy of life. It is also common to cite a mailing address, phone numbers, or a URL for a personal Web page in the signature.

The Signature Options are shown in **Figure 13.15**. A sample message with a signature is shown in **Figure 13.16**.

- *No signature*. Choose this setting if no signature is desired.
- *Text*. Choose this setting, and type your signature text in the box.
- *File*. Choose this setting if your signature text is to be read from a file.
- *Add signature to the end of all outgoing messages*. When checked, your signature is automatically appended to messages.
- *Don't add signature to Replies and Forwards*. When checked, the signature is added only to standard outgoing messages. When it is not checked, the signature is added to every type of message.

✔ Tip

- Add a blank or dashed line at the beginning of your signature to separate it from the message text.
- When the "Add signature..." option is not checked, you can still include your signature in the current message by choosing Signature from the Insert menu (see **Figure 13.17**).

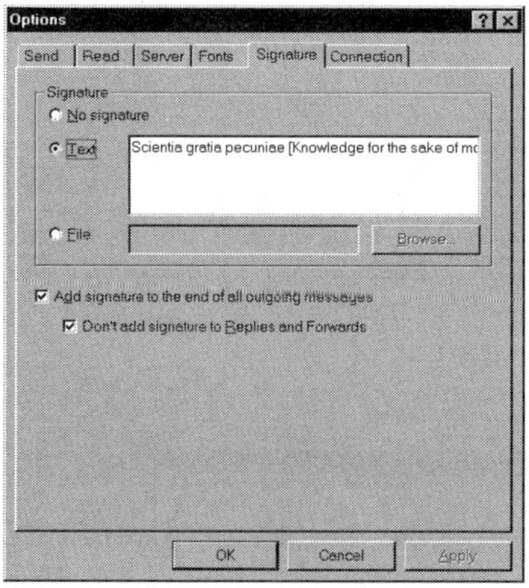

Figure 13.15 *Signature options for Internet Mail.*

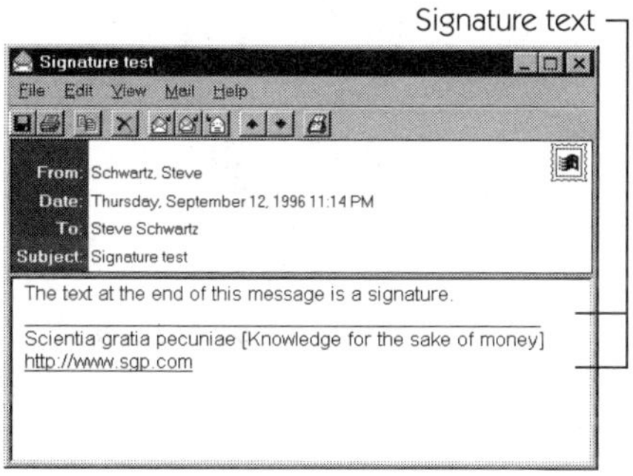

Figure 13.16 *A signature can provide any type of message or information that you want to convey.*

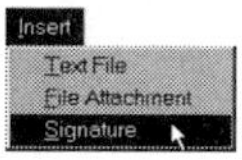

Figure 13.17 *Choose Signature from the Insert menu to manually add a signature to the current message.*

Connection Options

The Connection Options (see Figure **13.18**) specify the manner in which you connect to your mail server to send and receive e-mail.

- *I use a LAN connection.* Choose this option if you connect to your mail server through a local area network.
- *I connect manually.* Choose this option if you manually connect to the mail server before sending and receiving mail.
- *I use a modem to access my e-mail.* Choose this option if you connect using a connection defined in Dial-Up Networking. Select the appropriate connection from the pop-up menu.

  If you want to examine or change the settings for the selected Dial-Up Networking connection, click the Properties button. The dialog box in **Figure 13.19** appears.
- *Disconnect when finished sending and receiving.* Check this option to automatically close the connection after sending and receiving mail. Do not check it if you normally keep the connection open (enabling you to continue checking for mail and use other Internet programs, such as Explorer and News).

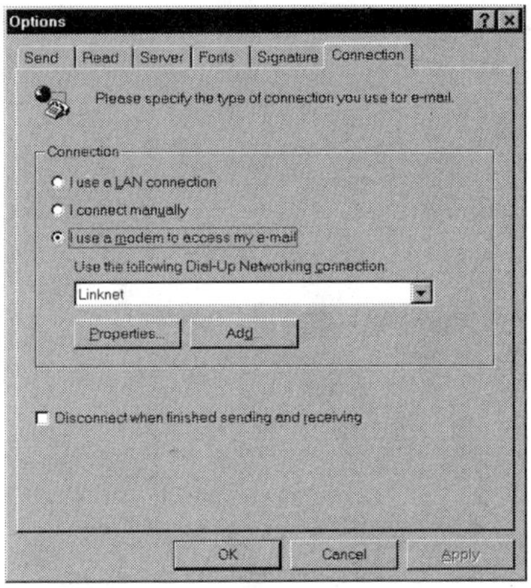

Figure 13.18 *Connection options for Internet Mail.*

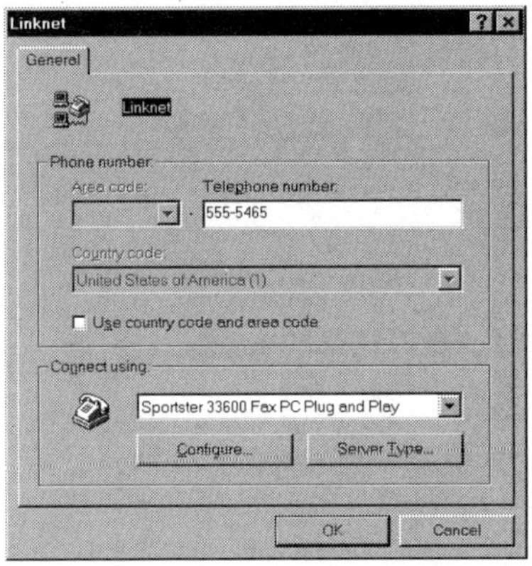

Figure 13.19 *You can view or change existing connections.*

✔ **Tip**

- For help in configuring a dial-up networking connection, see "Use the Following Dial-Up Networking Connection" in Chapter 7.

Part III: Internet News

14 Newsgroups and Internet News

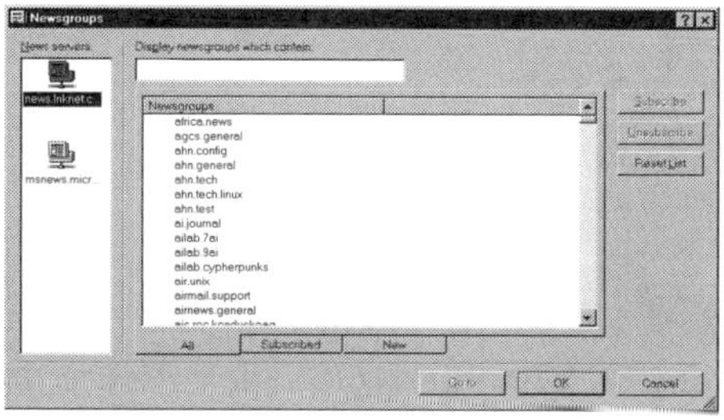

Figure 14.1 *This ISP carries more than 17,000 newsgroups.*

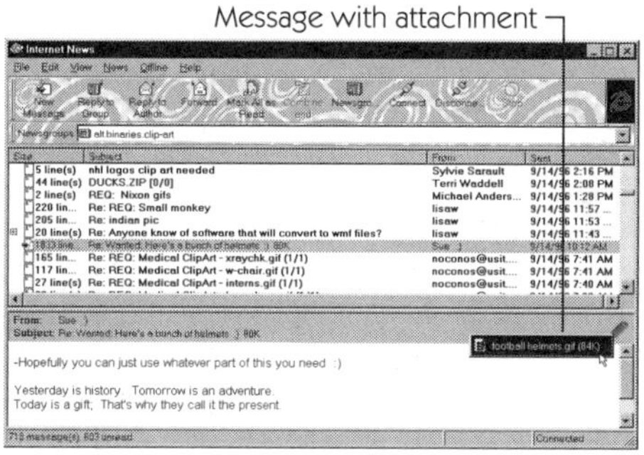

Figure 14.2 *Articles larger than a few hundred lines frequently contain encoded binary attachments, such as this clip art file.*

About Newsgroups

Newsgroups are collections of messages from people who share an interest in a topic, such as cars, Amiga computers, hang gliding, or flower arranging. Most news servers carry messages (called *articles*) from thousands of newsgroups (see **Figure 14.1**).

Newsgroup topics can be very broad (e.g., rec.crafts), narrowly focused (e.g., alt.games.duke3d), or somewhere in between. You're free to select, read, and post to every newsgroup that interests you.

Subscribing to Newsgroups

If you find a newsgroup that you want to read and participate in, you can *subscribe* to it. Subscribing is a news reader software feature, rather than a formal declaration of interest. When subscribing to a newsgroup, you are simply instructing your news reader to keep track of new posts.

Article Types

Although the majority of articles are text messages, they can contain attachments, as shown in **Figure 14.2**. There are graphics newsgroups, for example, filled with image files. When you post an article with an attachment, it is automatically encoded prior to being sent to the news server.

Article Threads

Articles for a newsgroup are grouped in *threads*, a series of messages in response to a post. Every new article can conceivably be the start of a new thread (see **Figure 14.3**).

For example, I might send a message named "What I like about Collies." Responses with the title "Re: What I like about Collies" would be part of the thread. You can configure your news reader to group articles by thread, so you can easily find all the ones on a topic that interests you.

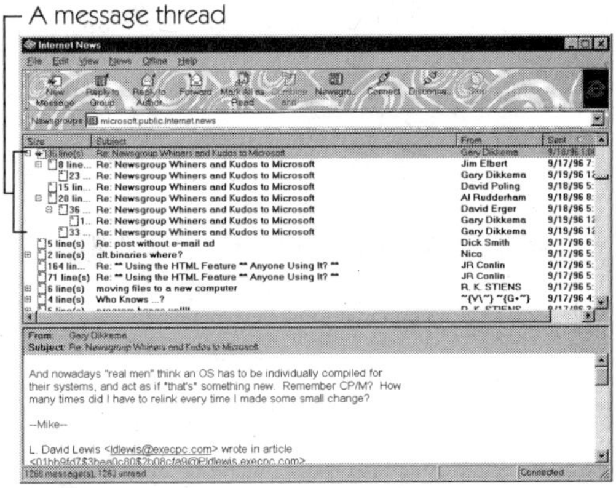

Figure 14.3 *To make it easy to follow a topic of conversation, articles can be grouped into threads. Articles in a thread are marked with a plus sign.*

Posting to a Newsgroup

Although you can gain a lot of information from reading articles, you can actively participate in newsgroups by posting new articles and responding to others. An article (see **Figure 14.4**) can be sent to the newsgroup—where it can be viewed by everyone—or it can be sent privately to the author of the original article (as e-mail).

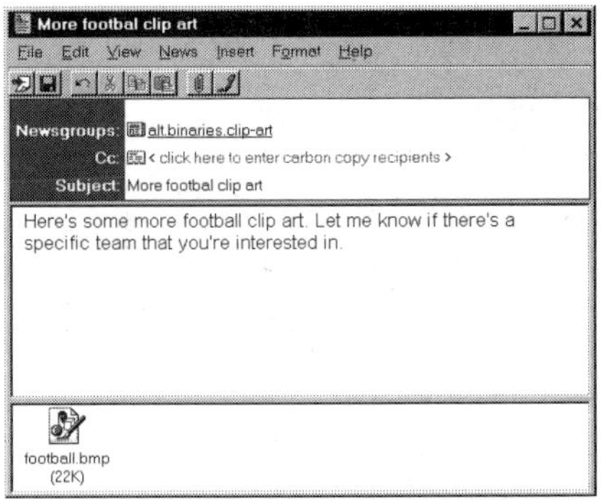

Figure 14.4 *Composing an article is the same as composing e-mail. Instead of addressing it to a person, however, you can send it to one or more newsgroups.*

About News Servers

The news server is responsible for tracking the newsgroups it carries. As new articles arrive from around the world, the news server makes them available to you and other users.

Many news servers track thousands of newsgroups. Some, on the other hand, handle only a small set of newsgroups. For example, Microsoft and Intel each has its own news server that covers company business and discussions about new hardware and software (see **Figure 14.5**).

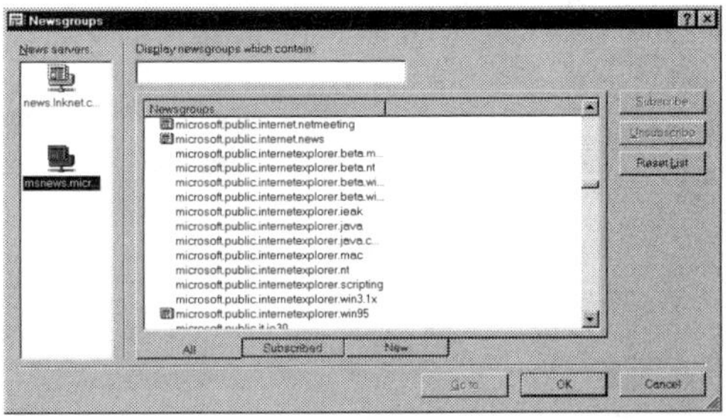

Figure 14.5 *Microsoft maintains its own news server.*

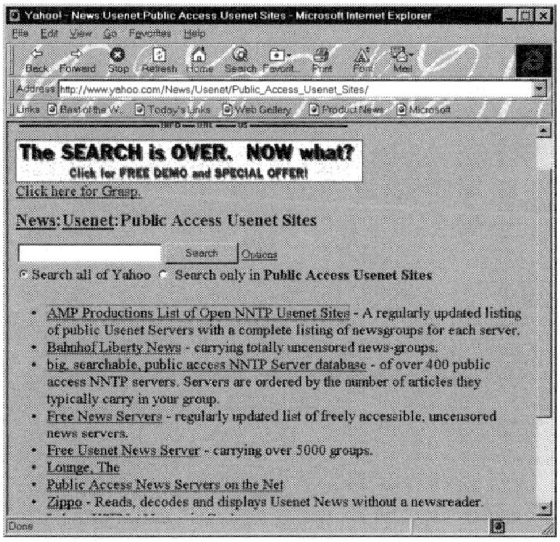

Figure 14.6 *This Yahoo! page is a good place to start when looking for public news servers.*

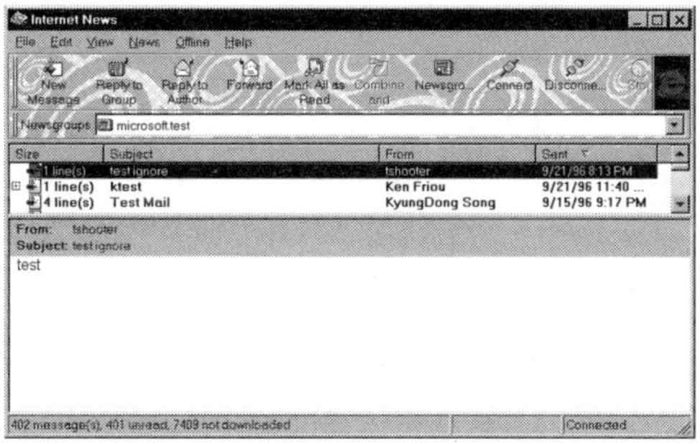

Figure 14.7 *Don't post test articles to normal newsgroups. You can find many newsgroups that are meant for test posts, such as microsoft.test.*

Your primary news server is usually the one provided by your ISP. In addition, there are many *public* news servers that you can use to gain access to newsgroups that are not carried by your ISP.

✔ Tips

- If your news server doesn't carry the newsgroups that you want (or you don't *have* a news server), you can use one of the Internet search sites to look for "public news servers." Or you can check this URL (see **Figure 14.6**):

  `www.yahoo.com/news/usenet/public_access_usenet_sites/`

  Note that while all public news servers allow you to *read* articles, not all of them allow you to *post*.

- When learning about newsgroups, you may want to make some test posts. Look for a newsgroup with *test* in its name. Such groups are specifically designed for testing (see **Figure 14.7**).

  To avoid warnings from the server when testing, include the word *ignore* somewhere in the Subject line of each test message.

- For the most part, newsgroups are not moderated or censored. Anyone can post an article about anything to any newsgroup, regardless of the newsgroup topic. Of course, you are free to read or ignore any article.

About Internet News

Internet News provides all the capabilities that most users will ever need to read and participate in newsgroups. Here are some of the major features and where you can learn about them:

- Subscribe to newsgroups on multiple news servers (Chapter 15).
- Search for newsgroups by keyword (Chapter 15).
- View all or only unread articles (Chapter 15).
- Sort the articles by the contents of any column in the article list (Chapter 15).
- Encode and decode binary attachments (Chapter 15).
- Combine and decode multipart posts (Chapter 15).
- Unscramble ROT13 articles (Chapter 15).
- Post replies to the newsgroup, the author, or both (Chapter 16).
- Cancel personal posts (Chapter 16).
- Work off-line, marking articles for downloading from multiple newsgroups (Chapter 17).
- Customize the message display and toolbar (Chapters 18 and 12).
- Automatically download all or a specified number of new article headers each time you connect (Chapter 18).
- Apply multiple levels of cache management (Chapter 18).

Reading and Managing Articles

15

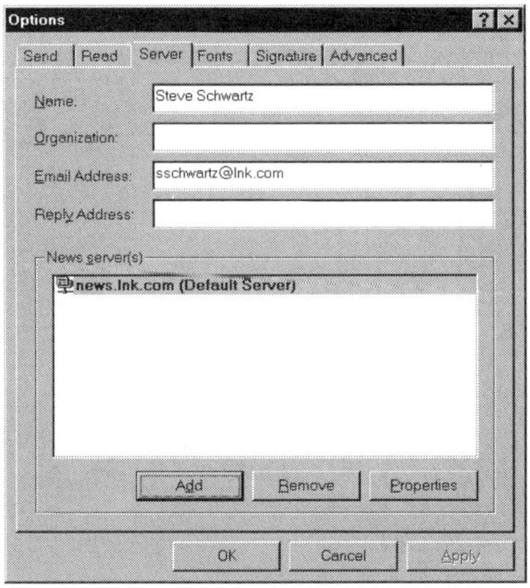

Figure 15.1 *You can add or remove news servers in the Servers section of the Options dialog box.*

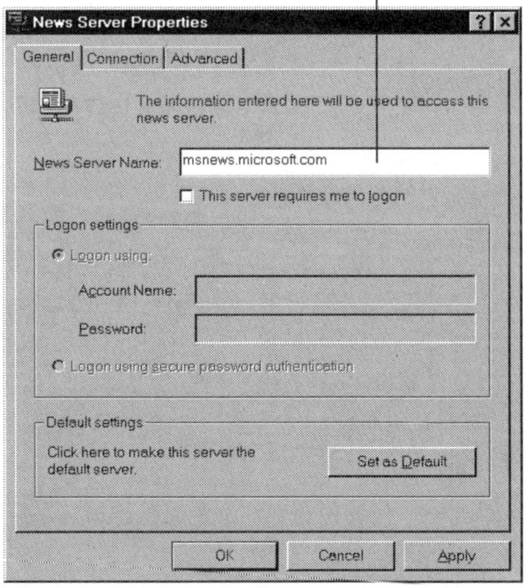

Figure 15.2 *In many cases, adding a news server to Internet News only requires entering its name.*

Before You Begin

If you're like most people, you'll spend much of your time in Internet News in an endless cycle of clicking headers, waiting for the message text to appear, and reading. However, there are a few preparatory steps you must take before launching into this routine.

Adding a News Server

Internet News can accommodate multiple news servers and subscribed-to newsgroups. Although you can add more servers whenever you wish, the first step is to specify at least one news server. Normally, this is done when you install the program.

To add a news server:

1. Choose Options from the News menu. The Options dialog box appears. Click the Server tab at the top of the dialog box, as shown in **Figure 15.1**.
2. Click Add. The News Server Properties dialog box appears (see **Figure 15.2**).
3. Enter the name of the news server in the News Server Name box.
4. If the news server requires you to log on (specifying an account name and password), click the check box and then fill in the Logon settings.
5. *Optional*: To make this server your default server, click Set as Default.

6. Click OK. A prompt appears (see **Figure 15.3**), asking if you'd like to subscribe to newsgroups from this news server.

7. Click Yes to download the list of newsgroups. The Newsgroups dialog box appears (see **Figure 15.4**).

8. You can subscribe to newsgroups now, if you wish (see "Subscribing to Newsgroups," below). When you're done, click OK.

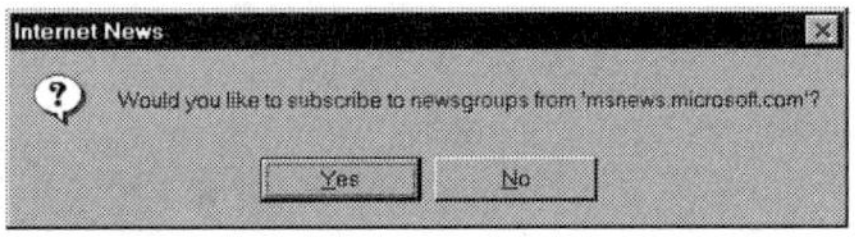

Figure 15.3 *Click Yes to download a list of newsgroups carried by the news server.*

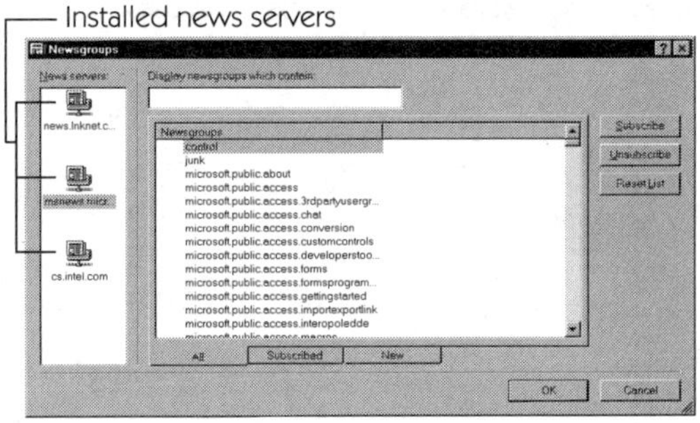

Figure 15.4 *You can subscribe to or unsubscribe from newsgroups carried by any server listed in the left side of this dialog box. Click a server icon to view its list of newsgroups.*

Subscribing to Newsgroups

There will undoubtedly be many newsgroups that you want to follow. *Subscribing* to these groups instructs Internet News to keep the article list up to date, always displaying only the newest ones.

To subscribe to a newsgroup:

1. Click the Newsgroups button in the toolbar, choose Newsgroups from the News menu, or press Ctrl W. The Newsgroups dialog box appears.

2. Select a news server from the list on the left. (Only servers that you have added will appear in the list.)

3. Click the All tab. All newsgroups available on the selected server are displayed in an alphabetical list.

4. Select a newsgroup that interests you, and click Subscribe. An icon is added to the left of the newsgroup name.

5. To unsubscribe from a newsgroup, select any newsgroup marked with the subscribed icon and click Unsubscribe.

6. When you're done, click OK.

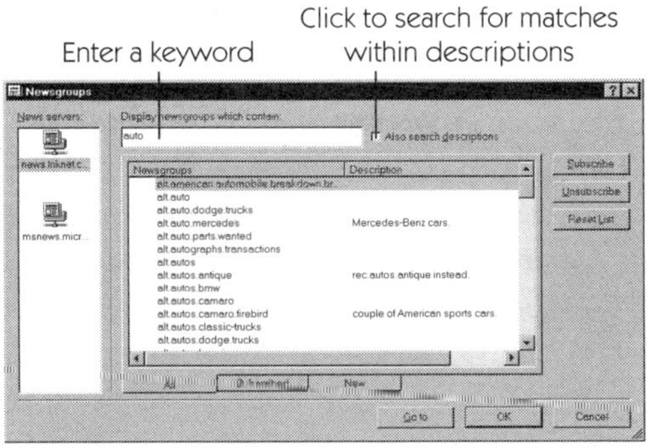

Figure 15.5 *To filter the newsgroup list, click All and type a keyword into the Display newsgroups box. To simultaneously search newsgroup descriptions, click Also search descriptions.*

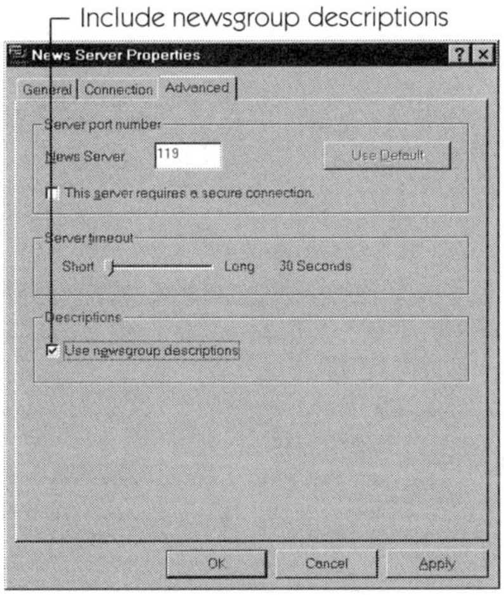

Figure 15.6 *The inclusion of newsgroup descriptions must be set on a server-by-server basis in the Server section of the Options dialog box. Select a server, click the Properties button, and click the Advanced tab.*

✔ Tips

- Double-clicking a newsgroup name toggles its status between subscribed and unsubscribed.
- To facilitate finding newsgroups of interest, type a keyword (such as *auto* or *explorer*) in the box at the top of the Newsgroups dialog box (see **Figure 15.5**). Only group names that contain the keyword will be listed.
- When selecting and managing newsgroups, you can restrict the list to show only subscribed groups (click the Subscribed tab) or only new newsgroups (click the New tab). Note that after the new groups have been viewed, they are merged with the All list.
- You can also download newsgroup *descriptions* if you set that option for a news server (see **Figure 15.6**). If the option is set after you have added the news server, click the Reset button in the Newsgroups dialog box to download a fresh list of newsgroups and their descriptions. (Not all newsgroups have descriptions.)
- You can view the messages of any newsgroup *without* subscribing to it. Click the Newsgroups button in the toolbar or choose Newsgroups from the News menu. The Newsgroups dialog box appears. Select a newsgroup, and click the Go to button. When you exit from the newsgroup, you will be asked if you want to subscribe to it.

Reading Articles

After you've chosen some newsgroups, you're ready to start reading articles.

To read articles in a newsgroup:

1. Select a newsgroup from the pop-up Newsgroups list in the main window. The list of article headers is displayed (see **Figure 15.7**).
2. If you are already connected to the Internet, the article list updates to reflect the new articles. If you are not connected, click the Connect button in the toolbar.
3. Click to select an article that interests you. The text of the article is downloaded to the cache, the header is marked with a new icon (see **Figure 15.8**), and the article appears in the preview pane.
4. After an article has been read, the boldface is removed from the header and the icon turns white.

To read other articles in the current newsgroup, repeat Step 3. To read articles in other newsgroups, repeat all of the steps.

✔ Tips

- You can continue clicking and reading articles as others download. To select multiple articles, Ctrl-click them.
- To view any article in a separate window (see **Figure 15.9**), double-click its header.
- If additional articles are available for the current newsgroup on the server, you can choose Get Next *xx* Headers from the News menu to manually retrieve them.

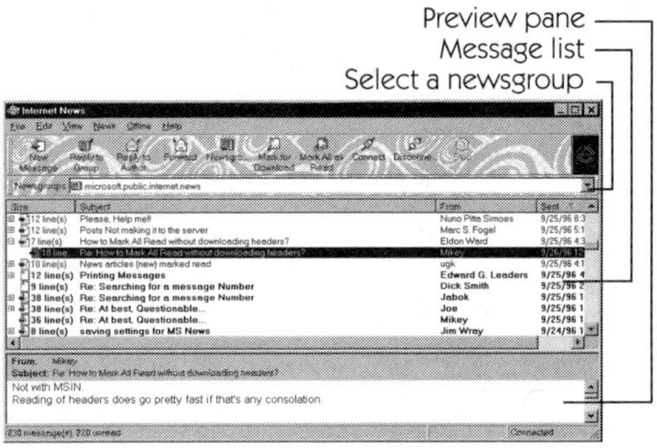

Figure 15.7 *The standard window for Internet News displays article headers in the top section and message text in the preview pane at the bottom.*

Figure 15.8 *This icon denotes an unread article that has been downloaded to the cache on your hard disk.*

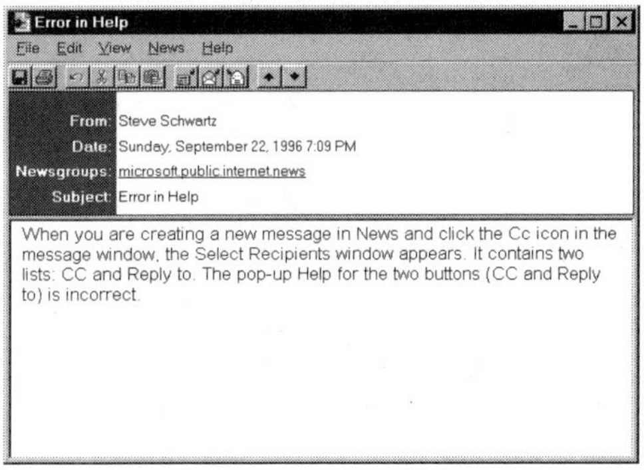

Figure 15.9 *Any article can be viewed in its own window.*

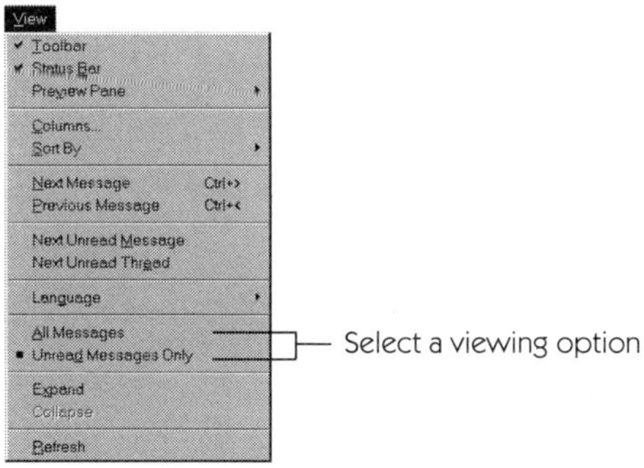

Figure 15.10 *You can view all articles or only the ones you haven't read by choosing a command from the View menu.*

Article Selection Tips

There are several techniques and procedures that you can use to make it easier to select and read articles:

- Don't use the up- and down-arrow keys to scroll through the article list. Each article that is highlighted will be downloaded. Instead, choose articles with the mouse.
- Choose Unread Messages Only from the View menu (see **Figure 15.10**) to limit the article list to unread articles.

  To see *all* current articles (including ones you've previously read), choose All Messages from the View menu. This is helpful when reviewing message threads.
- You can lessen the clutter in the article list by choosing Unread Messages Only, and then periodically choosing Refresh from the View menu. All articles read during the current session will be removed from the list.
- You can sort the article list by the contents of any column. Click a column heading to sort by that column. Click the heading again to toggle between an ascending and a descending sort. (You can also choose sort commands from the Sort By submenu of the View menu.)
- If the article list contains unread and read articles, you can move to the next unread article in the list by choosing Next Unread Message or Next Unread Thread from the View menu.

To move to the next or previous article (regardless of whether it has been read), choose Next Article or Previous Article from the View menu.

- To make it easier to follow article threads, select Group Messages by Thread from the Sort By submenu of the View menu. Otherwise, the articles will be scattered throughout the list, according to the current sort order.
- To expand or collapse a message thread, click the + or - symbol to the left of the article header. You can automatically expand *all* article threads by choosing Auto expand all conversation threads in the Read section of the Options dialog box.
- Keeping the article list to a reasonable size makes it easier to spot important new articles. You can eliminate articles that don't interest you by selecting them and choosing an appropriate Mark As Read command from the Edit menu (see **Figure 15.11**).
- To view a previously read article, choose All Messages from the View menu, select the article, and choose Mark as Unread from the Edit menu. When you switch back to Unread Messages Only view, the article will be visible.
- There are a variety of article marking options that you can employ by right-clicking a message, as shown in **Figure 15.12**.

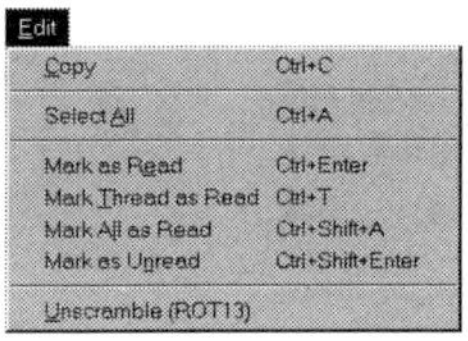

Figure 15.11 *You can use the Mark commands to manually mark articles as read or unread.*

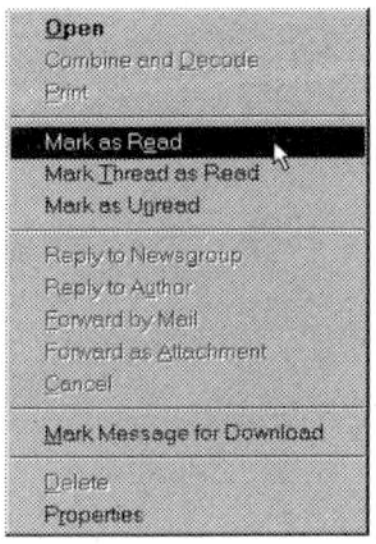

Figure 15.12 *This pop-up menu appears when you click an article header in the article list.*

Working with Attachments and Encoded Articles

Some articles contain more than a text message. Each requires a procedure to decode or use the non-text material, as explained below.

Article Attachments

Like e-mail messages, articles can contain binary attachments, such as graphic files, word processing documents, or computer programs. For assistance in opening an attachment, see "Working with Attachments" in Chapter 11.

Unscrambling ROT13 Articles

To make an article difficult to decipher, authors occasionally scramble the text using a simple protocol called ROT13 (see **Figure 15.13**). Letters in the message are shifted by 13 characters. To decode the scrambled text, select the article in the article list and choose Unscramble (ROT13) from the Edit menu.

```
Vafgnag Xyvatba, onfvpnyyl!
Instant Klingon, basically!
```

Figure 15.13 *A single line of text (top) was scrambled with ROT13. The Unscramble (ROT13) command can be used to make sense of it (bottom).*

Multipart Articles

Because of the size limits imposed on articles by many servers, you'll sometimes encounter an article than has been split into two or more parts. This is most common when sending large graphics, programs, movies, and .ZIP files. The article parts are usually listed as (1/2) and (2/2), for example.

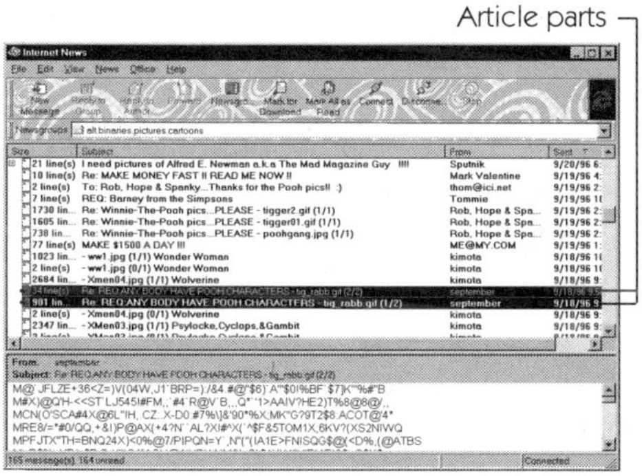

Figure 15.14 *Select the article parts that you want to combine.*

To combine a multipart article:

1. Download all the article parts.
2. Select the article parts in the article list by Ctrl-clicking, as shown in **Figure 15.14**.

3. Choose Combine and Decode from the News menu. The Order for decoding dialog box appears (see **Figure 15.15**).
4. Arrange the parts in the correct order, lowest to highest. (You can move parts by dragging them or by clicking the Move Up and Move Down buttons.)
5. Click OK. The parts are combined and decoded. The article opens in a new window. The non-text material is displayed as an attachment at the bottom of the window. For help opening the attachment, refer to "Working with Attachments" in Chapter 11.

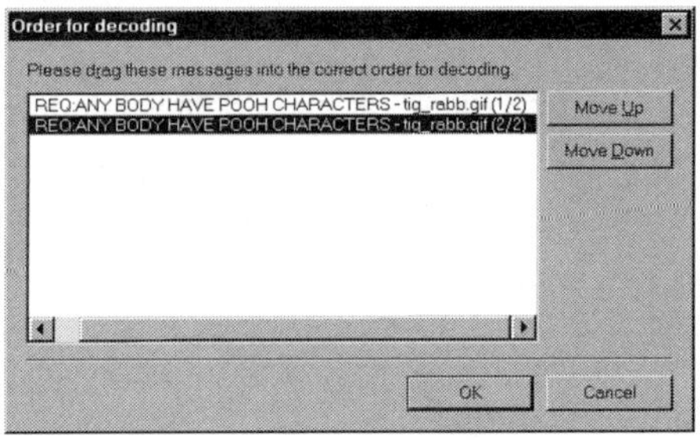

Figure 15.15 *Use the Order for decoding dialog box to specify the order in which the article pieces are to be arranged.*

✔ Tips

- ROT13 messages are rare. While ROT13 may fool Internet novices, it is no substitute for encryption. If you're interested in *real* security, buy an encryption program.
- There are several ways to tell if an article contains an attachment. First, look for a file name in the article header, such as boat.jpg or turkey.gif. Second, check the file size. Any file with more than 200 lines often contains an attachment. To make it easy to spot such files, you can sort by the Size column or rearrange the display, making Size the first column.

Article Management

After downloading articles and reading them, there are several actions you can take to manage the new information.

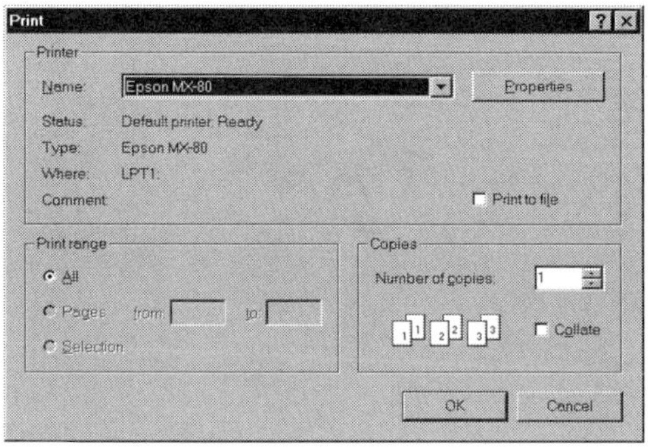

Figure 15.16 *Prior to printing, you can set print options in the Print dialog box.*

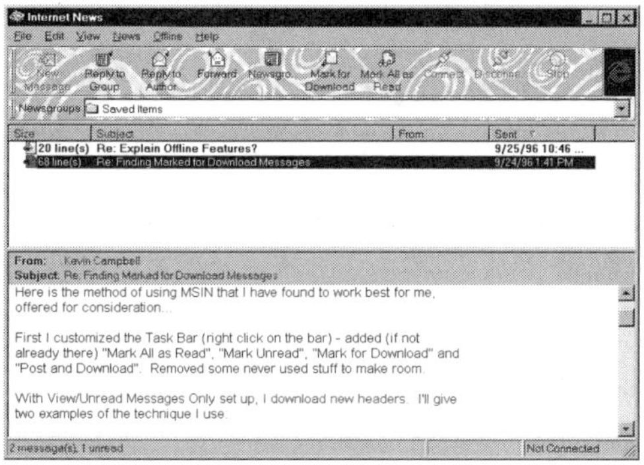

Figure 15.17 *To read a saved article, select Saved Items from the Newsgroups pop-up list, and select the article.*

Printing Articles

You can print any article that you've downloaded. Select the article in the article list or open it in its own window, and choose Print from the File menu (or press Ctrl P). Set options in the Print dialog box (see **Figure 15.16**), and click OK.

Saving Articles

Internet News provides a Saved Items folder in which to save important articles. Select the article in the article list or open it in its own window, and choose Save from the File menu (or press Ctrl S). A copy of the article is placed in the Saved Items folder (see **Figure 15.17**).

You can also save articles to any location on disk as Internet Mail or Internet News files. Select the article in the article list or open it in its own window, and choose Save As from the File menu. Choose a location and file type for the new file, and click Save.

Deleting Articles

Although you can't delete messages from the article list, you can delete articles that are stored in the Saved Items and Posted Items folders. To mark an article for deletion, select the appropriate folder from the Newsgroups pop-up list, and highlight the article. Then choose Delete from the File menu, press Del, or press Ctrl D.

Cleaning Up the Cache

There are two ways to free up the disk space that Internet News uses to store headers and article bodies:

- *Save space automatically*. As shown in **Figure 15.18**, Internet News can be set to automatically compact the caches whenever the specified percentage of disk space is being wasted.
- *Save space manually*. Click Clean Up Now in the Advanced Options dialog box (refer to **Figure 15.18**), or choose Clean Up Files from the File menu. Either procedure leads to the Local File Clean Up dialog box, where you can compact the caches, delete article bodies, or delete headers and bodies. See Chapter 18 for details.

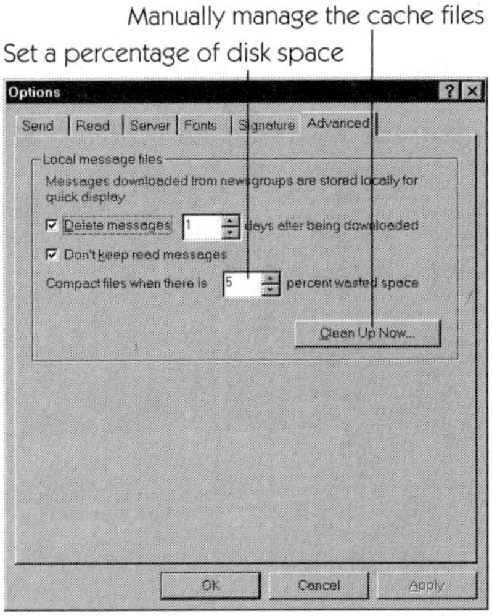

Figure 15.18 *To set cache management options, go to the Advanced section of the Options dialog box.*

16 Posting to Newsgroups

About Posting

If you want to *participate* in a newsgroup (rather than only reading other people's articles), you can post new articles to the newsgroup or reply to articles written by others.

All articles are composed in an Internet News or Mail message window (see **Figure 16.1**). You can post any of the following types of articles:

- A new article to a newsgroup. (The article is listed in the article list for the newsgroup and can be read by anyone.)
- A reply to an existing article. (The article becomes part of a thread.)
- A direct reply to an individual, sent as e-mail. (Only the author of the original article sees the reply. It is not sent to the newsgroup.)

In addition, you can forward any article that you read in a newsgroup as e-mail or as an e-mail attachment.

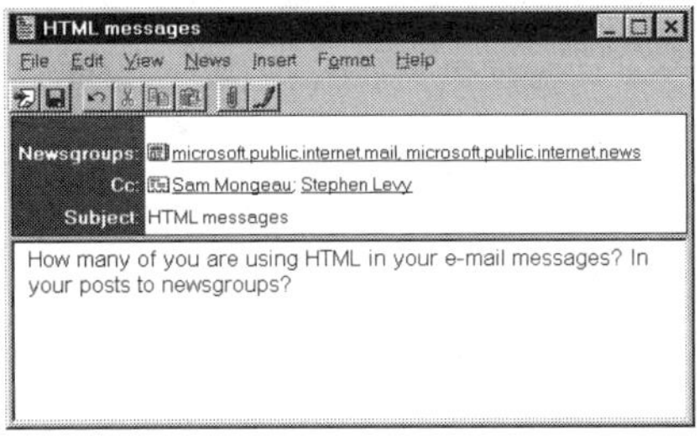

Figure 16.1 *Compose a new article for a newsgroup in a normal message window. As you can see, you can post an article to multiple newsgroups.*

✔ **Tips**

- When posting articles, send them only to appropriate newsgroups. An article about your gardening problems will not be well received in a computing newsgroup.
- You can add attachments to an article by clicking the Insert File button in the toolbar or by choosing File Attachment from the Insert menu.

Composing and Posting an Article

The process of composing and posting articles varies slightly, depending on whether you are sending a new message, replying to an existing article, replying directly to the author of an article, or forwarding an article as e-mail or an e-mail attachment.

To post a new article:

1. Choose New Message to Newsgroup from the News menu (or press Ctrl N). A New Message window appears.
2. Compose the article.
3. Fill in the necessary lines in the message header. (See "Addressing the Article," later in this chapter.)
4. Click the Post Message button (see **Figure 16.2**), choose Post Message from the File menu (see **Figure 16.3**), or press Alt S.

To post a reply to a newsgroup:

1. Select an article in the message list to which you want to reply (see **Figure 16.4**), or open the article in its own window.
2. Click Reply to Group, choose Reply to Newsgroup from the News menu, or press Ctrl G.
3. Compose the article.
4. Fill in the necessary lines in the header. (See "Addressing the Article," later in this chapter.)
5. Click the Post Message button, choose Post Message from the File menu, or press Alt S.

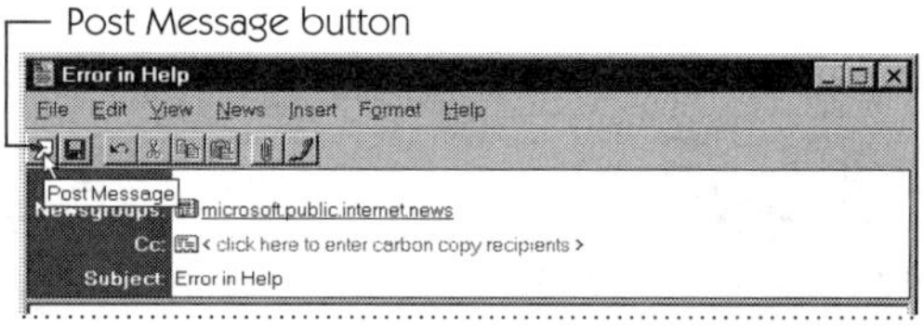

Figure 16.2 *To post the current article, click the Post Message button in the message window's toolbar.*

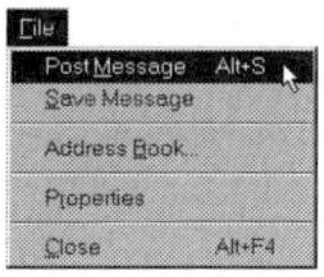

Figure 16.3 *Or you can choose Post Message from the File menu.*

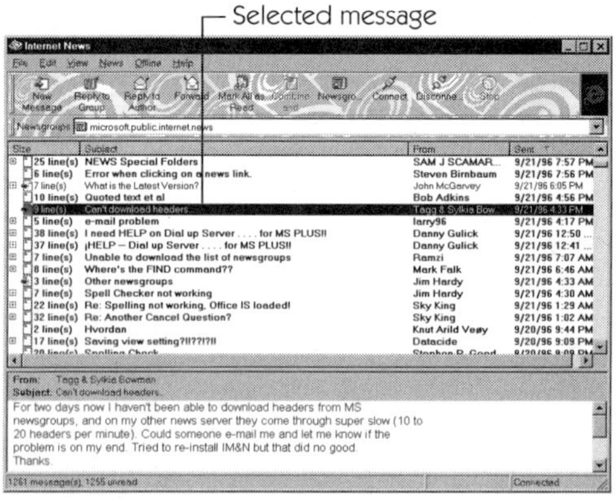

Figure 16.4 *When replying to an article, the first step is to select the article.*

To reply directly to an individual:

1. Select an article in the message list to which you want to reply, or open an article in its own window.
2. Click Reply to Author in the toolbar, choose Reply to Author from the News menu, or press Ctrl R.
3. Compose the article.
4. Fill in the necessary lines in the header. (See "Addressing the Article," later in this chapter.)
5. Click the Send button in the toolbar, choose Send Message from the File menu, or press Alt S.

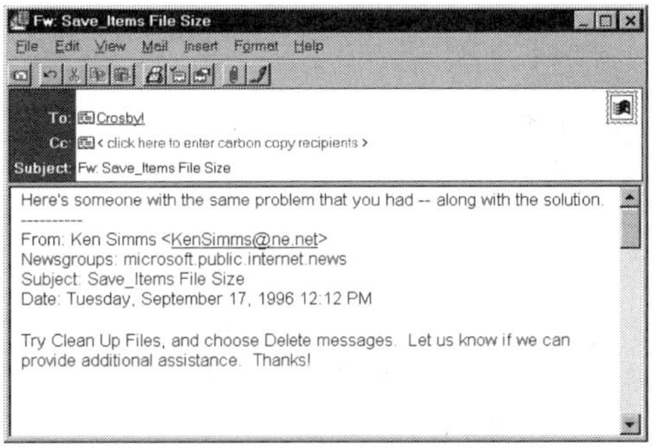

Figure 16.5 *A forwarded article appears at the bottom of the message. You can add your own comments, if you like.*

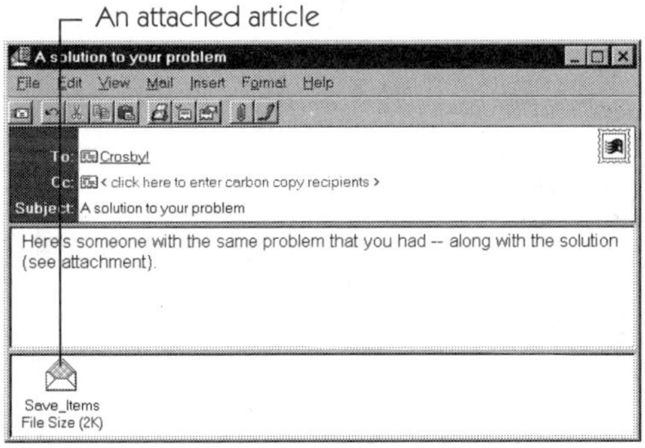

Figure 16.6 *The entire message area is initially blank when you forward an article as an attachment. Add your own message.*

To forward an article as e-mail:

1. In the message list, select the article that you want to forward, or open the article in its own window.
2. Click the Forward button in the toolbar, choose Forward from the News menu, or press Ctrl F (see **Figure 16.5**).

   or

2. Choose Forward as Attachment from the News menu, as shown in **Figure 16.6**.
3. Compose the article.
4. Fill in the necessary lines in the header. (See "Addressing the Message," later in this chapter.)
5. Click the Send button in the toolbar, choose Send Message from the File menu, or press Alt S.

✔ **Tip**

- To include your signature, choose Signature from the Insert menu.

Addressing the Article

When readying an article for posting, you must fill in some lines in the message header. The number of lines shown depends on whether Full Headers is chosen in the View menu of the message window (see **Figures 16.7** and **16.8**). There are also minor differences between posting or replying to a group, and replying to or forwarding an article to an individual.

The lines of the message header are as follows:

- *Newsgroups (appears when posting a new article or a reply to a newsgroup)*. Enter the names of the newsgroup(s) to whom the article will be sent, separated by commas. You can choose newsgroups by clicking the icon beside Newsgroups (see **Figure 16.9**) or by choosing Choose Newsgroups from the News menu.
- *To (appears when replying to or forwarding an article to an individual)*. Enter the names of the individuals to whom the article will be sent, separated by semicolons. You can choose names from your address book by clicking the icon beside To, clicking the Pick Recipients button in the toolbar, or choosing Choose Recipients from the Mail menu.
- *Followup-To*. An entry in this line specifies the newsgroup to which follow-up articles to your article should be posted. Normally, this line contains the name of the original newsgroup, but it can be used to redirect the discussion to another newsgroup.

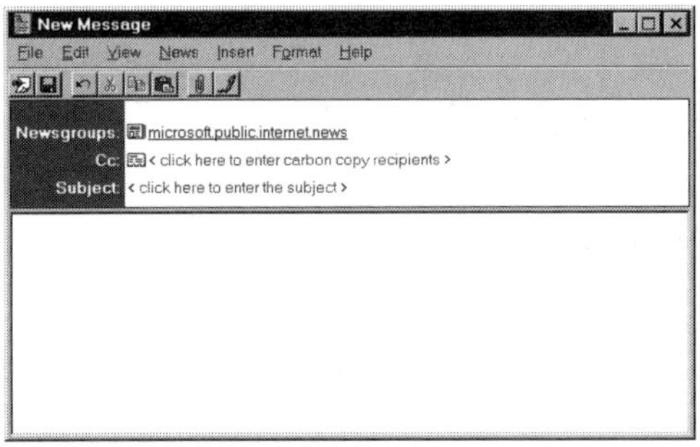

Figure 16.7 *A normal header contains three lines: Newsgroups (or To), Cc, and Subject.*

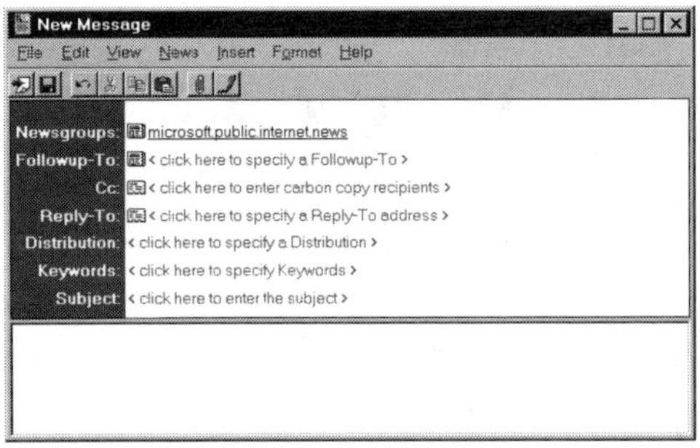

Figure 16.8 *A full header contains seven lines, many of which are optional.*

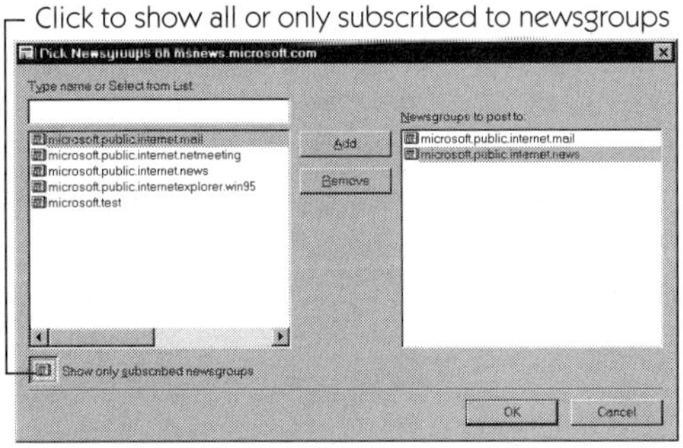

Figure 16.9 *The easiest way to select target newsgroups for an article is by using this dialog box. The button beneath the newsgroup list toggles between showing subscribed and all newsgroups.*

- *Cc*. Enter the names of individuals to whom a copy of the article will be sent. You can pick names from your address book by clicking the icon beside Cc or by choosing Choose Recipients from the Mail menu.
- *Reply-To*. If you want replies sent to a different e-mail address than your usual one, enter the address here. To select a Reply-To address from your address book, click the icon beside Reply-To.
- *Distribution*. Any entry found in the Distribution line is used to restrict the areas of the country or world to which the article is made available. You might enter Dallas, for example, to restrict the article distribution to the Dallas area.
- *Keywords*. Some news readers are able to sort or find articles based on keywords that have been assigned by the author. Keywords must be separated by commas.
- *Subject*. Enter a descriptive title for the article.

✔ **Tips**

- When replying to or forwarding an article, some header lines will be filled in for you.
- To make sure that an author sees your reply, choose Reply to Newsgroup and Author from the Mail menu (see **Figure 16.10**).
- You can post an article to several newsgroups, but only if they are on the same news server. To post to newsgroups on multiple servers, you must send a copy of the article to each news server.

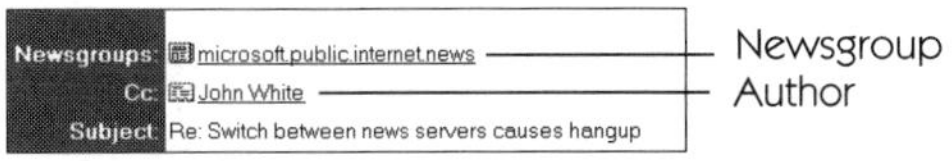

Figure 16.10 *The Reply to Newsgroup and Author command addresses the reply to the newsgroup, while sending a copy to the author.*

Cancelling an Article

Normally, when you post an article, it is available to newsgroup subscribers throughout the world until deleted from their news server. If, however, you discover an error in the article or no longer seek replies to it, you can cancel the article—removing it from the news server.

To cancel an article that you posted to a newsgroup, select it in the message list and choose Cancel from the File menu (see **Figure 16.11**).

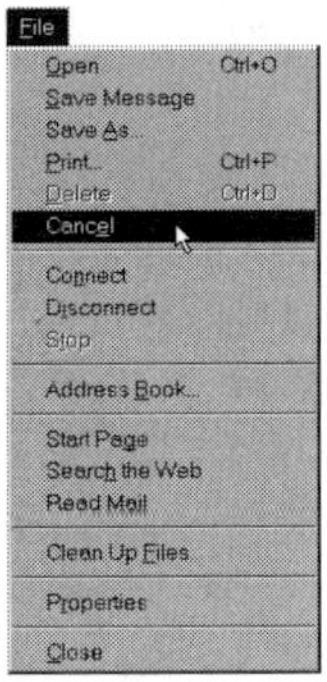

Figure 16.11 *You can cancel any of your posts to a newsgroup.*

17 Working Off-Line

About Working Off-Line

In addition to working interactively with Internet News (marking and reading articles on-line), you can also do much of your work *off-line*. The process is straightforward:

- While off-line, select the newsgroups that interest you.
- Instruct Internet News to download any new article headers for those newsgroups and log off.
- Examine the new headers (while off-line), and mark the articles that you want to read.
- Instruct Internet News to connect again, download the articles to your hard disk (see **Figure 17.1**), and log off.
- Read the articles at your leisure.

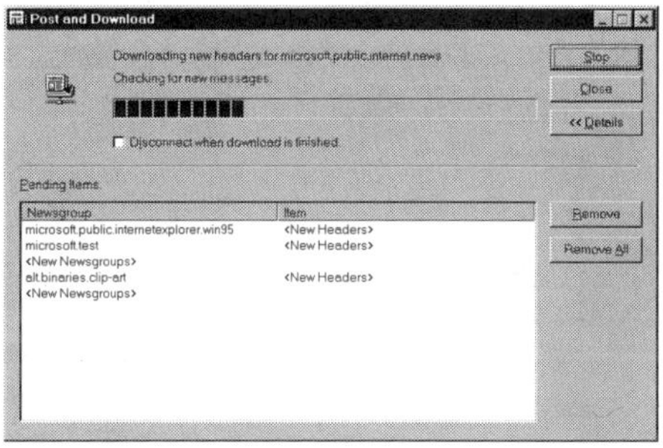

Figure 17.1 *All on-line time is spent doing one of two things: downloading the headers for new articles or downloading the articles themselves.*

Figure 17.2 *The status bar shows whether you are currently connected with the news server.*

If you pay for Internet access by the hour, this process keeps on-line time to a minimum. Rather than waste billable minutes reading messages while you're on-line, all connect time is devoted to downloading headers and articles.

✔ Tip

- If your goal is to minimize on-line time, be sure to check the status bar. It should read "Not Connected" (see **Figure 17.2**) while you are picking newsgroups to update and marking messages. If not, click the Disconnect button or choose Disconnect from the File menu.

Downloading New Headers

Unless you routinely read *all* articles posted to a particular newsgroup, the first step in most off-line work is to download the new articles headers. That way, your list of available articles will match that of your news server.

To download new article headers:

1. Choose Mark Newsgroups from the Offline menu. The Mark Newsgroups dialog box appears (see **Figure 17.3**).
2. To download all new headers from all subscribed newsgroups, click All Subscribed Newsgroups.

   or

2. To download headers from selected newsgroups, click Selected Newsgroups, and choose newsgroups to update.
3. Click Download headers only.
4. *Optional*: To set an age limit for articles, click "Don't download new messages posted more than *xx* days ago," and select a number of days.
5. Click Download Now. The Post and Download dialog box appears (see **Figure 17.4**), and the downloading process begins.
6. Unless you want to remain on-line, click the option to Disconnect when download is finished.

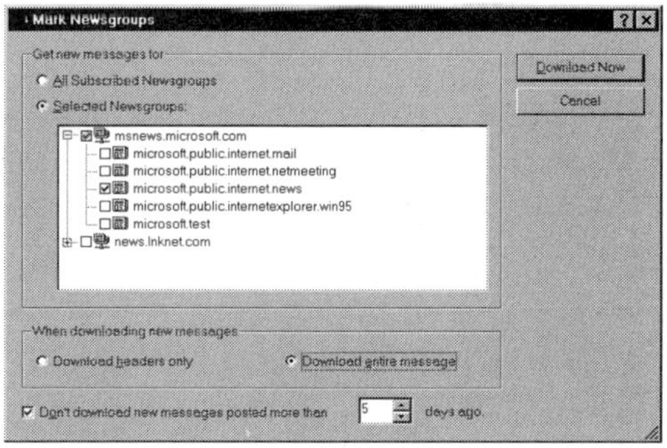

Figure 17.3 *You can download selected or all headers from multiple newsgroups on multiple news servers.*

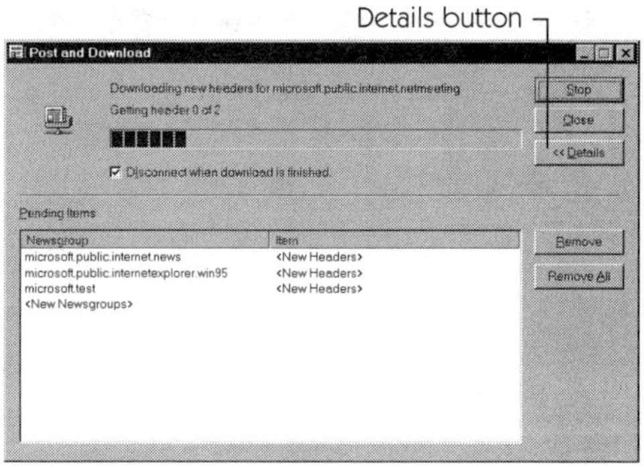

Figure 17.4 *To follow the progress of the download (as shown here), click the Details button to expand the Post and Download dialog box.*

✔ Tip

- The maximum number of new headers retrieved from each newsgroup is determined by a setting in the Options dialog box (see **Figure 17.5**).

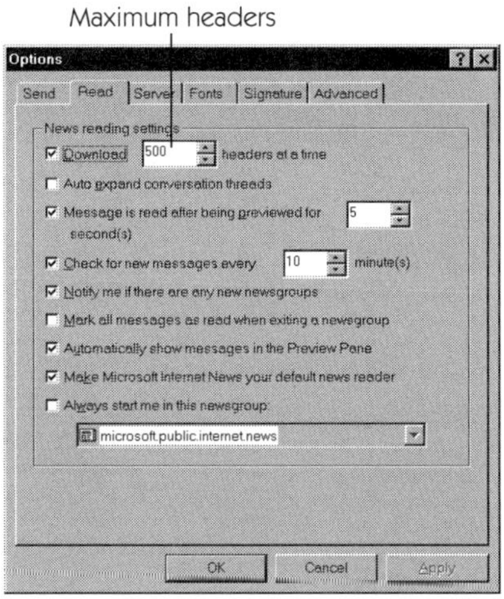

Figure 17.5 *You can specify the maximum number of headers to be downloaded from each newsgroup. Remove the check mark if you want to download all new headers.*

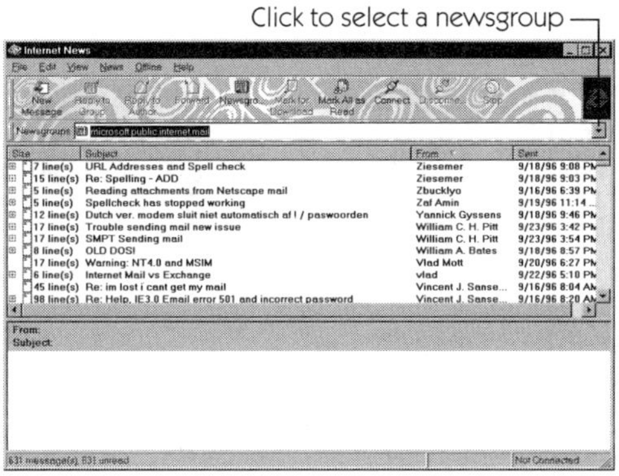

Figure 17.6 *To select a newsgroup, click the pop-up indicator at the end of the Newsgroups box to reveal the list of subscribed newsgroups.*

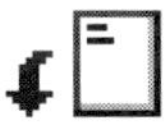

Figure 17.7 *Messages marked for downloading are indicated by a downward curving arrow.*

Downloading Articles

You can use the off-line capabilities of Internet News to download:

- All new articles from all or only selected newsgroups.

  or

- Selected articles (new or older articles in the message list) from one or more newsgroups.

Downloading All New Articles

The procedure for downloading all new articles from one or more newsgroups is done in the same manner as downloading the new headers. In Step 3 of the previous procedure ("To download new article headers"), click Download entire message.

Downloading Selected Articles

Unless you prefer to read every article in a newsgroup, you can download the ones that interest you—just as you do when you are working on-line. Instead of clicking and reading, however, you mark the messages you want and then send the list to the news server.

To download selected articles:

1. Select a subscribed newsgroup from the pop-up list of newsgroups (see **Figure 17.6**).
2. Select a message to download, and choose Mark Message for Download from the Offline menu (see **Figure 17.7**).

   Note that you can mark multiple messages at once by Ctrl-clicking them, and then choosing Mark Message for Download.

3. To mark a message *thread* for downloading (messages preceded by a + sign), select the outermost message and choose Mark Thread for Download from the Offline menu.

4. To download all visible messages in the current newsgroup, choose Mark All for Download from the Offline menu.

5. If you change your mind about downloading some of the marked articles, select them again and choose Unmark for Download from the Offline menu.

6. Repeat Steps 1 through 5 for additional newsgroups, as desired.

7. When you're ready to retrieve the selected articles, choose Post and Download from the Offline menu. Retrieved articles are indicated in the message list by the icon shown in **Figure 17.8**.

Figure 17.8 *Downloaded messages are indicated by this icon. It means that a copy of the article is in the cache on your hard disk.*

✔ **Tips**

- You can select contiguous groups of articles by Shift-clicking the first and last article.
- Time—especially on-line time—is money. You can save more time by combining posts and downloads in the same session. Prepare all outgoing messages, mark articles for retrieval, and *then* choose Post and Download.

Composing and Posting Messages

While off-line, you can also create new messages for newsgroups and write replies to articles (see Chapter 16). And rather than send them immediately, they can be held in your Outbox until the next connection with the news server is made.

To post articles:

1. Choose Post Message or Send Message from the File menu (the wording of the command depends on whether the article is a new message, a reply to a newsgroup, or a reply to an author).
2. The Post Article dialog box appears (see **Figure 17.9**). Click OK. The message is stored in your Outbox.
3. When you are ready to connect with your server, choose Post and Download from the Offline menu (see **Figure 17.10**). All outgoing messages are sent. Any header or message downloads that you have specified are also performed.

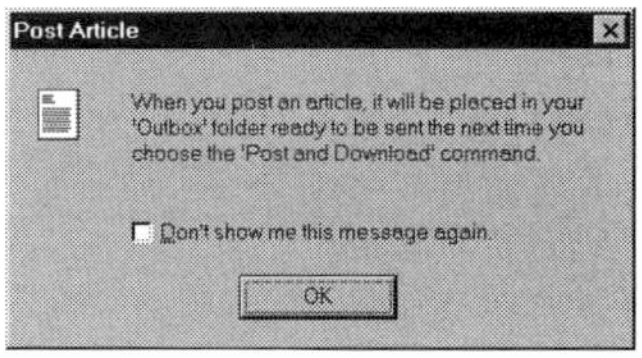

Figure 17.9 *Unless you have permanently dismissed this dialog box, it appears whenever you try to post/send a message while you are off-line.*

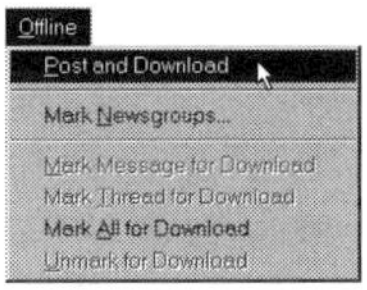

Figure 17.10 *To simultaneously send all messages in your Outbox and retrieve marked articles, choose Post and Download from the Offline menu.*

✔ **Tip**

- To avoid future appearances of the dialog box shown in **Figure 17.9**, click "Don't show me this message again," and then click OK.

Internet News Options

18

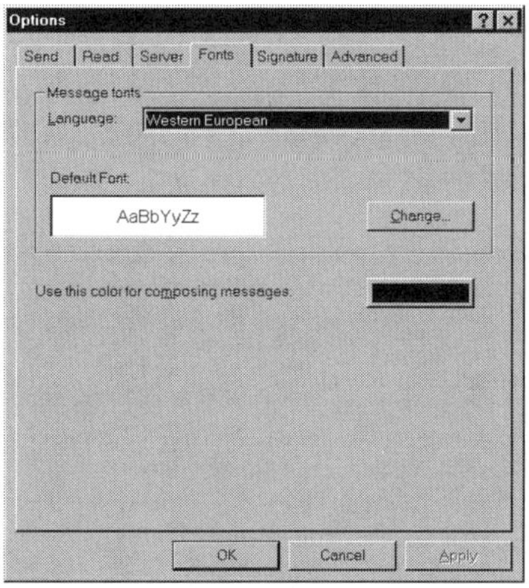

Figure 18.1 *Fonts options for Internet News.*

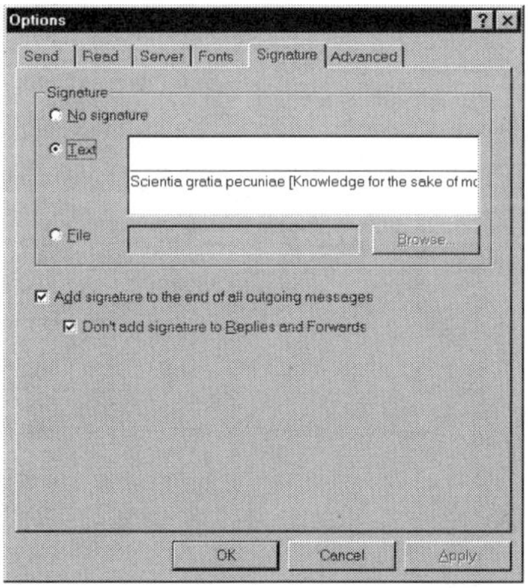

Figure 18.2 *Signature options for Internet News.*

About Setting Options

There are many preferences that you can set for Internet News. Choose Options from the News menu. The Options dialog box appears.

Option Categories

There are six option categories that correspond to the tabs at the top of the Options dialog box, as follows:

- *Send*. Settings for composing and posting messages.
- *Read*. Options to check for new posts and newsgroups, managing threads, and reading messages.
- *Server*. Specifying e-mail account and news server information.
- *Fonts*. Selecting a language, default font, and text color for posts.
- *Signature*. Specifying a signature line or file to optionally be appended to outgoing posts.
- *Advanced*. Options for managing the caches for newsgroup headers and messages.

The Fonts and Signature options (see **Figures 18.1** and **18.2**) are identical to those of Internet Mail. See Chapter 13 for information.

Customizing the Display

To customize the display and toolbar, refer to the instructions in Chapter 12, pages 118–122.

Send Options

For the most part, the Send options (see **Figure 18.3)** are the same as those for Internet Mail. For an explanation of these options, refer to "Send Options" in Chapter 13.

The first option ("When posting, save a copy in 'Posted Messages' folder"), however, is somewhat different. When checked, copies of all messages that you post to newsgroups are automatically stored in the Posted Items folder. Because it is easy to lose the original message (and, hence, not know to what another person is responding), checking this option ensures that you will always have a copy of your posts.

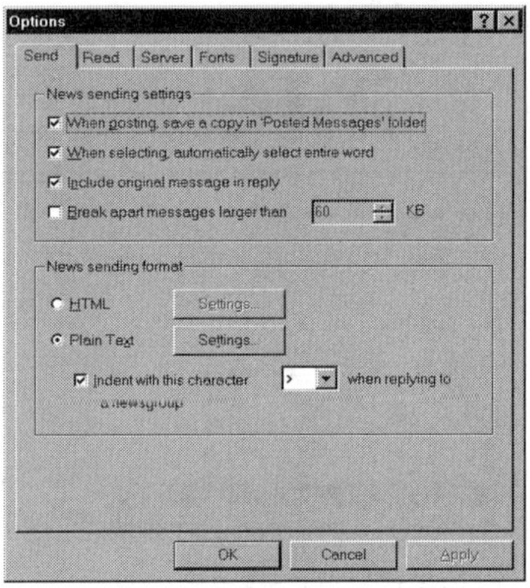

Figure 18.3 *Send options for Internet News.*

To review and manage posts:

- To review your posted messages, choose Posted Items from the folder pop-up (see **Figure 18.4**).
- To delete your copy of a posted message, open the Posted Items folder, select the message in the message list, and choose Delete from the File menu (or press Del).

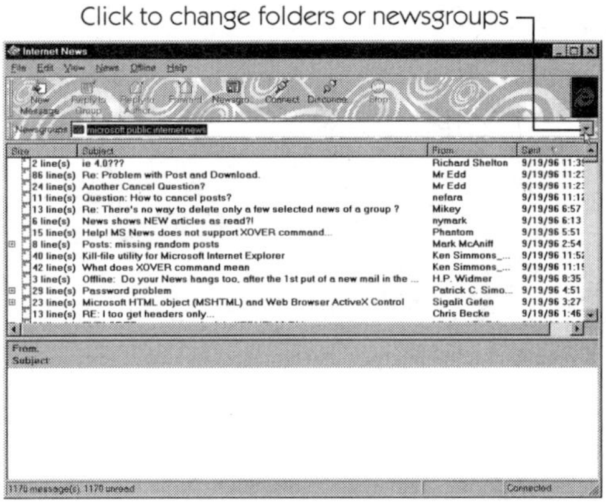

Figure 18.4 *To change to another folder or newsgroup, click the folder pop-up.*

✔ Tips

- Use Plain Text for posting to most newsgroups. All news readers can handle this format; few can display HTML-formatted messages.
- If you intend to send attachments (such as graphics), select Plain Text, click Settings, and choose Uuencode. Although MIME can be used, uuencode is the preferred format.

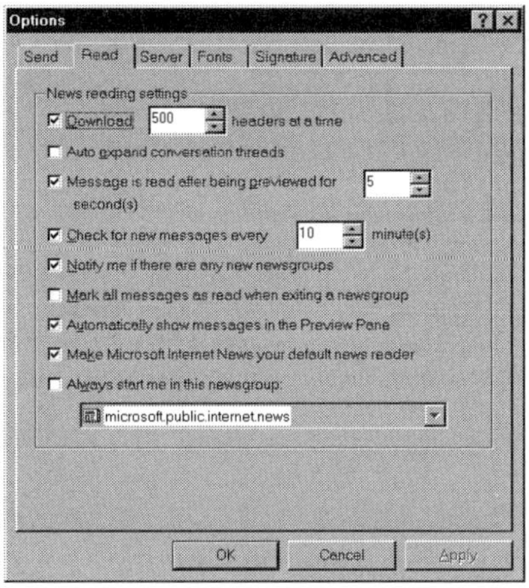

Figure 18.5 *Read options for Internet News.*

Read Options

Most of the Read options (see **Figure 18.5**) are unique to Internet News.

- *Download xx headers at a time.* Check this option to specify the maximum message headers (50–1,000) to be downloaded at one time. When unchecked, all new headers are downloaded each time you view a newsgroup.
- *Auto expand conversation threads.* Messages that are part of a thread are marked with a + symbol in the message list. When this option is checked, all threads are expanded; that is, you can see the headers for all messages in the thread. When unchecked, you can manually expand individual threads, as desired.
- *Message is read after being previewed for xx seconds.* See Chapter 13.
- *Check for new messages every xx minutes.* See Chapter 13.
- *Notify me if there are any new newsgroups.* The newsgroups that are available on a given server can change frequently. Check this option if you want to be notified when new newsgroups are added.
- *Mark all messages as read when exiting a newsgroup.* Check this option to see only new messages for each newsgroup, automatically eliminating the old ones each time you exit.
- *Automatically show messages in the Preview Pane.* When this option is checked and you select a message in the message list, the

Read Options

text of the message is displayed in the preview pane. If unchecked, you can still display messages by selecting them, and then pressing Spacebar (see **Figure 18.6**) or choosing Open from the File menu.

- *Make Internet News your default news reader*. When this option is checked and you click a Web link to a newsgroup, Internet News is launched. If you prefer to use another news reader for those activities, remove the check mark.
- *Always start me in this newsgroup*. If you have a preferred newsgroup, select it from the pop-up list (see **Figure 18.7**). Only groups to which you are currently subscribed appear in the list.

✔ Tips

- You can manually check for new newsgroups by clicking the Newsgroups button, selecting a news server (if you have more than one), and then clicking the New tab in the Newsgroups dialog box.
- Automatically marking all messages as read when exiting a newsgroup can have side effects, depending on your reading habits. It is most useful if you always want to see only the new messages in *every* newsgroup to which you subscribe.

  You can manually mark all messages in a *single* newsgroup as having been read by pressing Ctrl Shift A or by choosing Mark All as Read from the Edit menu.

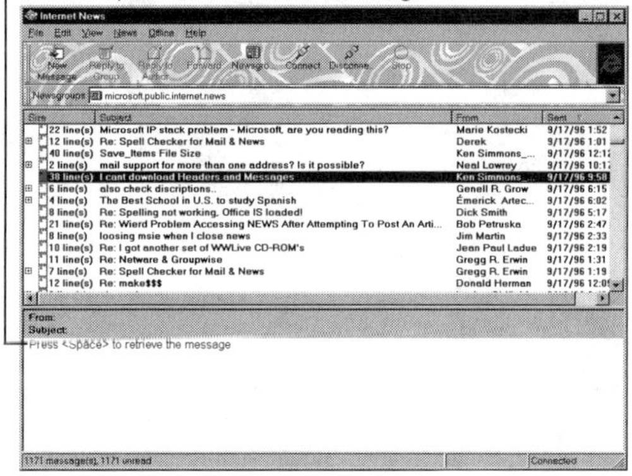

Figure 18.6 *If messages are not automatically downloaded to the preview pane, this reminder appears whenever you click a new message.*

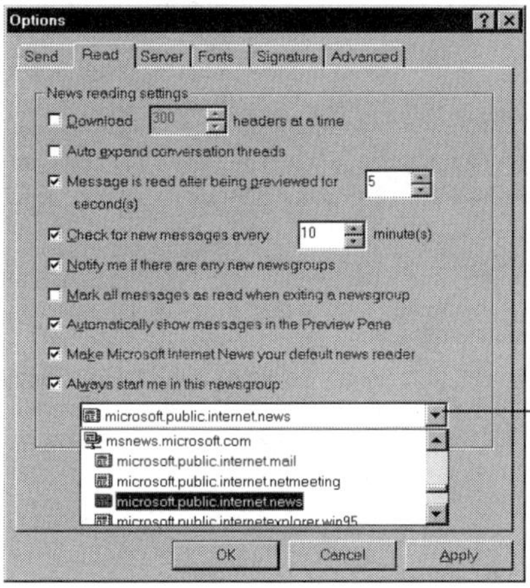

Figure 18.7 *You can select a newsgroup in which to start each session.*

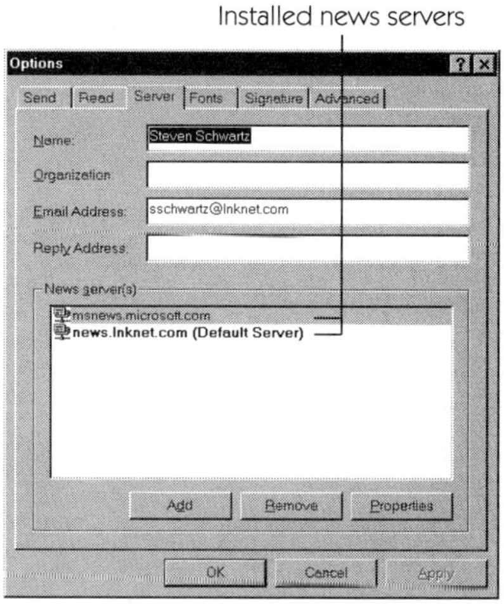

Figure 18.8 *Server options for Internet News.*

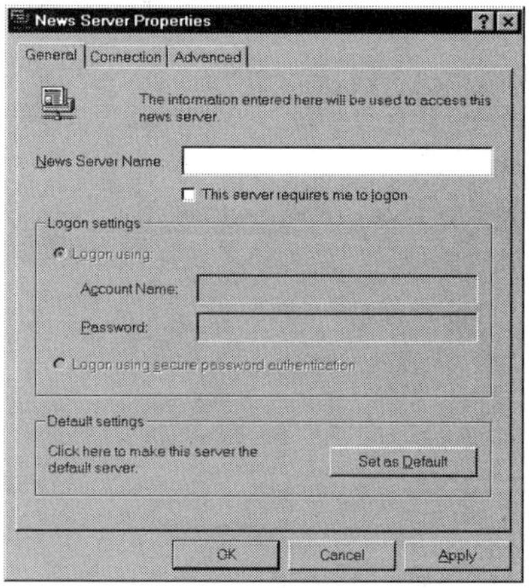

Figure 18.9 *General options in the News Server Properties dialog box.*

Server Options

You specify general information about your Internet account and news server(s) in the Server section of the Options dialog box (see **Figure 18.8**).

- *Name*. Enter the "friendly" name that will appear in the From line of all outgoing messages, such as Alice Sanders or The Prof.
- *Organization*. Enter a group or organization name, if desired.
- *E-mail Address*. Enter your normal e-mail address, such as jonas_smith@aol.com.
- *Reply Address*. If you want replies to your posts to be sent to a different address than the one above, enter another e-mail address here.

The first time you run Internet News, a Wizard guides you through the process of entering information for your primary news server. You can add and remove servers by clicking the Add and Remove buttons. You can examine the information for any installed news server by selecting its name and clicking Properties (see **Figure 18.8**).

Adding News Servers

To add a news server, click Add. The News Server Properties dialog box appears, as shown in **Figure 18.9**. The dialog box is split into three sections: General, Connection, and Advanced.

General Properties

In the General section of the dialog box, enter the exact name of the server in the News Server Name box, such as news.linkshare.com.

If the news server requires you to log on, click the check box and enter the information requested in the Logon settings section. (If you need help, contact your ISP.)

Connection Properties

In the Connection section of the dialog box (see **Figure 18.10**), specify a connection method by clicking a radio button. If you use a modem, select the appropriate Dial-Up Networking connection from the pop-up list.

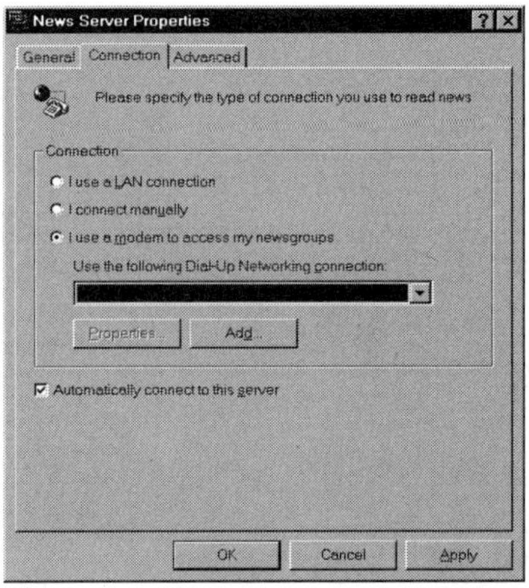

Figure 18.10 *Connection options in the News Server Properties dialog box.*

Advanced Properties

In the Advanced section of the dialog box (see **Figure 18.11**), you can set the following options:

- *Port number*. Change the default port number (119) only if advised to do so by your ISP.
- *Secure connection*. Most news servers do not require a secure connection. Contact your ISP if you're unsure.
- *Server timeout*. Move the slider to specify the time to allow a connection to be made. If you have a slow connection or a busy news server, you can allow more time.
- *Newsgroup descriptions*. To make it easier to identify the thousands of available newsgroups, check this option to download newsgroup descriptions.

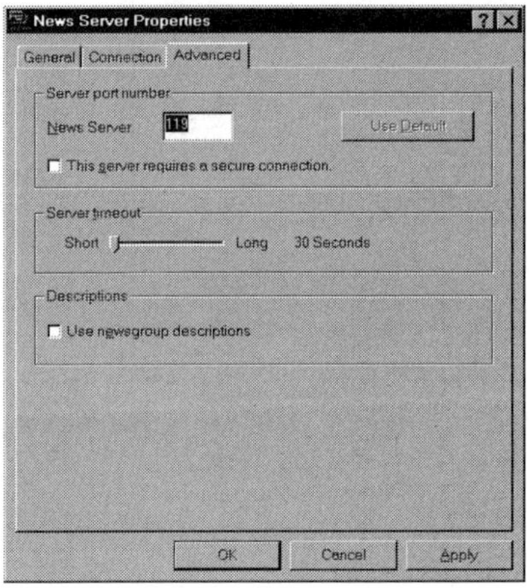

Figure 18.11 *Advanced options in the News Server Properties dialog box.*

✔ Tip

- There are many public news servers that allow anyone to view messages. For example, Microsoft has a public server for its newsgroups at msnews.microsoft.com.

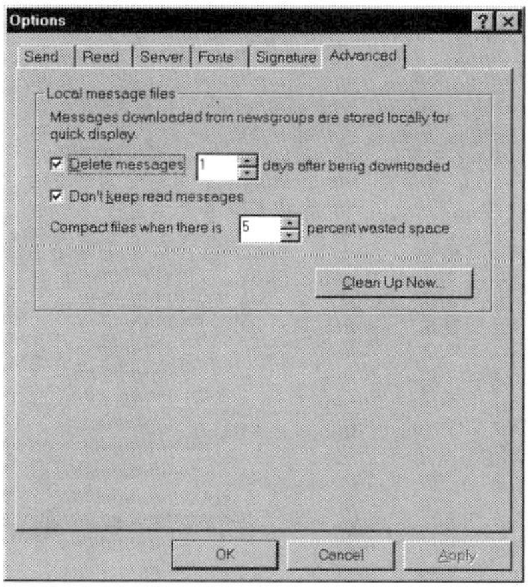

Figure 18.12 *Advanced options for Internet News.*

Advanced Options

The Advanced options (see **Figure 18.12**) enable you to manage the *cache* (areas of your hard disk where article headers and messages are stored). A cache is created for each news server and newsgroup to which you subscribe.

Whenever you open a subscribed newsgroup, the news server compares your cache with the current messages, and then updates the cache as necessary by transmitting new message headers.

Setting Advanced Options

You can set the following options:

- *Delete messages xx days after being downloaded.* When set, this option automatically deletes files from the cache.
- *Don't keep read messages.* If you usually don't reread messages, check this option to instruct Internet Mail to delete them from the cache each time you exit from the program.
- *Compact files when there is xx percent wasted space.* When the percentage is exceeded, the cache is automatically compressed to reclaim wasted space.

✔ Tip

- If "Don't keep read messages" is checked, you can retain selected read messages by marking them as unread before quitting.

Manually Managing the Cache

To manually clean up the cache, click Clean Up Now. The Local File Clean Up dialog box appears (see **Figure 18.13**).

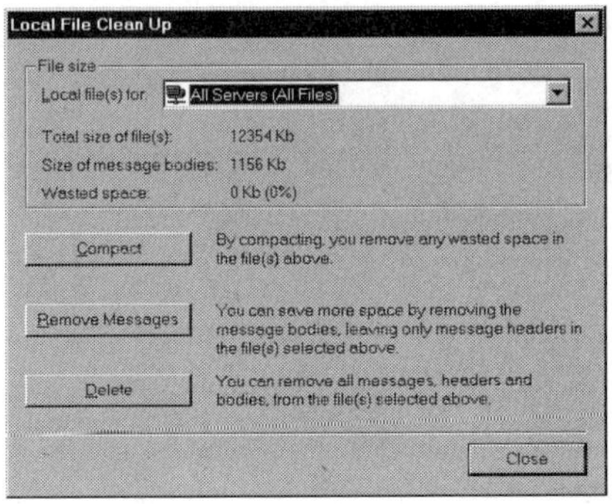

Figure 18.13 *You can clean the cache using the Local File Clean Up dialog box.*

Select a server or newsgroup from the Local file(s) for pop-up to determine the amount of space and "wasted" space each represents. You can then choose from the following options:

- *Compact*. Compress the selected cache(s) to reduce wasted space.
- *Remove messages*. Delete all messages—leaving only headers—for the selected cache(s).
- *Delete*. Purge the selected cache of all headers and messages. This option is useful for removing information for newsgroups in which you're no longer interested, or when you have no interest in the older messages.

✔ **Tip**

- Depending on your choice in the Local file(s) for pop-up list (refer to **Figure 18.13**), you can manage the cache for a single newsgroup, all newsgroups on a single news server, or all newsgroups on all news servers.

Advanced Options

Part IV: Appendices

Glossary

A

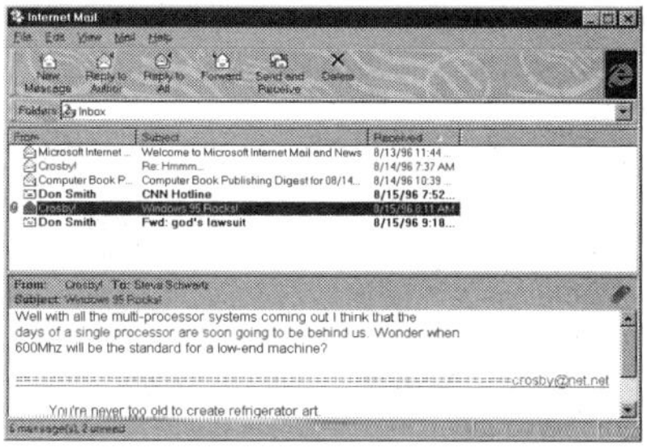

Figure A.1 *In Internet Mail, a message with an attachment is marked with a paper clip icon.*

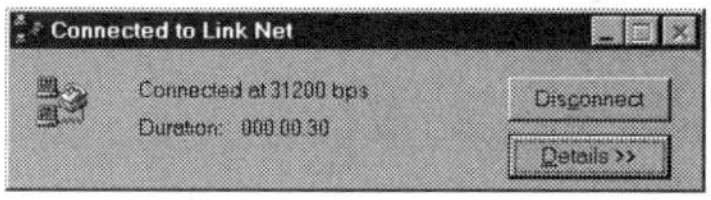

Figure A.2 *The Dial-Up Connection utility reports a modem's connect speed in bps.*

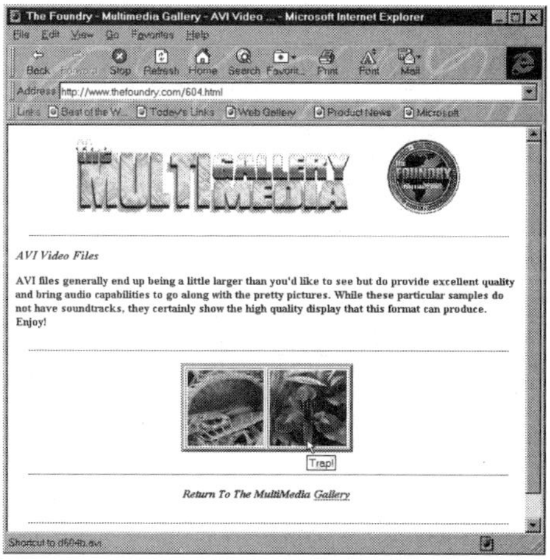

Figure A.3 *A browser enables you to experience the complex multimedia that is now commonplace on the World Wide Web.*

If you're new to the Internet and the World Wide Web, you'll find that there is a whole new language for you to learn. This appendix has definitions for many of the terms and abbreviations that you'll encounter.

address See **URL**.

attachment A file—such as a text or word processing document, graphic image, or program—that is sent along with an e-mail message (see **Figure A.1**). See also **e-mail**.

BBS Abbreviation for *bulletin board system;* an electronic bulletin board where users can exchange messages and download files. BBSs are often run by individuals out of their homes or businesses and often serve as on-line meeting places for computer users. Although frequently free, some BBSs charge a subscription fee based on usage or covering a period of time.

bookmark See **favorite**.

bps Abbreviation for *bits per second;* a measure of a modem's speed (see **Figure A.2**). A 28.8 modem, for example, can transmit up to 28,800 characters of data per second.

browser A program, such as Internet Explorer (see **Figure A.3**), that enables you to view information on the World Wide Web. Browser features are often extended to enable e-mail and newsgroup handling.

chat See **IRC**.

chat client A computer program, such as Comic Chat (see **Figure A.4**), that enables you to participate in on-line, interactive chat sessions where participants type messages to each other in real-time. See also **IRC**.

Figure A.4 *Microsoft's Comic Chat program turns chat sessions into comic strips. Each participant can select his or her own character.*

compression, file Files downloaded from and uploaded to the Internet, information services, and BBSs are often compressed in order to reduce their size and transmission time. The most popular compression programs are PKZIP and WinZip (PC) and StuffIt Deluxe (Macintosh). See also **self-extracting archive** and **.ZIP file**.

download To retrieve a text, data, or program file from another person's computer, an information service, BBS, or a location on the Internet (see **Figure A.5**). See also **upload**.

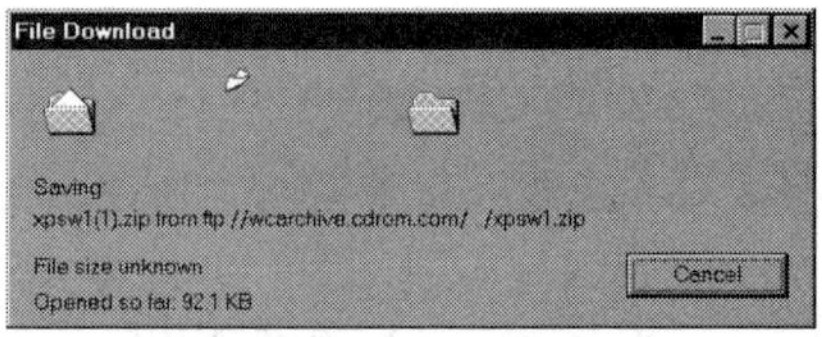

Figure A.5 *When downloading a file from an FTP site, Explorer displays a dialog box that shows the progress of the download.*

duplex (half and full) Some applications, such as NetMeeting, enable individuals to talk to each other over the Internet by using a microphone and a sound card. If both individuals have full-duplex sound cards, they can simultaneously send and receive sound—as occurs during a normal telephone conversation. If either user's sound card is only capable of half-duplex, the individuals must take turns talking to one another.

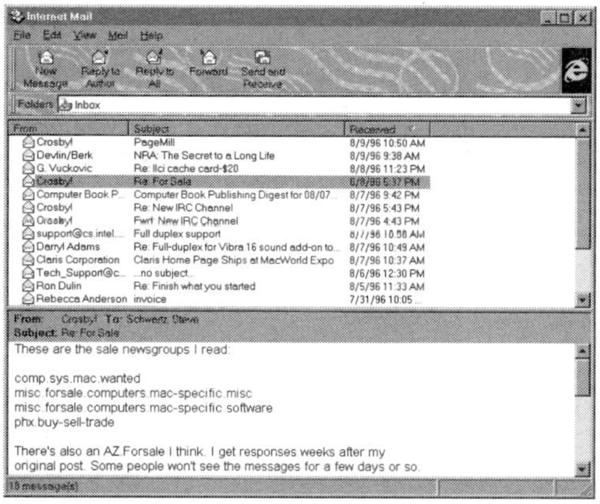

Figure A.6 *Internet Mail enables you to exchange messages with friends, associates, and total strangers.*

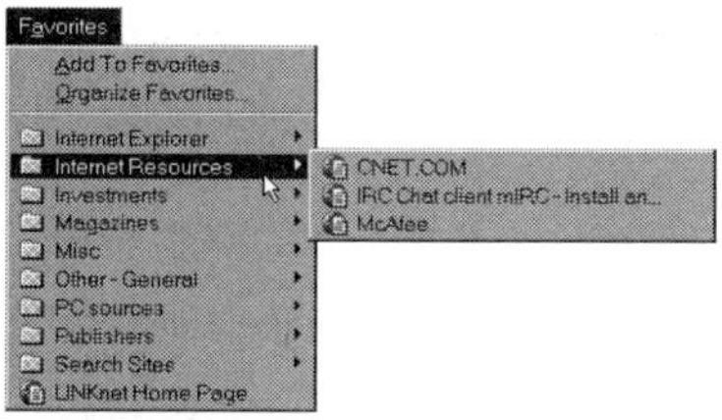

Figure A.7 *To quickly go to a favorite Web page, you can choose it from the Favorites menu.*

e-mail Short for *electronic mail.* E-mail messages are text notes created in an e-mail program, a browser, text editor, or word processing program and then sent over the Internet (see **Figure A.6**). Optionally, e-mail can include attachments, such as text files, word processing documents, graphic images, or even programs. See also **attachment**.

GIF file Abbreviation for *Graphic Interchange Format;* a popular format for creating compressed graphic files. See also **JPEG file**.

favorite A Web page that you visit frequently. Browsers typically provide features for recording and organizing favorites (see **Figure A.7**). Favorites are often referred to as *bookmarks* in other programs.

forward To send a copy of a received e-mail message to another user.

freeware Software that you may use for free. When redistributing such material, however, you must abide by the author's instructions.

FTP site The purpose of an FTP (*File Transfer Protocol*) site is to transmit and receive files. When you click a hypertext link on a Web page to download a program, for example, you may note in the status area that you are being transferred to an FTP site.

helper application A program that—when used in conjunction with a Web browser—enables particular types of files to be opened or otherwise handled. For example, you might configure a browser to automatically uncompress certain file types as they are received or to use a given graphics program to open JPEG files.

home page The first or starting page of a Web site; often referred to as the *index page.*

HTML Abbreviation for *Hypertext Markup Language;* the programming language used to create pages for the World Wide Web (see **Figure A.8**).

Internet A worldwide collection of interconnected computers.

IRC Abbreviation for *Internet Relay Chat;* a system that enables thousands of users to conduct chat sessions, typing messages to each other in real-time. See also **chat client**.

ISP Abbreviation for *Internet Service Provider;* a company that provides access to the Internet, usually for a monthly or hourly fee.

JPEG file Abbreviation for *Joint Photographic Experts Group;* a popular file format for creating compressed graphic files. See also **GIF file**.

log on, log off To connect or disconnect, respectively, from an information service, BBS, or Internet provider.

movies Motion picture files that can be downloaded from or played on the Web (see **Figure A.9**). Common movie files formats include AVI, MPEG, and QuickTime. Some browsers, such as Internet Explorer, can automatically interpret and play movie files. Others require a helper application. See also **helper application**.

plug-in An add-on module that gives a Web browser a new capability, such as the ability to play certain types of audio or video data or to display 3D graphics.

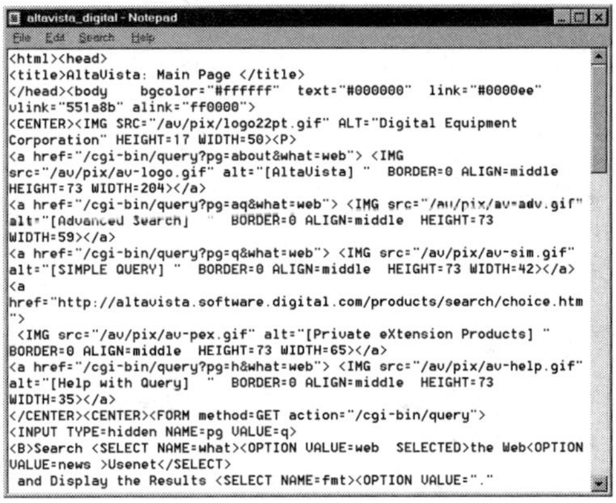

Figure A.8 *If you'd like to see how a Web page was created, choose Source from the View menu to display the HTML code for the current page.*

Figure A.9 *Movie files, such as this one of a frog investigating a Venus flytrap, are readily available on the Web.*

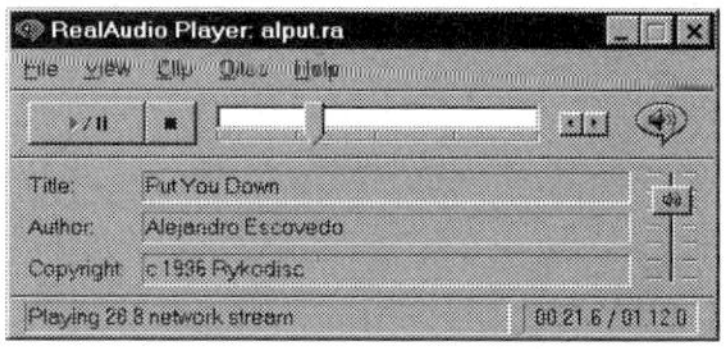

Figure A.10 *Internet Explorer's support for the RealAudio player enables users to listen to music and radio show clips over the Internet.*

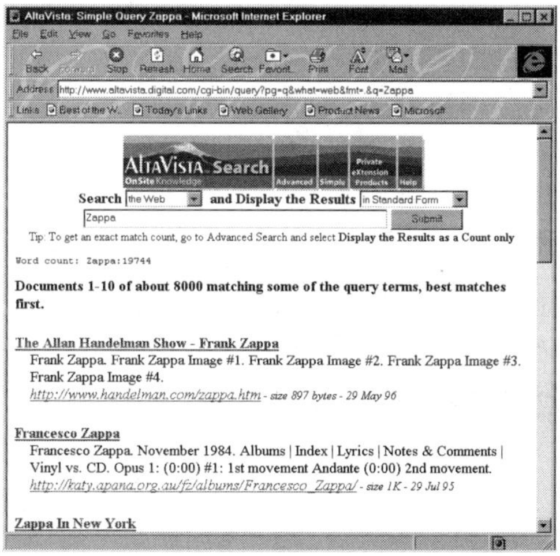

Figure A.11 *Every search site, such as AltaVista, employs one or more search engines to help you locate topics of interest on the Internet.*

newsgroup A message group organized around a specific topic, such as using a particular graphics program, computer equipment for sale, and games. To read or post messages to a newsgroup, you must have a newsgroup reader or a browser that supports newsgroups.

newsgroup reader A program, such as Internet News, that is designed specifically to read and post messages to newsgroups. Most such programs also provide features for sorting, archiving, and otherwise handling newsgroup messages.

RealAudio Player A popular browser add-in that allows audio data, such as music and news reports, to be received and played over the Internet (see **Figure A.10**).

search engine A software tool that enables a search site to retrieve and index information from the Internet (see **Figure A.11**).

self-extracting archive A compressed file that—when run—can automatically extract its contents. Unlike normal file archives, a self-extracting archive does not require a special extraction program. See also **compression, file** and **.ZIP file**.

shareware Software that you can "try before you buy." Shareware is distributed on the honor system. If you decide to keep it, you must send the author the requested fee.

TCP/IP Abbreviation for *Transmission Control Protocol/Internet Protocol;* A network communications protocol that is used to connect computers over the Internet.

upload To transmit a text, data, or program file to another person, bbs, information service, or location on the Internet. See also **download**.

URL Abbreviation for *Universal Resource Locator;* an address for an item on the Internet, such as a Web page or a file. Different types of addresses have different prefixes. For example, Web addresses are preceded by *http://* and addresses of FTP sites start with *ftp://*.

.WAV file A popular PC format for audio files.

Web page A page of information on the World Wide Web. Every Web page has a unique address that specifies the page's location. See also **URL**.

Web site A collection of Web pages created for a single company, organization, or individual.

Webmaster/Webmistress The person responsible for administering a given Web site.

World Wide Web An international system for linking text, graphics, and multimedia documents on the Internet; frequently shortened to the Web. CERN, the European Laboratory for Particle Physics, is considered the birthplace of the World Wide Web. The World Wide Web Organization is responsible for setting standards for the Web. A *www* in an address prefix (as in http://www) stands for World Wide Web.

.ZIP file A compressed file or group of files, where the compression protocol is compatible with the algorithm used by PKZIP, a PC program (see **Figure A.12**). See also **compression, file** and **self-extracting archive**.

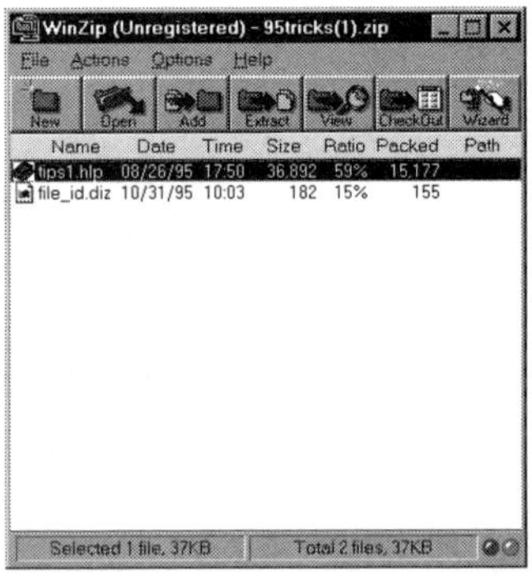

Figure A.12 *WinZip's simple interface makes it easy to extract compressed files from their archives.*

Internet Explorer Keystroke Reference

B

You can perform common tasks in Internet Explorer by pressing a single key or a combination of keys. These keyboard shortcuts can speed up your work and are often more convenient than searching for the associated menu command.

Table B.1. Web Page Navigation Shortcuts

Task	Keyboard Shortcut	Menu Command
Go to next page	Shift Backspace or Alt →	Go ⇨ Forward
Go to previous page	Backspace or Alt ←	Go ⇨ Back
Scroll the page up	↑	
Scroll the page down	↓	
Scroll the page up one screen	Pg Up or click blank area above the scroll box	
Scroll the page down one screen	Pg Dn or click blank area beneath the scroll box	
Scroll the page a specific distance	Drag scroll box up/down	
Scroll to the beginning of the page	Home	
Scroll to the end of the page	End	
Scroll page to the left or right	Drag scroll box at bottom of page to the left or right	
Move between frames	Ctrl Tab	
Move to the next link on the page	Tab	
Move to the previous link on the page	Shift Tab	

Table B.2. Editing Shortcuts

Task	Keyboard Shortcut	Menu Command
Cut selected text*	Ctrl X	Edit ⇨ Cut
Copy selected text*	Ctrl C	Edit ⇨ Copy
Paste text from clipboard*	Ctrl V	Edit ⇨ Paste
Undo last editing command	Ctrl Z	
Select all†	Ctrl A	Edit ⇨ Select All
Find text on this page	Ctrl F	Edit ⇨ Find

Note: In addition to editing URLs in the Address box, you can select the body text of any Web page and copy it using the Copy command.

*When editing a URL or file name in the Address box, you cannot choose editing commands from the Edit menu. You must use the keyboard shortcuts.

†The Select All command selects all text on the current page, while ignoring graphics. Select All cannot be applied to text in the Address box.

Table B.3. Miscellaneous Shortcuts

Task	Keyboard Shortcut	Menu Command
Open a new browser window	Ctrl N	File ⇨ New Window
Open Web page or disk file	Ctrl O or Ctrl L	File ⇨ Open
Open link in new window	Shift-click the link	
Close current browser window	Ctrl W	File ⇨ Close
Print the current Web page	Ctrl P	File ⇨ Print
Display a pop-up menu for a hypertext link	Shift F10 or right-click the hypertext link	
Display a pop-up menu for a graphic or other object	Right-click graphic or object	
Go to the selected link	Enter or Return	
Click the selected button	Spacebar	
Refresh the current page	F5 or Ctrl R	View ⇨ Refresh
Stop current page from loading	Esc	View ⇨ Stop
Open History folder	Ctrl H	Go ⇨ Open History

Table B.3 (Continued)

Task	Keyboard Shortcut	Menu Command
Organize Favorites	Ctrl B	Favorites ⇨ Organize Favorites
Open Favorites folder	Shift-choose Favorites ⇨ Organize Favorites	
Add current page to Favorites	Ctrl D	

Internet Mail Keystroke Reference

C

The following Internet Mail tasks have keyboard shortcuts:

Table C.1. Main Window Shortcuts

Task	Keyboard Shortcut	Menu Command
Open the selected message	Ctrl O, Enter, or Return	File ⇨ Open
Print the selected message	Ctrl P	File ⇨ Print
Delete the selected message	Ctrl D or Del	File ⇨ Delete
View properties of a message	Alt Enter	File ⇨ Properties
Go to the Inbox	Ctrl I	
Mark selected message as read	Ctrl Enter	Edit ⇨ Mark as Read
Mark selected message as unread	Ctrl Shift Enter	Edit ⇨ Mark as Unread
Find next	F3	Edit ⇨ Find Next
Copy selected text	Ctrl C	Edit ⇨ Copy
Select all messages or text	Ctrl A	Edit ⇨ Select All
View next message in list	Ctrl >, Alt →, or ↓	View ⇨ Next Message
View previous message in list	Ctrl <, Alt ←, or ↑	View ⇨ Previous Message
View first message in list	Home	
View last message in list	End	
Scroll messages down one screen	Pg Dn	
Scroll messages up one screen	Pg Up	
New message	Ctrl N	Mail ⇨ New Message
Reply to author of message	Ctrl R	Mail ⇨ Reply to Author
Reply to all	Ctrl Shift R	Mail ⇨ Reply to All
Forward selected message	Ctrl F	Mail ⇨ Forward
Send and receive mail	Ctrl M	Mail ⇨ Send and Receive
Help	F1	Help ⇨ Help Topics

Table C.2. Message Window Shortcuts

Task	Keyboard Shortcut	Menu Command
Send current message	Alt S or Alt Enter	File ⇨ Send Message
Print the current message	Ctrl P	File ⇨ Print
Close the message window	Alt F4 or Esc	File ⇨ Close
Find next instance of text string	F3	Edit ⇨ Find
Undo last edit	Ctrl Z	Edit ⇨ Undo
Cut selected text	Ctrl X	Edit ⇨ Cut
Copy selected text	Ctrl C	Edit ⇨ Copy
Paste text from clipboard	Ctrl V	Edit ⇨ Paste
Select all text	Ctrl A	Edit ⇨ Select All
View next message	Ctrl > or Alt →	View ⇨ Next Message
View previous message	Ctrl < or Alt ←	View ⇨ Previous Message
Go to beginning of message	Ctrl Home	
Go to end of message	Ctrl End	
Go to start of current line	Home	
Go to end of current line	End	
Scroll up one screen	Pg Up	
Scroll down one screen	Pg Dn	
New message	Ctrl N	Mail ⇨ New Message
Reply to author of message	Ctrl R	Mail ⇨ Reply to Author
Reply to all	Ctrl Shift R	Mail ⇨ Reply to All
Forward selected message	Ctrl F	Mail ⇨ Forward
Check spelling of document*	F7	Mail ⇨ Check Spelling
Check names in To and Cc lines	Ctrl K or Alt K	Mail ⇨ Check Names
Help	F1	Help ⇨ Help Topics

Note: Not all commands and procedures are available in all message windows. For example, when reading incoming mail in a message window, most editing commands are unavailable.

*The Check Spelling command is only available when you are creating outgoing mail and only if you have installed Microsoft Office 95 or a compatible spell-check program.

Internet News Keystroke Reference

D

Work in Internet News consists of three activities: viewing messages in the main window, viewing messages in their own windows, and composing messages. The following tables list keyboard shortcuts for these three activities.

Table D.1. Shortcuts for Viewing Messages in the Main Window

Task	Keyboard Shortcut	Menu Command
Open the selected message	Ctrl O, Enter, or Return	File ⇨ Open
Print the selected message	Ctrl P	File ⇨ Print
Delete saved or posted item	Ctrl D or Del	File ⇨ Delete
View properties of message	Alt Enter	File ⇨ Properties
Mark message as read	Ctrl Enter	Edit ⇨ Mark as Read
Mark message as unread	Ctrl Shift Enter	Edit ⇨ Mark as Unread
Mark thread as read	Ctrl T	Edit ⇨ Mark Thread as Read
Mark all messages as read	Ctrl Shift A	Edit ⇨ Mark All as Read
Copy text in preview pane	Ctrl C	Edit ⇨ Copy
Select all messages	Ctrl A	Edit ⇨ Select All
View next message in list	Ctrl >, Alt →, or ↓	View ⇨ Next Message
View prev. message in list	Ctrl <, Alt ←, or ↑	View ⇨ Previous Message
Expand a message thread	→ or +	View ⇨ Expand
Collapse a message thread	← or −	View ⇨ Collapse
Refresh headers and articles	F5	View ⇨ Refresh
View first message in list	Home	
View last message in list	End	
Scroll down one screen	Pg Dn	
Scroll up one screen	Pg Up	
Move between window areas	Tab	

Table D.1 (Continued)

Task	Keyboard Shortcut	Menu Command
View newsgroup list	Ctrl W	News ⇨ Newsgroups
New message to newsgroup	Ctrl N	News ⇨ New Message to Newsgroup
Reply to newsgroup	Ctrl G or Ctrl Shift R	News ⇨ Reply to Newsgroup
Reply to author of message	Ctrl R	News ⇨ Reply to Author
Forward selected message	Ctrl F	News ⇨ Forward
Help	F1	Help ⇨ Help Topics

Table D.2. Shortcuts for Writing, Replying, and Forwarding Messages

Task	Keyboard Shortcut	Menu Command
Post or send message	Alt S	File ⇨ Post Message
View properties of message	Alt Enter	File ⇨ Properties
Close the message window	Esc or Alt F4	File ⇨ Close
Undo last edit	Ctrl Z	Edit ⇨ Undo
Cut selected text	Ctrl X	Edit ⇨ Cut
Copy selected text	Ctrl C	Edit ⇨ Copy
Paste text from clipboard	Ctrl V	Edit ⇨ Paste
Select all text	Ctrl A	Edit ⇨ Select All
Find text in message	F3 or Ctrl Shift F	Edit ⇨ Find
Scroll down one screen	Pg Dn	
Scroll up one screen	Pg Up	
Go to start of message	Ctrl Home	
Go to end of message	Ctrl End	
New message to newsgroup	Ctrl N	News ⇨ New Message to Newsgroup
Check names in message	Ctrl K or Alt K	Mail ⇨ Check Names
Check spelling of message	F7	Mail ⇨ Check Spelling
Help	F1	Help ⇨ Help Topics

Table D.3. Shortcuts for Viewing Messages in Individual Windows

Task	Keyboard Shortcut	Menu Command
Print the selected message	Ctrl P	File ⇨ Print
View properties of message	Alt Enter	File ⇨ Properties
Close the message window	Esc or Alt F4	File ⇨ Close
Copy selected text	Ctrl C	Edit ⇨ Copy
Select all text	Ctrl A	Edit ⇨ Select All
Find text in message	F3 or Ctrl Shift F	Edit ⇨ Find
View next message in list	Ctrl > or Alt →	View ⇨ Next Message
View prev. message in list	Ctrl < or Alt ←	View ⇨ Previous Message
Scroll down one screen	Pg Dn	
Scroll up one screen	Pg Up	
Go to start of message	Ctrl Home	
Go to end of message	Ctrl End	
Move between window areas	Tab	
New message to newsgroup	Ctrl N	News ⇨ New Message to Newsgroup
Reply to newsgroup	Ctrl G or Ctrl Shift R	News ⇨ Reply to Newsgroup
Reply to author of message	Ctrl R	News ⇨ Reply to Author
Forward message	Ctrl F	News ⇨ Forward
Help	F1	Help ⇨ Help Topics

Index

Note: Some entries are followed by bracketed letters, indicating that they refer to a specific program, as follows: [IE] Internet Explorer, [IM] Internet Mail, and [IN] Internet News.

C

D

E

F

G

H

I

P

Q

R

S

T

U

V

W